To MaryElla,
Happy travels through
life

Ooh-la-la Land

Escapades on the French Riviera

Stephen Foey

Stephen Foey

Library and Archives Canada Cataloguing in Publication

Foey, Stephen, author
Ooh-la-la Land – Escapades on the French Riviera

Includes bibliographical references.
Issued in print and electronic format.
ISBN 978-0-9693889-1-3 (pbk.) -- ISBN 978-0-9693889-2-0 (pdf)

1- Foey, Stephen, — Travel. 2- Riviera (France) — Description and travel. I. Title

DC608.3F64 2015   914.49   C2014-907993-1
                                         C2014-907994-X

Published in Canada by WorkPoint Ventures
E: **workpointventures@shaw.ca**

Copyedited by Lucy Kenward
Cover Design by Andrew Bagatella
Maps by Stephen Foey

Back cover sunglasses image: "Woman in a Bikini" by shutterstock
Front cover sunglasses image "The French Riviera"—courtesy of
Science & Society Picture Library, Science Museum Group
Exhibition Road, London, SW7 2DD, England

Also by Stephen Foey

"I Know, I've Been There"

To my beautiful wife,
the one true love of my life.

Special thanks to:

Jesse Finkelstein, Page Two: Strategic Publishing

Jesse & Shelley James

John Sawyer

Sheila Schroeder

Catherine Wynn

FRANCE

PROVENCE

and the

Côte d'Azur

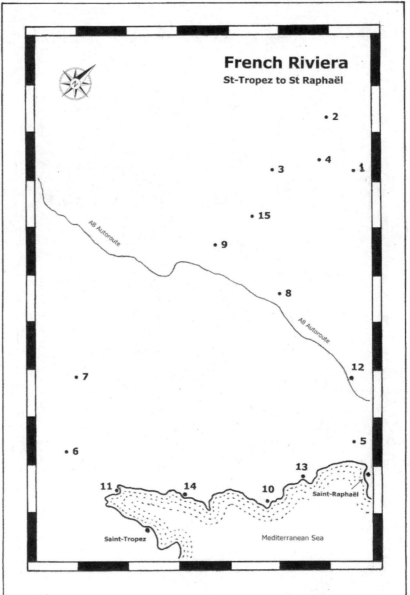

French Riviera

St-Tropez to St Raphaël

1 Callas	6 Grimaud	11 Port Grimaud
2 Châteaudouble	7 La Garde-Freinet	12 Puget-sur-Argens
3 Draguignan	8 Le Muy	13 Saint-Aygulf
4 Figanières	9 Les Arcs	14 Sainte-Maxime
5 Fréjus	10 Les Issambres	15 Trans-en-Provence

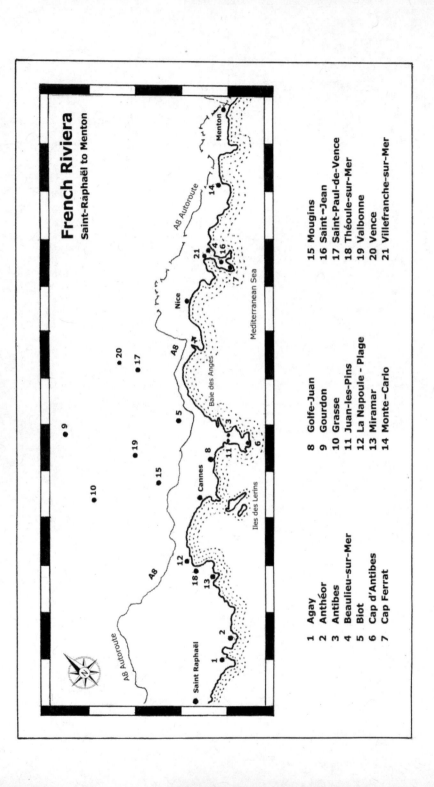

French Riviera
Saint-Raphaël to Menton

1 Agay	8 Golfe-Juan	15 Mougins
2 Anthéor	9 Gourdon	16 Saint–Jean
3 Antibes	10 Grasse	17 Saint-Paul-de-Vence
4 Beaulieu-sur-Mer	11 Juan-les-Pins	18 Théoule-sur-Mer
5 Biot	12 La Napoule – Plage	19 Valbonne
6 Cap d'Antibes	13 Miramar	20 Vence
7 Cap Ferrat	14 Monte–Carlo	21 Villefranche-sur-Mer

Contents - Titles

Part Three

Contents – Places

Villages / towns / cities in *italics*
were travelled through en route to
planned destinations.

Preface

Are You Going to Skip This?

As the author, I cannot assume that you will read this, my Preface. Should you choose to skip it, I strongly recommend that you don't skip my Introduction. I thought of asking the critically acclaimed author Bill Bryson to write a Foreword, but then I thought that that would be too forward of me. I considered writing a Prologue, but it was suggested that, if I did, I should also write an Epilogue and insert it after the climax, to tighten up any loose knots and to round out the storyline. But I couldn't think of one. What's more, although I'm confident that you'll find my book entertaining, I doubt you'll be in awe of its climax. But then *Ooh-la-la Land* is not an intriguing murder mystery with a clever and unexpected twist at the end. Besides, I thought it best that you draw your own conclusions as to what transpires. I'm sure you'll find a loose knot or two, but that is how I prefer to wear a tie. If the knot is too tight, it restricts my movements, even my thoughts.

My "Why?" for writing this book is to entertain, inform, and inspire. Why? You need a break from the daily bombardment of negative news: wars, terrorist attacks, natural disasters, diseases, abuses, and more. You deserve a time out to smile, even laugh. You're curious to know more about the French Riviera, and you need to be inspired to plan a holiday there. So sit back, kick off your shoes, loosen your tie, shut out all negative news, and escape with me and my wife to Ooh-la-la Land.

I hope you'll be happy you did. Now, I realize that you may not be striving to become an impressionist, but I believe that, by the end of the book, though you may be disappointed there's no Epilogue, you'll be happy to have developed the ability to speak English with a French, German, Italian, Australian, and North American accent.

If you read my book, *"I Know, I've Been There"*, which I published years ago, you would have read the following disclaimer:

"... that the opinions, observations, and philosophies expressed herein are mine alone, and I trust that no individual, family, company, religion, race, or nation's people will be offended by them."

Likewise, you can ditto that sentence for this book, but insert:

"... and hotel and Gîtes de France proprietors and their staff..."

And add:

"And that most of the characters described herein bear little to no relation to any living persons."

If you recognize, or even suspect, an incongruous reporting of events—chronologically, that is—you'll be correct, as the escapades storied within have been compiled from several holidays in Ooh-la-la Land. However, most of them we experienced while on a recent trip during which we stayed at three different base camps—two hotels and a Gîtes de France hobby farm—each described and separated in Parts One, Two, and Three.

In *"I Know, I've Been There"*, I share the late Andy Rooney's sentiments about writing, which he describes in his book *Word for Word*. These sentiments still hold true and are worth echoing:

Ooh-la-la Land

"Writing is difficult.... Writing isn't like mathematics where what you've put down is either right or wrong.... How come every day I think that for the first time I'm beginning to get the hang of writing but when I reread it the following day I realize I still have a ways to go...? I have finally come to the sad realization that I will never write anything today that looks as good as it should to me tomorrow.... It's the writer who makes a fool of himself and reveals how shallow he is by putting every thought he has on paper, where everyone can see it, read it and put it away to read again tomorrow. Those who merely speak their thoughts are safe. The spoken word drifts away and evaporates in the air, never to be held against the speaker.... The writer may not think much but he has to know what little he thinks to get it down on paper at all. If someone knows what he's doing, he ought to be able to tell you, and if someone knows what he thinks, he ought to be able to write it down. If he can't, the chances are he doesn't have a thought...."

I hope that this Preface and all that follows—including the climax—looks okay to you today and to me tomorrow.

Introduction

Stories Are To Be Shared:

So Come Along with Us to Ooh-la-la Land

There are those who say that the excitement of a vacation doesn't begin until they've reached their resort, unpacked, taken a shower, and changed out of their blue jeans and turtleneck sweater into shorts and a colourful singlet. But I disagree. Looking forward to a holiday, the mere anticipation is exciting.

I began to get excited the moment I picked up the phone to book our flight to Nice. And even more so when my wife whispered, "Darling, it's pronounced *niece,* as in your sister's daughter, not *nice,* as in, 'That's a nice bikini'." Her last two words raised the excitement.

Even the thought of me, a linguistically challenged Canadian-Brit, experimenting with my forty-word French vocabulary was exciting.

Then there was the excitement while packing.

"Why do you need four pairs of dress shoes, three pairs of sandals, two pairs of flip flops, and two pairs of sneakers?" I asked, frowning.

"You're not taking *that* shirt, are you?" my wife questioned.

"Sixteen tops! You packed sixteen tops last time but only wore half of them. The rest hung in a closet collecting dust. It doesn't make any sense at all!"

"You *really* need to buy some new underwear. These briefs are gossamer-thin and fraying. I'm throwing them out!"

You can sense the excitement building.

Ooh-la-la Land

Getting to the airport was exciting. Our taxi broke down on the Lions Gate Bridge during rush hour and we stood in the rain waiting for another to be dispatched.

Being informed by the ticket agent that one of our suitcases was five kilograms overweight, while noticing that the giant of a guy checking in alongside us was at least twice my weight, and then trying to argue the point (as I visualized my wife packing eleven pieces of footwear and sixteen tops) created more excitement, of a sort.

Then, after passing through Security, my wife asked me if I'd remembered to turn off the stove, the seed of doubt gnawing at me until after my first inflight drink. And the excitement continued.

Do you consider yourself to be a good traveller? I must rephrase that. Do you and your companion travel well together? I don't mean on a seven-day, all-inclusive holiday at a resort-hotel that sits in a fenced compound by a beach—a package deal that includes airport transfers. No, I'm talking touring, just the two of you, in a country with a foreign language, different culture, and strange customs. Do you remain calm and patient, and think rationally when tired or hungry, or when things don't go quite according to plan? Do you tend to argue or present a "cold shoulder" when your companion disagrees with you, or says or does something annoying?

Are you the leader or the follower? My wife is far more intelligent than me, and that is why she lets me believe that I'm the leader. Combine her high IQ with her outgoing personality, spirit of adventure, pretty face, curvy body, and natural powers of persuasion, and "*Voilà!*" I have a perfect travelling companion—a follower who guides me almost every step of the way.

A case in point: We had parked our car overnight on a side street in Cap d'Antibes in clear view of our third-floor hotel room. After breakfast, while getting ready to depart, my wife anxiously shouted that she'd spotted a parking enforcement officer making his way along the row of parked cars. Concerned that we'd find a parking ticket stuck under a wiper blade, I feverishly threw our clothes into our suitcases and rushed for the door. Then I noticed that my wife had filled the bathroom sink with soapy water, placed a foot in it, and commenced shaving her legs—one at a time, of course.

"Surely, you're not going to do that now, are you?" I asked.

"Yes, I have to. I *can't* be seen with hairy legs."

"But we'll be in the car all day."

"It doesn't matter. They need doing."

"Why didn't you just slip on a pair of jeans?"

"It's too hot. You go on ahead."

Exasperated, I arrived at our car as the officer was about to put pen to ticket. Using my extremely limited vocabulary and inept charade gestures, I tried to explain that we were Canadian tourists, that we'd rented a French-made Renault, and that we'd be spending copious amounts of euros on goods and services, all of which would be heavily taxed. The officer frowned as I attempted to convey that a small percentage of the taxes would be transferred from the French Treasury to pay his salary. His gaze shifted to our licence plate, his pen poised.

"*Bonjour, Monsieur. Parlez-vous anglais, s'il vous plaît?* Do you speak English?" my wife asked Monsieur Meter-man as she arrived decked out in a colourful singlet, skimpy shorts, and shaven legs—like the cavalry coming to the rescue—not that the cavalry wear…

"Yehz, juz a leetle. Are you weez thiz man?" asked the officer.

(To be honest, I thought she hesitated a little too long.)

"Please don't write a ticket, *please*," she pleaded, and feigned biting her bottom lip like all innocent girls with hairless legs do.

Monsieur Meter-man looked at my wife. (To be honest, I thought a little too long.) Then he smiled and put away his pen. *Fait accompli!* Case dismissed! Got the picture? Then come along to Ooh-la-la Land.

Part One

1

The Flight:

Getting There is Half the Fun

The sky was the richest shade of blue, but then it usually is at cruising altitude. Scrunched together against the window at 16A, we peered down in excited anticipation at the jagged coastline and the shimmering Mediterranean. The south of France, or to be more precise the Côte d'Azur, lay patiently awaiting our arrival, eager to exchange our Canadian dollars for fewer euros.

Except for the pain inflicted upon me by the zombie to my right in 16C and the incessant screeching of a doting mother directly behind me in 17B, the flight had been very enjoyable. The morning had been beautiful and clear, and I hoped, mostly for the sake of the zombie with the flying phobia, that it would remain that way for the rest of the flight. Moreover, I hoped that by late afternoon I would regain the full manipulation of my right hand. Like most people, I too prefer to start vacations pain free and, perhaps with the exception of enduring an occasional hangover, to continue that way until it comes to its scheduled end.

Still, from our vantage point—jetting along and yet seemingly suspended at 35,000 feet—we saw no clouds, not even a small puffy one casting its shadow for momentary relief over sunbathers on the beaches, decks, and patios below. For *that* I was particularly thankful, as clear skies gave me some assurance that there'd be no turbulent bumps, no flashes of lightning, and no need for an instrument landing.

Ooh-la-la Land

These events would only have added to the zombie's already mounting anxiety as we began our descent to the promise of safety on solid ground—*la terre ferme*.

Fred 'oskins, as he'd pronounced it, was the name of the ashen-faced giant of a man beside me. We'd introduced ourselves, and I'd shaken his sweaty palm while settling into our seats. Then, as the aircraft began pulling away from the gate, Fred grabbed my right hand—to my surprise and excruciating pain—and almost crushed it. On hearing me gasp, he released my crumpled fingers in exchange for the solid anchor of the armrest and, from that moment on, he'd sat motionless, staring straight ahead with his seatback upright, his seatbelt tightly fastened, and a white-knuckle grip of both armrests.

I heard the reduction in pitch of the engines, and immediately sensed our slight deceleration and descent. A moment later, the seatbelt signs came on. We'd soon be touching down, and we were thrilled at the thought of stepping into the sunshine of the French Riviera, the fabled playground of the rich and famous, and the place of origin of the expression, "Ooh la la!" or, *en français*, "*Oh là là!*" And though we were neither rich nor famous, we were itching to be driving along the "coast of blue" with its spectacular promenades and sandy beaches.

A voice came through our headsets: "Ladies and Gentlemen, the captain has switched on the seatbelt signs as we are now on our final approach to Nice airport. Please return to your seats, fold up and secure your tray tables, ensure that your hand luggage is safely stowed in the overhead bins or under the seats in front of you, bring your seatbacks to the upright position, and fasten your seatbelts in preparation for landing. Thank you."

Fred didn't move—he had no reason to. He remained transfixed, his eyes wide open and glued to the back of the headrest in front of him. As we complied with the instructions, I realized that we'd been listening to a recording. I'd understood every word and each had been enunciated perfectly, which was more than could be said for what I'd heard on the flight until that point—the exception being, of course, the words spoken by my eloquent wife. It's not as if we were on a long-haul flight out of Beijing; we were not. Our flight had originated in Liverpool, at John Lennon Airport.

Sitting directly behind me in 17B was a thirty-something woman, and next to her in the window seat 17A was a young girl, whom I assumed to be her daughter. Whenever Mother spoke, which was for most of the flight, regardless of whether she was speaking to her daughter or to a passing crew member, she did so in a high-pitched, baby-talk diction. After being subjected to several minutes of Mother's shrill, one-way conversation with her daughter, I began to wonder if her child had a hearing impairment—possibly deaf to all normal pitches other than her mother's voice and dog whistles.

Having made a concentrated effort to tune in to Mother's mother tongue, I managed to decipher, with a degree of astonishment I might add, that she was actually speaking English, albeit drowning in a strong, north-country accent. Even cranking up the inflight music did little to drown out Mother's shrill gibberish.

"Luvvie, 'ere's yer crayuns and 'ere's yer dolly. Now be a good girl won't yer, luvvie? If yer play nicely, al get yer a drinka pop when the nice lady comes. Int flyin' grairt? Der yer like it, luvvie?" Mother screeched in upper-range decibels.

Judging by his accent, I guessed that the guy sitting in the aisle seat beside Mother was a young, bilingual Frenchman, probably a student returning home. Speculating that he'd studied English at Oxford University and had spent countless hours listening to BBC Radio, I wondered if he could understand the high-pitched gobbledygook coming from his neighbour. Surely, at some point he must have been curious to know her native language, which part of the world she was from, or from which planet. Perhaps she was an alien.

Only once during the two-hour assault on our eardrums did my wife look up from her book, turn to me with raised eyebrows, and exhale a deep sigh of irritability. I nodded in agreement, then cocked my head and rolled my eyes in the direction of 16C (where the zombie hadn't blinked in ninety minutes) and whispered, "I think he's dead."

Overwhelmingly intrigued by the reticence of the alien's daughter, and with a growing curiosity to see if the girl was, sadly, a deaf three-year-old, I peered over my left shoulder and was surprised to see a normal, cute-as-a-button, six-year-old. She wasn't playing with crayons or her dolly, but was engrossed in the inflight magazine. She glanced up and caught me peeking between the headrests. I winked and said, "Hi." Adding to my surprise, she smiled sweetly and winked back at me. "Hello," she said and returned to her magazine—oblivious to my surprised expression and the ear-piercing drivel coming from 17B.

By touchdown, with ears still ringing and hand still throbbing, I began to seriously question the adage, "Getting there is half the fun."

2

Nice Airport:

Aromas, Customs, and Captain Good-Looking

As we walked along the telescopic passageway that had reached out to greet our plane, there was the unmistakable smell of jet fuel. Entering the terminal building, I was struck by the sheer brilliance of the sun's rays blazing in through its glass walls. Then, as we walked—or should I say hiked—the three kilometres from the gate to passport control, I was amazed to see hundreds of people massing around the dozen or so cafés on the other side of the glass partition that keep departing and arriving passengers separate. Most of the departing passengers looked healthy, their tanned faces contrasting vividly with those of the harried café staff and shopkeepers who looked in need of a week at the beach.

As we hiked on, it was impossible to miss the tantalizing aroma of coffee being carried off on the vapours of dozens of overworked espresso machines to the four corners of the airport and beyond, up to heaven itself. The scent of pine trees and the holiday-magic fragrance of salt air wafted in through open windows on the warm, summer breeze. What a wonderful welcome back to France, I thought, as we pressed on along zigzagging corridors, up and down escalators, and over hand-railed bridges—like little tokens being moved along in a life-sized game of Snakes and Ladders. I detected the not-so-pleasant odour of disinfectant as we passed several washroom doors, and signs upon these displayed the two most important words for an Anglophone to remember: HOMMES and DAMES.

Ooh-la-la Land

Without question, cigarette smoke was the most pungent odour. In the designated smoking areas, nearly every adult was in some stage of smoking: lighting up, puffing in, puffing out, flicking ash, or butting out. Some were leaving their cigarettes to smoulder between fingers and lips, and on the edges of filthy ashtrays. Smoke puffed forth, accumulating in layers of haze, and assaulted nostrils indiscriminately. How wonderful it must be for smokers to partake of their life-threatening addiction without having non-smokers around mumbling complaints and fanning smoke away from their frowning faces. It seemed to me that Nice's terminal building was a smoker's paradise, the ultimate destination where a consumer of nicotine-coated tobacco could come to sit back and relax in the comfort of a lounge, drink delicious coffee, and inhale toxins to their heart's content, or until it stopped beating, whichever came first.

In the shuffling line at passport control, I opened our English-French phrasebook at "Lesson 2: Everyday Expressions," and began repeating, "*Bonjour, Monsieur. Parlez-vous anglais, s'il vous plaît?*" Not that I rehearsed this salutation and question with the intention of trying to impress anyone, but rather to generate a little more holiday excitement by experimenting with the host language. What's more, with Canada being a bilingual country, I felt it my duty to make an effort to use my French, a knowledge perhaps sufficient to converse with a four-year-old Francophone. Regardless, I knew that any attempt to *parler en français* would be appreciated by the officer in the booth ahead. The broad-shouldered man was wearing a uniform, a pistol, and a severe expression. Inching closer, I began to feel nervous. I was certain that our passports were valid and, after all my rehearsing, I felt confident of the correct pronunciation of "*Bonjour, Monsieur. Parlez-vous anglais, s'il vous plaît?*" But had I completed the customs form accurately? Quickly, I reread it and checked my answers. No, we had not been on a farm and mingled with cows on our visit to England. No, we were not carrying over 100,000 American dollars. No, we were not in the business of importing surface-to-air missiles.

All was in order. So why was I nervous? Considering that customs officers are able to stare deep into the soul of each inbound traveller, I knew that the simplest question directed my way would trigger feelings of guilt. Had I *really* forgotten to declare that packet of smoked salmon and that bottle of rye whiskey that I'd carefully hidden away in my suitcase the last time we visited France? Had that parking ticket *really* blown off the windshield of our rental car in Paris?

Taken aback by the officer's abrupt, "Next!" we presented ourselves and proffered our documents. Transfixed by his scrutiny of my face and my passport photograph, and disappointed that he hadn't called out, "*Au suivant!*" or something else in French, I croaked, "Hello" through clenched teeth—like a ventriloquist suffering from stage fright. The officer chose to ignore me. But when my wife smiled and said, "*Bonjour, Monsieur,*" his eyes shifted to her. He smiled, assessed her paranoia-free behaviour and overall body type, rubber-stamped our passports, gave a casual salute to the peak of his cap, and with a soft, "*Merci, Madame,*" waved us on our way. As we headed towards the baggage claim area, I felt compelled to glance back. Our interrogator was still smiling, but his eyes remained focused on the knapsack that hung to my wife's lower back and swayed from side to side in time with the movement of her denim-clad hips. No doubt he was wondering about the contents packed tightly therein.

While crowding around the baggage carousel, where fellow passengers looked on expectantly at the empty conveyor going around and around, I spotted a row of baggage carts parked alongside a wall nearby. After elbowing my way out of the mob, a sign informed me that coins were required to release a cart. Without a coin, I failed to force a cart free then fought my way back to the carousel, dismayed at the prospect of having to carry our two heavy suitcases—bulging with guidebooks, bottles of sunscreen, and my wife's eleven pieces of footwear and sixteen tops—all the way to the rental car counter.

I don't know how long we stood waiting for our bags, but it was too long. I was convinced that our pilot had flown back to John Lennon Airport (perhaps with the luggage still aboard) and was sitting at home watching the evening news or out with his wife at Yoko Ono Shopping Plaza. Eventually, the first bag appeared and a collective, "Ah!" went up as we all surged closer to the carousel.

To my astonishment, I saw Fred 'oskins smiling and chatting with everyone around. I couldn't believe how charming, animated, and convivial the former flying zombie had become as he grabbed suitcases off the conveyor for his fellow travellers. Watching him reminded me of that TV commercial for a luggage company that boasts the most robust products on the market. The star performer was a gorilla that tossed suitcases about as if they were ping pong balls.

At the other end of the carousel, but still within hearing range, was Mother (the alien) from 17B talking excitedly to her daughter. Her high-pitched voice—approaching wine-glass-shattering level—carried over the commotion to the far end of the customs hall, where a drug-sniffing dog suddenly barked and jerked to attention with its snout "pointing" directly at her.

"Wan tit a grairt flight, luvvie? Did yer like it, luvvie?"

Sitting on the rim of the carousel, her not-so-dumb, cute-as-a-button daughter was excited too, but for a different reason. She'd found an English edition of *Time* magazine and was deeply immersed in an article—likely one written by the geopolitical science editor—and was oblivious to Mother's prattling.

Though I attend a gym in Vancouver and participate in a strength-building class that the muscle-bound bodybuilders have dubbed "Weekly Workouts for Weaklings," my arms felt as though they were about to drop off as we left the baggage claim area. As we entered the sunny, smoky lobby of the Arrivals level, our objective was to find the Renault rental car counter amid the pandemonium around the cafés, shops, and information booths. In need of direction and a much-needed rest, I stopped a man in a business suit coming our way. *"Pardonnez-moi, Monsieur. Parlez-vous anglais, s'il vous plaît?"* But Mister Businessman sidestepped me and walked on without blinking an eye. Could it have been my pronunciation? Surely Mister Businessman hadn't chosen to ignore a visiting Anglophone's request for help. No, a Frenchman would never do that.

Snubbed by Mister Businessman, the decision to turn right or left would have been easier if I'd had a coin to toss. Unfortunately, we almost circumnavigated the lobby before coming across our rental car counter. For the last fifty metres, I'd dragged our cases along the floor and swept up an abundance of paper coffee cups and cigarette butts. Perspiring profusely, I faced the man behind the counter and asked, *"Bonjour, Monsieur. Parlez-vous anglais, s'il vous plaît?"*

The man replied, "Yehz, I am pleaz to—juz a leetle."

What a relief, I thought. Then, as I looked for our reservation papers, I heard the man say, *"Enchanté.* My nom ees Jean-Claude. Eet ees my privi-large to be of ser-veece."

I looked up to see that he'd reached for my wife's hand and was placing a kiss on the back of it. My wife sighed. My eyebrows rose before realizing that his kiss was our reintroduction to the French culture and that Jean-Claude was just welcoming us to France.

I studied Jean-Claude as he entered our information into a computer. Why wasn't he in uniform? Perhaps he hadn't had time to change into the one hanging on the door behind him. It was a white uniform similar to those worn by naval officers in warm climates. To the right of the computer was a bunch of keys. The key fob displayed an emblem of a black stallion on a yellow background with *Ferrari* written below. So, he was a Frenchman who drove an Italian sports car and could speak some English, albeit with a lilting French accent that some women would describe as sexy. He was tall, dark, tanned, and square-jawed. He wore a tight-fitting T-shirt and tight-fitting blue jeans, and I thought it a minor miracle that this combination didn't prevent his blood—obviously struggling to circulate his cardiovascular system—from grinding to a halt. And, I supposed, some women would describe him as handsome. Yes, he had piercing blue eyes, long dark eyelashes, perfectly shaped white teeth, and manicured fingernails, but I was convinced that his five-o'clock shadow, hairy chest, and heavy gold necklace would be a huge turnoff for many. In support of that notion, I noticed that he wasn't wearing a wedding ring and, therefore, began to suspect that he had a big problem—probably many. Poor guy!

With the forms signed and the paperwork put away, Jean-Claude excused himself, grabbed his uniform, and then disappeared into the back room. Reappearing a few minutes later—looking like a movie-star captain about to lead the Sixth Fleet to victory in the South Pacific—he took my wife by her right arm and led her out of the terminal building, across the access road, and into the parking lot. Meanwhile, I staggered behind carrying our luggage—like an old pack mule coming to the end of its days and destined for the glue factory.

Having circled the car to inspect for scratches and dents, I kicked one tire a couple of times and then signed the release form. Disguised as an officer and a gentleman, Jean-Claude held the front passenger-side door open while my wife manoeuvred into place. He then set about adjusting her seat and seatbelt, showed her where the glove compartment was and how to open it, and how to access the mirror on the back of the fold-down sun visor. It was quite a performance. All part of the "ser-veece," I thought, and all done with lots of smiling and flashing of teeth.

Meanwhile, I was left to load the luggage, get familiar with the controls, and make final adjustments to my seat and mirrors. Before starting the car, I asked Captain Good-Looking if he would come around to my side of the car and give me directions to Antibes. Without making eye contact, he just handed me a map and continued to assist my wife. "And thiz ees 'ow you o-pen the win-dow," said Captain Good-Looking as I almost threw up over the steering wheel.

I studied the map. Ahead was a complicated route of twists and turns and one-way streets just to get off airport property. Eager to get moving, I revved the engine and set off. The passenger-side door slammed shut, my wife smiled and sighed, and we left Captain Good-Looking at the curb, waving bon voyage and flashing his teeth.

3

En Route to Cap d'Antibes:

Philosophies and Suicidal Drivers

When people say, "We're off to the Riviera," they're usually going on holiday to the French or Italian Riviera. However, *riviera* applies to any coastline, especially one that is sunny, has a sandy beach, and is popular with tourists. The Côte d'Azur, which is often known as the French Riviera, is the Mediterranean coastline of the southeast corner of France, and it includes the sovereign state of Monaco. There is no official boundary, but the French Riviera is usually considered to extend from Menton, at the Italian border in the east, to Saint-Tropez. Some contend that the boundary stretches as far west as Marseille.

With its casinos attracting gamblers from all over the world, its beaches and cabaret clubs offering excessive indulgence in sensual pleasures, and Monaco providing a haven for income tax refugees, I can understand why William Somerset Maugham, the English playwright, novelist, and short story writer referred to the French Riviera as "a sunny place for shady people." But then for someone so gifted with the use of the English language, yet peculiar enough to go through life preferring to be called by his middle name, Somerset, had, to my way of thinking, qualified as a shady character himself.

Although my wife and I had agreed to a general philosophy of avoiding big cities and their frenetic pace, we still researched the attractions of Nice and Old Nice. Both offer pleasant pedestrian streets, colourful markets, excellent shopping, first-rate museums, non-stop nightlife, and lodgings galore. But its summertime population of over one million convinced us not to use Nice as a base from which to explore the coast. And although my niece says Nice is nice, Nice has a not-so-nice pebbly beach, and we prefer sandy ones.

Our plan was to enjoy a quiet, stress-free vacation in small towns and villages. Moreover, we didn't want a structured itinerary. We wanted the freedom to do as we pleased, where we pleased, and when we pleased. If we so chose, we could do absolutely nothing other than rest and relax. This approach, we hoped, would mellow away our angst, lift our spirits, and rejuvenate our bodies. We looked forward to idling away hours sitting at outdoor cafés sipping on coffee or wine, and watching people, dogs, and pigeons—life itself—pass by in front of us. We would enjoy picnics in the shade of palm trees, read books on the beach, and go for long, barefoot walks in the sand at the water's edge. Away from the beaches, we'd hike in the countryside while taking in its beauty, and we'd listen to the quiet being broken only by a bird singing, a dog barking, or a church bell ringing out across a valley. We would savour the earthy smell of rich soil, the sweetness of newly cut hay, the delicious aroma of bread baking in a stone cottage, the fragrance of blooming flowers, and the heady scent of pine trees. In slowing down to "smell the roses," we would witness the wonder of nature itself and, we hoped, experience a profound sense of serenity.

The reality, however, was quite different. Battling heavy traffic and avoiding maniacal drivers seemingly intent on committing suicide on the N7 heading towards Antibes compressed those warm and fuzzy philosophies into bits of grey matter and stuffed them into the tiny crevices of my brain. Within minutes of setting off in our Renault Twingo, I knew for certain that we were not on the right road to a profound sense of serenity. We had definitely missed *that* turnoff.

Driving along the Côte d'Azur on a beautiful afternoon was indeed exciting, but doing so in French Riviera traffic was beyond exciting; it was nerve-wracking. Motorcycles and scooters zipped in and out of lanes, missing us by inches. Cars sped about as though part of an unofficial Grand Prix race. Horns blew, headlights flashed, tires squealed, and hands gestured from open windows as I tried to convince myself that it was all part of the excitement of being in France.

When we stopped at one red light, we looked on in disbelief as several scooters raced by on either side. The riders, seemingly oblivious to the red light, threw me questioning looks: "Why has he stopped? Does he think he can park there?"

Motorcyclists-turned-daredevils would rev their engines while waiting impatiently for the green light to appear and, while doing so, would check out my wife who was looking cool in trendy sunshades. The instant the light turned green, they'd race off down the road doing wheelies. In most places around the world, professional stuntmen perform such death-defying tricks at carnivals and for the film industry, but not without bales of straw, safety apparatus, and a Medevac helicopter standing by. We now know where the stuntmen are trained.

While focused on the road ahead, manoeuvering to avoid certain death, I managed to catch glimpses of palm tree–lined avenues and flowering shrubs flourishing on median strips. I noticed many six-floor, stone-fronted apartment buildings and classic hotels with early 1900s Provençal architectural features: decorative wrought-iron railings at balconies; pastel-painted shutters at windows; steep, grey-slate roofs; parapets and turrets; huge wooden doors with gleaming brass knockers and nameplates; and colourful awnings.

The roadsides were chock-a-block with cars, almost all parked at meters. Beach supply shops were plentiful and obvious by the colourful array of goods stacked outside, enticing tourists to come in and buy. Each had racks of postcards, nets bulging with beach balls, bins of beach mats, flip flops, swimwear, and fold-up chairs. And hanging from each awning was an assortment of inflated plastic sun beds, snorkel sets, buckets and spades, and every other imaginable item a family could need for a week at the beach—things, inevitably, left behind in hotel room garbage cans.

There were cafés and restaurants galore. On their patios were tables covered with white linen tablecloths, and set upon those were folded napkins, sparkling glasses, and shining cutlery. Waiters wearing white shirts, black pants, and white aprons scurried from table to table carrying bottles of wine, plates of steaming food, bowls of ice cream, trays of glasses of cold frothy beer, and baskets loaded with sliced baguettes. There were many shops with signs above their windows: BOUCHERIE, POISSONNERIE, PARFUMERIE, CRÊPERIE, PÂTISSERIE, FROMAGERIE, RÔTISSERIE, and BRASSERIE, to name just a few. They all sounded so foreign—so French. If only I knew what was sold in each. Keeping my phrasebook handy would be essential, especially when shopping for a birthday present for my wife. Otherwise, I'd likely step inside a brasserie in search of a lace-trimmed bra only to find shelves of sandwiches, pizzas, and pickled eggs.

Captain Good-Looking, who we'd last seen flashing his teeth back at the Renault parking lot, had managed to turn his attention away from my wife just long enough to advise me that there were only five litres of fuel in the tank. With the fuel gauge indicating almost empty, I pulled over (like a Monaco Formula 1 Grand Prix racing driver manoeuvring into the pits) and stopped at a *station-service* to fill up, and to give my blood pressure a chance to drop below hypertension level. When I stopped at the pump, I was surprised that a pit crew didn't rush out and jack up the car, change the wheels, top up all liquids, and clean my sunglasses, which had become smeared with perspiration during the tense three-kilometre drive.

Having read the sign, I deduced that SERVEZ-VOUS meant we were at a self-service station. And though I understood the grades: NORMALE, ORDINAIRE, SUPER, and GAS-OIL, I didn't understand the French instructions for operating the pump. While struggling to interpret the wording, I noticed the sullen-faced attendant in the front office gazing out at me. Determined to demonstrate to him that I knew what I was doing, I thought I'd start by removing the fuel tank cap. But where was it? After a nonchalant stroll around to the other side of the car, I found it, but it was locked. With Monsieur Expressionless still staring in my direction, I reached back inside the car for the keys, then unlocked and unscrewed the cap. So far so good, I thought. But then, after a confident stride back to the pump and an authoritative pull of the fuel spout, I discovered that the hose wasn't long enough to reach the tank nozzle.

Cracking a weak smile in the general direction of Monsieur Expressionless, I got back into the car and repositioned it closer. Still not knowing how to activate the pump, I turned to the office window, shrugged my shoulders, and made an eyebrow-raised pouting expression. Little did I know that that simple sequence of gestures was well practiced in France, and that we'd be on the receiving end of it many times. In that moment of helplessness, Monsieur Expressionless didn't move from his seat, but he did manage to summon the energy to smirk. Enraged, I started off in his direction, scanning the immediate area for a misplaced tire iron. He shot off his chair and out through the door. That's more like it, I thought. There comes a time in every man's life when he has to get tough. And *this* had been one of those times.

In the meantime, my wife had stepped out of the car, flicked her hair back over her shoulders, adjusted her sunshades to above her forehead, and, using the pump's chrome side panel as a mirror, she had begun applying a fresh coat of lipstick to her pursed lips. Monsieur Expressionless, obviously aware that I'd continued my threatening stare, had become Monsieur Animated, bursting with vigour. After filling the tank, he wiped all the windows, ran to and from his office, and finally presented the bill, together with a bonbon on a little tray, to my wife. Given my threatening stare, I was not surprised that he handed the tray to *her*. Clearly, he remained fearful of making eye contact with me. I'd stared him down and he'd choked. After accelerating out of the pits onto the N7 racetrack, I choked too—the cost of the fill-up was nearly twice what we'd pay in Canada.

I had read that Le Cros de Cagnes, La Brague, Antibes, and Juan-les-Pins were once small seaside towns and ports, quite distinct and separate. However, continuing westbound, with no sign of a black-and-white chequered flag and faithfully believing that the road signs were heading us in the right direction, I found it impossible to discern where one town ended and the next began. If not for the black-on-white boundary signs spelling out the name of each town, I would never have known that we'd arrived at someplace else on the map. If the sign had a red diagonal line stretching from corner to corner, crossing out the name within it, that indicated we were leaving the town, and not, as I had first mused, that the town had been assessed by the Bureau de Tourisme as a place not worth visiting. Had the latter been the case, then Le Cros de Cagnes and La Brague could well be deserving of the red diagonal line.

Wide-eyed and tense behind the wheel, ready to brake or swerve at any moment, I realized that I'd missed the turnoff for Antibes. Adjusting our route, I began to get a good feeling about the town of Juan-les-Pins. The main street was quite charming with a variety of specialty shops, outdoor cafés, and beach supply shops, and though it was busy with shoppers and traffic, both moved unhurriedly. Customers read newspapers and sipped drinks at cafés. Women carried rattan shopping baskets filled with groceries and little yappy dogs. Every third person on the street had a baguette tucked under an arm. Tanned, athletic youth, wearing not much more than sunscreen and smiles, shouldered knapsacks and carried rolled-up towels and bottles of Perrier. Baskets of flowers hung from lampposts, and more flowers bloomed in window boxes and in large pots on railed balconies. At the end of the street was the PLAGE, as many road signs had indicated. Unashamedly, I'd misinterpreted the first of these to mean *plague*, which brought about a fleeting concern that we had arrived during an epidemic, the signs directing people to quarantined areas.

Another common road sign that I'd misinterpreted at first sight was TOUTES DIRECTIONS. Posted at every multi-spoke junction, where cars, motorcycles, and scooters converge from all directions; where no one seems to care who has the right of way; where chaos reigns; and where horns blow incessantly, I interpreted the sign to mean: Toot your horn no matter the direction you're headed.

☼

Feeling a little more confident at the controls of our Renault Twingo—
I'd stopped frowning, perspiring, and cursing—I began to relax and
enjoy the scenery as we drove alongside Juan-les-Pins' two-kilometre
seafront of hotels, fine-sand beach, and tall pine trees. Then, keeping to
the scenic route of boulevards Edouard Baudoin and Maréchal Juin, we
headed south down the west coast of Cap d'Antibes.

It was late afternoon and the sun was still bright and the beaches
and promenades full of life. The sea looked clear and inviting and,
judging by the many bathers frolicking about in its surf, it was warm as
well. With Twingo's air-conditioning switched off and its windows
rolled down, it was wonderful to hear the crashing waves, children's
laughter, and squawking seagulls, and to see so much fun being had by
so many people in so little clothing.

And as the road wound its way around the edge of beautiful rocky
bays and small coves that shelter sandy beaches, the older, multi-floor
apartment buildings and hotels of Juan-les-Pins gave way to a less
densely populated residential area of luxurious villas and beautifully
landscaped gardens. Dotting the route, marinas and harbours
accommodated a variety of pleasure craft, providing their owners
excellent access to their favourite beachside restaurants and sundecks.

We turned inland on boulevard John F. Kennedy, then headed to
the east coast on boulevard de la Garoupe, and our excitement grew as
we neared our hotel. The reduction in volume of traffic was dramatic—
the day's Grand Prix qualifying race had ended. I was whistling by the
time we arrived at La Garoupe Plage, a small half-moon bay with a
fine-sand beach. Built out over the bordering rocks were several
restaurants and sundecks crowded with semi-clad people sitting under
colourful umbrellas. We turned onto Chemin de la Plage, and there, on
the left, was an empty parking space beckoning us to stop right in front
of our first base camp: *Hôtel Miramar.*

4

Cap d'Antibes:

Stripes and Smiles

Set back from the road several metres, Hôtel Miramar looked modest
yet quite charming: a two-level building with light beige stucco walls
and freshly painted lime green window shutters. Complementing the
shutters were lime green wrought-iron railings running the length of the
balconies. Beige-and-green striped awnings above the upper windows
provided shade, as did the matching canopy that cantilevered out above
the dining room windows and patio to the left of the entrance. Thriving
on either side of the entrance was a shoulder-high hedge. Climbing
from the patio to the balconies were vines of bougainvillea blooming in
their red splendour. Palms of different varieties and sizes flourished in
terra cotta pots casting shadows of their fan-shaped fronds. Smaller
pots filled with flowers sat on several beige patio tables, and hanging
plants spilled down from corners of the balconies. The cushions on the
patio chairs were also striped in beige and green.

Standing behind the reception desk, attending to a pile of
paperwork, was a man wearing khaki shorts, brown sandals, and a
white, short-sleeved shirt with an epaulette at each shoulder and button-
down flaps over its breast pockets. I guessed he was in his late forties.
He had wavy, black hair with just a hint of grey at his temples, and
bushy, black eyebrows. Every square centimetre of his skin was
bronzed to perfection. He looked up and beamed the warmest smile, as
one would with old friends not seen in years. His dark brown eyes
sparkled and, despite a few wrinkles, he radiated a youthful glow. His

voice was soft and melodic as he welcomed us enthusiastically, *"Bonjour, Madame et Monsieur. Bienvenue à Hôtel Miramar. Je m'appelle Michel."*

Michel stepped up to my wife, placed his hands gently above her elbows, and kissed her—once on each cheek. "Oh! Here we go again. Another attractive Frenchman kissing my wife," I thought. But then he stepped up to me and placed his hands gently above *my* elbows. My body stiffened like a soldier standing to attention as he leaned in and planted a kiss on either side of my silly grin. Well, okay, it wasn't a real kiss. It was merely his cheek touching mine, followed by the sound of a kiss between puckered lips.

Smiles, hugs, and kisses embodied this man's approach—and Hôtel Miramar's mission statement—to building excellent customer relations. Having lived most of my life in North America, I felt immediately awkward and was suspicious. But I had to remind myself that I was in France. Besides, Michel's smiling, uninhibited personality was so contagious that I began to feel it was time to loosen up. Why not give the guy a hug and a kiss? So what if he's a stranger and I don't speak his language.

Noticing my startled expression, my rigid stance, and my failure to respond in French, Michel said, *"Oh là là!* You moost be Mee-ster and Mee-ses Vancou-vair, of that I am cer-tain. *Oui?"* His sexy French accent was the finishing touch to his incredible charm.

"Yes," I said, followed by a barely audible *oui.* And then, "Yes, we are the couple from Vancouver."

Still smiling, Michel sat down at his computer, checked our reservation, asked us to fill out a registration card, and handed over two keys. Meanwhile, I'd retrieved my credit card and passport. Michel looked at them and smiled. *"Merci,* they are not *nécessaire.* I know you weel not leave Miramar weez-out pay-eeng, of that I am cer-tain. *Eh bien.* Pleaz, come thiz way. Your rum ees up 'ere. Your bag-arge I weel 'elp you la-ter. Pleaz, Mee-ster and Mee-ses Vancou-vair, follow me."

Dumbfounded that a hotel proprietor was so trusting, we thanked him and smiled. I was beginning to really like this guy who couldn't stop smiling and who greeted his guests cheek to cheek. Michel led us to the second floor and along a landing to our room. He unlocked the door and pushed it open. "Thiz ees your rum. I 'ope you are very 'appy 'ere. *Entrez, s'il vous plaît.*"

Michel dramatically drew back the beige-and-green striped drapes with a *"Voilà!"* like a magician concluding a mind-boggling illusion. Brightness flooded the small room. The queen-sized bed had a lime green headboard and a beige-and-green striped duvet that invited us to flop onto it and take a nap. The two bedside tables were lime green also, as was the rattan matting that covered the inner surface of the door. I suspected it had been installed as acoustical insulation to deaden the sound of fellow guests walking by and, more likely, of ooh-la-la moments inside the rooms, which might echo around the adjacent atrium of the cozy, family-oriented hotel. The window looked out onto a small garden, but a tall bush of soft green leaves and deep pink flowers obscured most of the "garden view." From the doorway, the window looked like a beautiful floral oil painting hanging on the wall, its luminescence created by a powerful spotlight: the late afternoon sun.

To the right of the window was the bathroom. Well, it was not exactly a bathroom. It had no bath and it was short on room. More aptly, it was the ablution space. It comprised a toilet, a bidet, a wash basin, and a shower cubicle. All had been shoehorned into place by a double-jointed plumber who, I imagined, revealed buttock cleavage under sinks by day and, as an exotic contortionist, in cabaret clubs by night. Michel smiled as he brought our attention to the room's accessories: an electrical shaving socket, a built-in hairdryer, a rattan basket containing shower caps and soaps, an extractor fan, and an emergency pull cord—the last of these provided for larger, less-agile guests who might find themselves trapped in, on, or between fixtures, and in need of help to extricate themselves. Peering around the retracted concertina-style folding door, I noticed that the shower curtain and towels were also striped in beige and green.

While checking in, I'd read one of Hôtel Miramar's colourful and attractive English brochures. Along with an understated "A *friendly welcome awaits you,"* a few typos communicated a sweet and naïve charm. Michel had certainly delivered on the promise of a friendly welcome, and he also delivered on his promise to bring our luggage to the room. With a polite knock on our open door, there he stood, slightly out of breath and beaming a huge smile. Thankful for his service, I reached inside my pocket and pulled out my wallet.

"Merci Monsieur, that ees not *nécessaire*, for that I am cer-tain. Eet ees my ple-zure to be of ser-veece. Eef you need no-thing at all, pleaz I weel do for you," Michel said.

Knowing what he really meant, I smiled, thanked him, and closed the door. We dumped our bags in a corner, and then freshened up in the ablution space. Although I took a couple of flying elbows to my ribs as my wife brushed her teeth, we didn't once get stuck in, on, or between fixtures—avoiding the embarrassment of having to pull the emergency cord. And despite being momentarily wedged between the basin and the shower cubicle while standing with one foot in the bidet and my face close to the mirror, I managed to shave without inflicting a single razor nick.

Leaving the hotel lobby, we headed down to the beach. The sun was low and there was a warm breeze. It felt good to be outdoors dressed only in shorts, a summer shirt, and sandals. The sand was clean, soft, and golden, and the intimate half-moon bay cupped a gentle sea of clear water. Behind were rolling hills covered in pines and dotted with splendid villas. Even though it was early evening, many people were still playing on the beach, swimming in the sea, and setting up picnics on the rocky outcroppings. We tiptoed tentatively into the gently trailing ripples and were delighted to discover lukewarm water.

At the west end of the beach, past the prominent sundecks and restaurants, a footpath led off around the rocky shoreline. With the promise of a good view of the bay and a magnificent sunset, we linked arms and set off along the path. Away from the holidaymakers, we were better able to appreciate the sound of the lapping waves and the changing colours of the craggy shoreline as the sun neared the horizon. We peered into tide pools contained in the rocks' current-sculpted depressions, and spotted several colourful sea creatures making the best of their temporary homes before being swept out to sea again. In that quietness, out of earshot of man-made clatter and clank, we shared a few sumptuous moments of calm—a taste of tranquility and serenity.

Unfortunately, this peace was shattered by a couple of tourists speaking in raised voices. As they drew nearer I caught a few words of German. For all I knew, they were passing pleasantries about their love of the local birdlife. The couple stopped in front of us, and the tall, barrel-chested man shouted, "Zahre ist notting at zee end of dis pass. I vaulk mit my frau for von hour in zat direkzion und zee notting. You must go back zat way."

I thanked him and nodded, and then willed him to leave us alone by gazing out to sea. "Itz gud spot here, yah?" he boomed. "Nice and pizful avay from it all."

"Hmmm," I replied, and for a full ten seconds the four of us stood gazing out to sea, bonded and united by the wonder of it all.

His wife then said something in German that must have translated to, "Let's move on, these people are freaking me out," because with a loud and decisive, "Ve vill go now," they set off towards the beach. And as they marched away, Hans and Heidi resumed their conversation, scaring the living daylights out of every winged creature within a two-kilometre radius.

By the time we returned to Hôtel Miramar, we were hungry. We found Michel behind the reception desk and asked him to recommend a restaurant for dinner. "*Oui*, I know *exactement*. Le bistro Chez Michel. The nom ees like me. Eet ees ama-zing. Eet ees in Antibes. Only three kilometres from 'ere. Eet ees fantas-teek. You moost go there and eat; you 'ave to. 'Ere ees a plan, and 'ere ees Chez Michel." Michel circled the street on a tourist map with his red pen and then smiled at us. "Go. You weel lurve eet. *Absolument!*"

How could we not act upon his recommendation? And so, after more smiles and my feeble attempt at pronouncing: "*Merci beaucoup, Michel. Au revoir*," we started the car, waved back at him, and drove off in search of fine French cuisine.

5

Antibes:

Bistros, Tee-Hees, and Titters

The short drive up the east coast to Antibes was as scenic as our drive earlier down the west coast from Juan-les-Pins. Although the sun had just set, promenade lights had been turned on along plage de la Salis and others were beginning to twinkle from across the bay where Antibes lay protected by its fortified walls. It was still light enough to see the fine villas and their beautifully landscaped gardens, and people picnicking on the sands, rocky outcroppings, and grassy areas beneath the tall pines. Approaching Antibes, the villas gave way to shops, low-rise apartment blocks, and office buildings—fishing and tourism the only signs of industry. At the outskirts of town, looking out for a vacant parking space, I felt giddy at the prospect of exploring the labyrinth of narrow streets in search of Chez Michel.

We'd gleaned from our guidebook, before leaving Vancouver, that Antibes has beautiful sandy beaches, impressive 16th-century ramparts, a large attractive harbour, and a charming old town of narrow streets, flower-bedecked houses, and oodles of cafés, bars, and restaurants. We also read that it is far less crowded than Nice and yet offers as many tourist attractions, that it has become a flower-growing centre, and that over the years it has attracted such artists as Pablo Picasso, Max Ernst, and Nicolas de Staël.

Most guidebooks explain when a town or city was first settled, the derivation of its original name, the major events during the following centuries, the role the Romans played after they came, saw, and conquered, the name of the wealthy family that ruled the region with an iron fist from 1384 to 1608, the 11th-century Romanesque tower that houses a museum, and the name of the gardener who recently thrust his spade through a priceless Gallo-Roman artefact while digging in a field at a local vineyard.

I'm not *that* interested in reading detailed historical information. Facts relating to the 4th century BC may interest me momentarily, but only until I've turned the page and begun reading about the most popular eateries and beaches, the most stunning scenic sites, and the date and place of the annual bikini contest. And yet I may go out of my way to visit impressive architectural structures: a 1st-century aqueduct, a 5th-century tower, a 9th-century fortress, a 12th-century cathedral, a 19th-century wine cellar, or a 21st-century pub. However, given my frustration at having spent fifteen minutes in search of a parking space, I would have been more appreciative of our guidebook had it provided a detailed map showing the location of each of Antibes' parking lots.

Back in the days of centurions and chariots, when all roads led to Rome, similarly, although lost in Antibes, we discovered that all roads led to a huge parking lot adjacent to the harbour. After parking and purchasing a ticket, we walked into the old-town quarters through Porte Marine: a huge arched entranceway in the massive stone rampart. Once inside the Vieille Ville of narrow streets and flower-bedecked houses— just as our guidebook had reported—we found ourselves on pedestrian-only streets. Throngs of happy, suntanned people roamed hither and thither and dined *al fresco* at the crowded restaurants, cafés, and bars. Eating, drinking, smoking, talking, laughing, flirting, and people-watching seemed to be the main activities of evenings in Antibes' Vieille Ville.

As we strolled hand-in-hand, soaking in the charm of the place, I couldn't help but notice several men swivelling around on their bar stools, staring at us as we passed by. And when I heard the first wolf whistle, I supposed I'd become part of their evening's entertainment. From the moment I'd slipped on my shorts, I'd become quite self-conscious of my lily white legs and knobbly knees. Fortunately, my wife, smiling, was oblivious to it all.

After several twists and turns down narrow streets and across a cobblestone square, we found Chez Michel just where we were told it would be. The bistro was bustling with happy customers and sprightly waiters. A tall, slim maître d' greeted us at the door and ushered us to one of the few empty tables. As we sat down and a mouth-watering aroma drifted from the open kitchen at the back, we grinned at each other. The sound of an acoustic guitar was coming from a dimly lit corner, and on each table were a single rose in a small vase and a candle dripping wax down the sides of an old wine bottle.

Chez Michel was romantic and intimate. The tables were so close together that we could hear every word spoken by our neighbours. Eager to start eating, I reached for the basket of bread that straddled the gap between our table and the one to my right. But a raised eyebrow and a short, muffled cough from the distinguished gentleman sitting diagonally opposite me were his tactful signals to retract my hand and wait for our own basket of bread. The two young lovers to my left were holding hands across the table and staring into each other's eyes, unaware of the commotion around them. I didn't understand a word, but I knew that they were whispering sweet nothings, and that their tee-hees and titters would, undoubtedly, lead to sweeter "somethings" later.

While trying to interpret the menu, I glimpsed a blur of a waiter, and then, as if by magic, a basket of warm bread and a carafe of water appeared on our table. Because we had no idea what would arrive if we ordered *socca*, *mesclun*, or *bouillabaisse*, not to mention *pissaladière*, *aïoli garni*, or *daube de joue de boeuf à la provençale*, we chose the menu of the day because it was the easiest dish to pronounce: *"Deux plats du jour, s'il vous plaît."*

Not bothering to write down the order, our waiter asked, *"Et vin?"* Noticing my befuddled expression, he waited impatiently while I retrieved my phrasebook to look up *"Et vin."* But before I'd found "Lesson 12: At the Restaurant," he repeated his question in English with an Australian accent. "D'ya want wine, mate? If so, d'ya want red or white?"

Even though I was disappointed that Pierre was an impostor from Down Under, somewhere between Wollongong and Burragorang, the evening was superb. Two hours seemed to disappear in a flash, and by the time the impostor presented me with the bill, we too were holding hands across the table and whispering sweet nothings. Happy with his tip, Pierre rushed over and made the attentive gesture of helping my wife push back her chair as we got up to leave. Then, expecting him to bid us farewell with, "Thanks, mate. Good on ya, cobber. I 'ope everything was tickety-boo, fair dinkum, and no worries, mate," we were pleased to hear, "*Bonsoir, Madame et Monsieur. Merci beaucoup. Au revoir.*"

Ignoring a couple of loud wolf whistles coming from the crowded café patios, we sauntered back through the cobbled streets to Twingo. Following CAP d'ANTIBES signs, we found our way onto the coast road, and en route to our hotel we laughed at discovering Pierre was actually Bruce and sheared Provençal sheep on his days off. And as I recalled the saga of the starry-eyed couple whispering sweet nothings, I knew that *our* tee-hees and titters would, undoubtedly, lead to sweeter "somethings" within the hour—behind a closed door lined with lime green acoustical insulation.

6

Cap d'Antibes:

Where Movie Stars Rendezvous

No alarm clock rang to startle us and no clock radio came on with get-up-and-go music. Instead, we awoke to the smell of freshly brewed coffee that had drifted out of the dining room, wafted up the stairs, and penetrated our bedroom door and its insulated panel. The sound of chirping birds came in through the open window—as did shafts of blazing sunlight—as we left the comfort of our bed and set about adapting to the confines of our ablution space. Being cognizant of each other's exact whereabouts and having the wherewithal to anticipate each other's next move was of paramount importance in avoiding injury while completing the obstacle course of porcelain fixtures. Injury-free, we went downstairs in search of breakfast.

The clink and clatter of cutlery and crockery, together with the excited chatter of guests, greeted us as we opened the glass door to the dining room. A fragrant breeze wafted in through large French windows at both ends of the room, one of which opened onto another patio. It, too, was furnished with beige tables, chairs, and sun lounges, and if you've guessed that the cushions and umbrellas were striped in beige and green, you'd be correct. Towels, bottles of sunscreen, paperback books, and sunglasses lay on several of the sun lounges, placed there by early risers determined to stake their claim for a sand-free day in the sun. More palms and flowers in terra cotta pots decorated the patio's four corners. In the centre of the patio was an ornate, three-tiered fountain.

Michel greeted us with a hearty, *"Bonjour,* Mee-ster and Mee-ses Vancou-vair. Come, pleaz, you moost seet 'ere," he said, as he guided us to a table set with a white tablecloth and a small vase of fresh flowers. "'ow was eet last night? Le bistro Chez Michel, 'ow was eet? *Très bon? Magnifique,* yehz?" We smiled and nodded, but he had already moved to another table, smiling at other guests.

I had expected a continental breakfast, but when we glanced at the menu card in its silver holder in the middle of the table, we were enticed by the choice of a buffet—a selection of cereals, eggs, ham, crêpes, yogurts, fresh fruit, and an assortment of pastries. Disguised amid a few curlicues of fancy graphics was a number—the price in euros. Even without a caffeine boost, I managed to convert the amount into Canadian dollars and realized that it was going to cost the equivalent of a down payment on a mid-sized Alberta cattle ranch. I exaggerate, of course, but suffice to say that to keep within our budget, we'd stick to a continental breakfast for the remainder of our stay.

Feeling that we'd overindulged, we got up from our table and waved goodbye to Michel, who rushed over and asked, "So, Mee-ster and Mee-ses Vancou-vair, where are you go-eeng today?"

Our plan was to spend the day relaxing on the beach at Juan-les-Pins. It was a simple plan. We knew how to get there and what to do once we arrived. The only problem, which became apparent when I responded to Michel's question, was that I hadn't a clue how to pronounce it correctly. So when I said, "Jew-an less Pins," Michel looked bewildered. I tried again but failed to generate the slightest sign of understanding. I repeated it slower and louder, stressing each syllable: "JEW-AN LESS PINS." No response. Having attracted the attention of several bemused guests and a curious waiter, I pointed to the name in our guidebook. Michel's smile returned. *"Oh là là!* You mean, *Szhu-an lay pan.* The town juz down the road. Yehz?"

Sensing my embarrassment, Michel escorted us to the lobby and, placing his arm around my shoulder, said, "Eet ees okay. You are from Vancou-vair, you 'ave no understand-eeng. You moost go 'ave a good day een—'ow you say?—JEW-AN LESS PINS. But first, you moost viz-eet Hôtel du Cap. Eet ees on the way. Eet ees *magnifique*. Eet ees where movie stars rendezvous. Eet ees poss-ee-bla that Brad Peet and Angelina Jolie weel be there. You weel lurve eet. *Au revoir*." Still smiling, Michel returned to his guests.

One kilometre along boulevard Kennedy, we drove through the grand gateway of Hôtel du Cap-Eden-Roc. Well hidden behind a thick screen of shrubs and trees, the hotel sat amid beautiful gardens. The four-storey building, with peach cream walls, lavender blue window shutters, and blue-grey slate roof, looked extremely impressive as we approached along its tree-lined driveway. Neatly pruned cedar bushes on either side of the cream marble stairway, which led to the brass-framed glass main doors, provided a central focal point to the grand, symmetrical structure of exquisite architectural details.

I stopped the car at the foot of the marble stairway, unsure where to park. As we got out, a young man burst through the front doors and skipped down the steps towards us. He was dressed in a bright red jacket, tight beige pants, a black top hat, and knee-high black boots. Assuming he was a Master of Foxhounds rushing out to a local fox hunt, I turned around and scanned the property for horses and a pack of hounds. Accustomed to greeting guests arriving in Rolls-Royce Silver Ghosts and full-sized Mercedes, the doorman might have thought we were tradespersons who had missed the hidden service entrance. But before he had the chance to suggest we turn around and leave, or before he could blow his horn and shout "Tally ho!" my wife smiled and said, "Hi there. Please park our car while we make some enquiries inside." We got out of the car, I tossed him the keys, and, like a well-trained foxhound wanting to work and eager to please, he obeyed her request without question.

Once inside the well-appointed grand lobby, we took on the air of a wealthy couple intending to check in and headed straight to *Réception*. Behind the counter was a stunningly beautiful woman who, I decided, was a budding starlet hoping to be noticed by the discerning eyes of

Steven Spielberg while he was on a weekend getaway. Captivated by her sparkling eyes, luscious lips, and sultry voice, I caught only bits of what she was saying: "Hôtel du Cap-Eden-Roc is the finest hotel on the Côte d'Azur... two hotels in one... in a twenty-two-acre park... dating back to 1870... magnificent and romantic... ultimate in quality and charm... and Hôtel Eden-Roc... a modern resort hotel overlooking the beach... air-conditioned suites... heated swimming pool... private jetty... fitness club... clay tennis courts..."

With a not-so-subtle jab to my ribs—compliments of my wife's bony elbow—I stopped gawking at Hollywood's future sex symbol and redirected my eyes to the brochure in front of me.

Leading from the rear of the lobby was another cream marble stairway that descended to a tree-lined driveway that cut through more beautiful gardens and painstakingly manicured lawns. The driveway and the gardens were deserted. Only the birds and the breeze whirling through the tall pines could be heard as we strolled the 200 metres to the modern, cliffside Eden-Roc resort. From a patio to the left of the white-walled building, we had a splendid view of the incredibly beautiful setting. And it was evident, by the many scantily clad people, that this was where most guests spent most of their time. The swimming pool, tanning decks, and cabanas were at one level, an outdoor restaurant and patio at another, a sundeck and jetty lower down, and a fine-sand beach and crystal-clear sea at the foot of the craggy cliffs.

Keen to capture the setting, I took out our camera and framed a shot of the swimming pool, tanning decks, and the surf crashing beyond. I was just about to depress the shutter button when I heard a man shout, "*Non! Non! Monsieur, no photographie, s'il vous plaît.*"

I turned around. A man dressed in a grey pinstripe suit was walking towards me, staring sternly and wagging his right index finger. Pinned to his jacket's breast pocket was a badge with a photograph of a face on it, which I assumed was his. Realizing we were Anglophones, he repeated his order in perfect English. He informed us that there were several VIPs in and around the pool and that it was his job to ensure no prying paparazzi sneaked shots of them in their next-to-nothings, next to someone they should not be seen next to.

Not one to argue with a security guard with a neck as big as my waist, I summoned the courage to shrug my shoulders and pout a little, French-style. But my wife smiled and complimented him on his flawless English. Then she explained that we'd travelled all the way from Vancouver just to see the hotel, and that if we were fortunate to stay there one day, we too wouldn't want any Tom, Dick, or Harry shooting compromising photos of us lying by the pool, and that we totally understood the reasoning behind his request. She added that since setting off from Canada we hadn't had a photo taken of the two of us together, and as we didn't speak French we were embarrassed to ask someone. Smiling now and showing genuine concern, the security guard acquiesced and suggested that one photograph wouldn't hurt. He took a quick look around. I handed him the camera. We stood in front of the pool. He shouted, "*Fromage.*" We smiled. He took the shot: the two of us in the foreground, and Brad and Angelina in the background.

"*Merci beaucoup,*" I said. I couldn't have done a better job myself.

7

Juan-les-Pins:

Pay-and-Display and Pay-as-You-Lay

The twisting coastal road heading into Juan-les-Pins would be the perfect setting to film a Renault commercial: An attractive couple in their easy-on-fuel, easy-to-park, easy-to-drive, sub-compact Twingo hatchback, smiling to the sound of saxophones and electric guitars as they speed through a sunny paradise of fine-sand beaches, pretty coves, and gently swaying pine trees. What else could a director or an attractive couple wish for? Well, there was one thing: a place to park. Evidently, you can drive through paradise, but you can't park in it. And after driving around Juan-les-Pins's centre several times, I realized that parking Twingo was going to be a daily challenge.

The thrill of finding a parking space was like winning a six-figure lottery. Not that I've ever won a six-figure lottery. Then there was the thrill of discovering that PAYANT, painted in white on the road alongside parking space markings, was an upper-case reminder to purchase a ticket from a dispensing machine and display it, print-side up, on the dashboard. You park then *pay and display*. That may sound simple enough, but there was more to it. First, you have to search for a ticket-dispensing machine, figure out how to operate it, and have sufficient euro coins ready to insert. Then you have to rush back to your car in the hope that it hasn't been towed or broken into. Once you've placed the ticket on your dashboard, you check that you've left nothing inside that isn't bolted down, close the windows and lock the doors, and fold back the door mirrors. Interestingly, I found the whole process quite gratifying. Even if I wasted away the remainder of the day, I could always reflect on having parked Twingo with a satisfying sense of accomplishment.

Tourists have been known to change their entire holiday plans after finding a parking space. "Yeah, we were scheduled to fly from Nice to Athens and connect with a fourteen-day cruise and escorted tour of the antiquities of the Med, but we found this great parking space in Juan-les-Pins that we just couldn't give up. So we stayed at the beach for two weeks instead. Yeah, it was a fantastic parking space. Would you like to see a photograph? I have one in my wallet."

We'd read that Juan-les-Pins is popular for its beautiful two-kilometre sandy beach, its many restaurants and bars, and its superb nightlife. That is why its streets are packed in summer with young people seeking sun, fun, and sex—but not necessarily in that order. Apparently, big-time partying began in the town in the late 1920s when American jazz musicians arrived with their swinging music and ooh-la-la swimsuits.

Also in the late 1920s, the suntan became fashionable. Apparently it was Coco Chanel who popularized tanning one's skin, and encouraged her high society clientele on the Côte d'Azur to look as healthy as any Provençal farmer—with the aid of her expensive sun cream, of course. And as the fad caught on, clothes came off, and the upper class no longer chose to look cool while sitting in the cool shade.

Even though we'd planned to avoid large towns and crowds, we found ourselves irresistibly drawn to bathing in our skimpiest on a sun-drenched beach with thousands of others. It was easy to rationalize. It would be restful and relaxing, it would reintroduce my lily white skin to the sun, and after liberal applications of Coco Chanel's tanning lotion, I'd develop a Provençal farmer's tan, and thereby discourage wolf whistles. Besides, if we were to leave, we'd have to give up our fantastic parking space.

☼

Ooh-la-la Land

On the short walk to the beach, we stopped at a beach supply shop to buy two roll-up mats. It was a simple transaction. I pointed at the mats with one hand, raised two fingers of the other, and then passed over some euros. Using hand gestures and nods, and without speaking a word of English or French, the store assistant might have thought we were visiting from Kazakhstan or that we were deaf and dumb. Regardless, he seemed accustomed to speechless sales. He didn't smile, didn't say hello or thank us for our business, and I got the distinct impression that he would have preferred that we hadn't come into his shop and interrupted his work on a crossword puzzle.

With roll-up mats in hand, we searched for a section of public beach rather than part with a small fortune to enter one of the private, *pay-as-you-lay* bathing operations. Most of the beachfront was covered with these full-service facilities built on concrete patios and wooden piers that protruded into the shallow surf. And I was amazed by their uniformity. All the umbrellas were set out in straight rows, and each row was parallel to the next. Two chairs per umbrella were set an equal distance from the centre pole, a side table was set in line with each chair, and an ashtray had been placed to the left of center on every table. Furthermore, the backs of all the chaise lounges had been adjusted to the same angle, and every row of chairs faced the same direction and was aligned within millimetres of the next.

Synchronized sunbathing didn't look like much fun, especially when all the action was only metres away on the sand and in the sea, where nothing had order. And each deck had its neat-and-tidy rules, which were enforced by a roving attendant. "Ahem! When you stood up to adjust your chair, you did so to the incorrect angle and then your rear end broke the laser beam. Having contravened several rules of this establishment, you are henceforth banned from this deck."

The seafront promenade bustled with life, which was mostly made up of throngs of holidaymakers heading in opposite directions. I found myself continually weaving in and out of bodies and hopping out of the way of wayward baby strollers, meandering toddlers, muscle-bound beach bums, and aloof poodles. Unperturbed by the masses, my wife gracefully moved through the crowd, stopping occasionally to allow me to reappear from out of her wake. Business proprietors were smiling, especially the street vendors who sold their wares from temporary stalls. We took refuge at one stall where, along with a group of pretty, young women, we examined inexpensive necklaces, rings, and bracelets—knock-offs of brand-name jewellery—neatly displayed on black, velvet cushions. At an adjacent stall, handsome, young men pretended to be looking at racks of sunglasses and wristwatches but they were actually scrutinizing the pretty, young women standing all around me. Or, perhaps, they were scrutinizing my wife.

Eventually, we came to a public section of beach. We tiptoed over and around glistening bodies to one of the few vacant spaces on the sand and claimed it by laying down our beach mats. Even though my head was close to a guy's large, smelly feet, and my navel was within ash-flicking range of the bare-breasted woman smoking a cigarette to my right, it felt wonderful to soak in the sun.

T.O.B. is the abbreviation for top-optional beach. Once referred to as a *topless beach*, a top-optional beach more aptly describes (to female bathers) a swimwear option. Apparently, the decision to endorse top-optional beaches remains controversial. Many women strongly object to other women going topless, and only 97 per cent of men are in favour of it. I'm with the men on this one. However, I'm not a fan of seeing women with large tattoos or multiple body piercings—an earring in each lobe being the exception. Call me old-fashioned, but the sight of a fire-breathing dragon tattooed across a shoulder, or a stud screwed through an eyebrow, a nostril, a lip, or a nipple does nothing to turn this man on. For some, such fads seem to have no boundaries. How far will they go? Hopefully, no farther than a half-inch diameter, stainless steel bolt through a slender neck, with a couple of washers and locknuts as finishing touches. What will the future bring? Will T.O.B.s one day become B.O.B.s? Now there's a scary thought.

From our roll-up base on the sand, we were close to two women wearing nipple rings. As a fond admirer of female breasts, I wonder what motivates women to attempt to enhance their beauty with these so-called adornments. Mother Nature must cringe and her eyes water at the thought of threading a loop of metal through the ends of them. Am I the odd man out here? Perhaps it's my engineering background, but I would only consider having a nipple ring installed if there was a practical reason. At a stretch of the imagination, I could clip a chain and anchor to one while floating on an air mattress. If I drifted off to sleep, it would prevent me from drifting out into the Mediterranean's shipping lanes.

8

Juan-les-Pins:

Beach Life, Picnics, and Pétanque

By lunchtime, my skin was radiating a warm glow and exhibiting a pinkish hue. Having put our trust in the protection of our factor-15 sunscreen, I felt confident that by dinnertime there would be evidence of the first stages of a Provençal-farmer tan. During the morning's bronzing process, we'd left our beach mats several times to cool down in the sea. Each time, we left our clothes, guidebook, and sunscreen in two separate heaps on our mats, and covered each with a Hôtel Miramar beige-and-green striped towel. For extra security, I cupped a handful of sand onto each corner—a proven deterrent to theft.

Even exercising my extraordinary foot-eye co-ordination—first applauded from the sidelines of muddy soccer fields when I was a child in England, and years later on the polished floors of discothèques—it was impossible to avoid stepping on someone's beach towel, hand, or cigarette pack, as I picked a path to the water's edge. In spite of my limited French, I know fellow sunbathers were cursing me as I trod on their body parts and their children's sandcastles.

Tiptoeing into the sea, I was relieved to feel that the water was not cold. Moreover, it was crystal clear. I'm not a strong swimmer and, as a confidence builder, I need to see what I'm about to step on, swim into, or float over. The challenge of overcoming the fear of drowning is great enough without having to be concerned about sea urchins, seaweed, rocks, and man-made flotsam. Even though the sea was lukewarm, clear, and inviting, it was my responsibility to hold our camera and the travel pouch that contained our documents, cash, credit cards, and keys. So, while I was limited to wading around in knee-deep surf with the toddlers and grandparents, my wife freestyled her way through the waves to a raft that bobbed up and down some 300 metres offshore.

While standing in the shallow surf with the three-year-olds and the eighty-three-year-olds, I slowly turned to observe the panoramic vista. The beach was crowded. Umbrellas, floppy hats, and sunscreen were being put to good use. An endless row of seafront hotels and apartment buildings ran on to adjacent bays and beyond. Off to the west was the outline of the 600-metre-high red rocks of the Massif de l'Estérel and, beyond them, the 800-metre-high, hazy blue profile of the Massif des Maures, which stands guard over Saint-Tropez. Looking southwest, out over the sea, lay the Îles de Lérins: islands of pine forests, scattered with several chapels and boasting one of Europe's most celebrated monasteries. And to the southeast was the picturesque coastline of Cap d'Antibes with its extremely powerful lighthouse (Phare de la Garoupe) prominently placed on the highest point at the tip of the peninsula, and below that, lay the wealthy villas and Hôtel Miramar. In every direction was a wonderful sight to behold.

One such sight was my wife wading through the shallows. But she was not alone. Accompanying her was the bronzed hulk of a lifeguard who declared that it was all part of his duty to escort her back from the raft to safer waters. Safer waters! All part of his duty! Sure! *He* was her biggest threat—the only shark to swim in the Med!

"Thank you," I croaked as I reached to shake Superman's hand.

"No. No. Eet ees my ple-zure. Eet ees my doo-tee," he replied, as he shook my hand and almost crushed it—producing pain reminiscent of that inflicted upon me by the flying zombie.

For lunch, we walked into town and bought groceries for a picnic. Although I communicated for the most part by pointing and nodding, I occasionally tried a little French. In one store, I asked for a baguette and actually had one handed to me. Some items, however, were more difficult to ask for than others—like ordering half-a-dozen slices of salami in a *boucherie*. I said to the butcher, *"Saucisson, s'il vous plaît."* I pointed to the salami, raised six fingers, and made a chopping gesture. The butcher smiled and nodded. He wiped his hands on his apron, opened a pantry door, and retrieved six long salami sausages. He'd missed my chopping gesture. I ran through the charade again.

We ate our picnic on a park bench in the shade of pine trees just back of the beach. Together with a baguette and six slices of salami, we'd bought a little brie cheese, a tomato, two peaches, and two small fruit tarts. We'd also bought a bottle of rosé wine, which, we were delighted to discover, cost less than a cup of café au lait. Using my Swiss Army knife, I created several sandwiches and then popped the cork on the wine bottle with the handy little corkscrew. As I did so, I wondered what kind of war the Swiss army had envisioned fighting when they added the corkscrew. Then, without plastic glasses or paper cups, we had no option but to sip the wine from the bottle, which raised the eyebrows of a passing priest and the hopes of a drunken beggar.

Talking of picnics and food, we'd read that Provence grows superb fruits and vegetables, which is why it's widely known as "the garden of France," and that menu dishes ending with *à la provençale* are prepared with garlic-seasoned tomatoes. The region is also known for its production of olive oil and goat cheese. And vast areas are used to grow flowers, chiefly for the perfume industry. The scent of millions of blossoms attracts millions of bees and, *"Voilà!"* honey production.

With our hunger satisfied, our mood mellowed by rosé wine, and our thoughts turning to napping in the sun, we ambled back in the direction of the beach. I'd read that locals spend much of their spare time playing pétanque (a game of bowls) in the shade of plane trees and sipping pastis (an anise-flavoured apéritif) in the shade of cafés. Soon we came across a group of craggy-faced old men bowling their cannon balls at a smaller white marker ball. The constant smiles and glassy eyes made it obvious that *these* guys combined their two pastimes. And so with that in mind, we stood well back from the marker ball to avoid taking a direct hit amidships. Seeing a dead pigeon a few metres away, its feet pointing skyward, I thought it unlikely that our travel insurance would cover costs associated with injuries incurred by metal balls thrown by drunken old men. So we sauntered back to the safety of the beach.

We were relieved to find our belongings lying exactly as we'd left them, securely wrapped in our towels—the corner sand piles still in place. The beach was even busier, and the sun's ever-changing position had brought about a mass reorientation of beach mats, towels, and sun chairs to enable fellow sunbathers to continue to catch its rays square on. We relocated our mats likewise. Not that that constituted anything like the synchronized sunbathing practiced up on the pay-as-you-lay decks. It was merely a matter of moving so that the head of the neighbour to my right wasn't inches from my crotch and that my vision wasn't obscured by the *derrière* of the neighbour up the beach from me. Our guidebook had cautioned that during mid-summer Juan-les-Pins' sandy beaches are crowded with visitors lying cheek to jowl. Interestingly though, even in those cramped, almost-nude confines, people still demand a fair degree of privacy.

After a fresh application of sunscreen, we lay back on our towels, closed our eyes, and listened to the soothing surf, the cries of gulls, the laughter of children, and the romantic babble of French conversation. The only annoyance as I was dozing off, was the sound of cell phones ringing. More perturbing, it took me back to the world of work, the world we'd just escaped from—life on the occupational treadmill. And for some strange reason, those using their phones spoke louder than normal. Really, who needs to hear someone agreeing to pick up a baguette and six slices of salami on their way home? However, as most of the offenders were speaking French, it was easier for me to forgive and ignore.

But before dozing off completely, I began to think of other words that were prefixed with the word *French*. French fries came to mind, then French chalk, French curves, French dressing, French windows, a French horn, a French kiss, a French Canadian, and a French letter. The plural of the last of these would be spoken quietly by a person in Britain when requesting condoms from the local pharmacy. I doubt if anyone would hear *that* request being spoken loudly into a phone on a packed beach.

9

Juan-les-Pins:

Casino and Picasso

Other than the beach and the main street, we really hadn't seen anything else of Juan-les-Pins. So, instead of heading straight for the car, we decided to stroll along the seafront promenade and then zigzag our way back through the side streets to our fantastic parking space. After passing many more pay-as-you-lay establishments, we came upon a casino at the end of the beach. Parked at the front were a couple of sports cars and several limousines with tinted windows. A small group of chauffeurs stood talking and smoking cigarettes. Even though the sun was still shining, the front of the casino was lit up with a thousand light bulbs and several neon signs. Most of the people exiting were dressed in shorts, singlets, and sandals, but those entering were dressed a little more formally—getting an early start on their evening's entertainment. Two large doormen dressed in tuxedos, starched-white shirts, and black bow ties stood guard at the front doors like a pair of huge penguin bookends scrutinizing everyone who entered.

We rarely go to casinos. Why? We don't like leaving them with less money than we had when we arrived, especially when we know that our hard-earned cash is being grabbed by the two-armed bandits that run the places. But we were on holiday on the French Riviera. We looked at each other and asked, "Why not?" Even if we lost a little, the flashing lights, ringing bells, whirring sirens, and the dink-dink-dinking of coins being dispensed from winning one-armed bandits would entertain us. And there's the free booze served by pretty women wearing short skirts and fishnet stockings. I looked at one of the penguins for permission to enter the den of iniquity. I thought he spent far too long scrutinizing my wife but he finally waved us on our way along the pathway to hell.

We took a long escalator ride down to a cavernous, windowless room full of flashing, ringing, dink-dink-dinking one-armed bandits, gaming tables, and roulette wheels. The place was packed with people carrying little plastic buckets into which they poured their winnings—if they were lucky enough. Most of them moved robotically and wore trance-like expressions—like Fred 'oskins. I expected to bump into the Devil himself, but he was busy in the back room counting the money, pulling the strings, fixing the wheels, marking the cards, and scheming more ways to cheat. Or maybe he was whipping the big-time losers stoking the fires.

It seemed that nearly everyone gambling was smoking. Some sat with their cigarettes hanging from their lips, the ash falling into their plastic buckets. Several guys were smoking cigars and looking like high-rolling, big-time spenders. The room was stifling hot. Obviously, the Devil had turned off the air conditioning and was preparing everyone for hotter, smokier times ahead.

After one slow, head-spinning circuit of the stuffy facilities, we realized that we may not survive Dante's inferno without falling victim to the temptation of dropping a lot of money on the tables, or, worse still, falling victim to the heat and smoke and dropping flat on the floor. In search of fresh air, we made our way back to the escalators and escaped to the street without needing mouth-to-mouth resuscitation from a giant penguin. I was going to suggest to the penguins that they add "respirator" to their dress code, but I recalled that a flight home in a coffin was twice the price of flying first class, and would leave my wife (and sole beneficiary of my "estate") sitting next to a handsome, sweet-talking opportunist.

☼

Ooh-la-la Land

Strolling away from the casino, Juan-les-Pins became a spider's web of narrow, busy streets brimming with cafés, bars, restaurants, shops, hotels, and nightclubs that provide fun, food, and lodging to mainly the young and unsophisticated crowds. Apéritifs were being served and consumed at all the outdoor bars, which were jam-packed with people wanting to watch others and wanting to be watched by others. At Pam Pam, a *rhumerie* on boulevard Wilson, good-looking, tanned waiters, and shapely, semi-clad waitresses rushed around the tables carrying trays of colourful drinks decorated with tiny paper umbrellas, swizzle sticks, and wedges of fruit. Their pockets, bulging with tips, grew bigger each time a satisfied customer paid his or her bill. "Happy Hour" in Juan-les-Pins more aptly describes the mood and timeframe of those who are serving than of those who are being served.

Not far from our fantastic parking space, we stopped at a bookstore that advertised in its window: ENGLISH BOOKS SOLD HERE. With time to spare and postcards to purchase, we entered and browsed awhile. Drawn to the tourist information section at the back of the shop, I leafed through several internationally acclaimed guidebooks and a few local tourist brochures, and was surprised by the amount of interesting text afforded the recent, famous artists who had lived and worked in the region for many years. Pablo Picasso, in particular—his achievements and idiosyncrasies—took many paragraphs. Moreover, much praise was written of the Picasso Museum, which is located in Antibes' old town and houses over 300 of his works.

I'm easy to please when viewing paintings and, regardless of the subject matter, I believe I have a good appreciation for colour, texture, use of light, and degree of detail. I also believe that I have a general understanding of the artists' techniques. But sometimes, when I study a Picasso painting, I wonder if, contrary to the curator's directives, the gallery staff hung his piece upside down by mistake. Unquestionably, his avant-garde works present more for me to wonder about than they do to simply view and admire. From what I read that afternoon, many of his contemporaries thought he was one of the biggest con artists ever to apply paint to canvas. And the negative critiques of his social life took many paragraphs also. He was anti-social, decadent, and degraded the women who loved him. According to one brief extract, Picasso's last wife shot herself, one of his mistresses committed suicide by hanging herself, and another went mad. Evidently, Picasso was not the kind of guy that a gal would want to find herself with on a blind date.

Reading on, I learned that Picasso and the French painter, Georges Braque, introduced Cubism to the world, and that Cubism is a method of creating a three-dimensional image on a flat surface without the proper use of perspective. Later, Picasso added collage, in which paper, string, wood, wire, and bits of flotsam became important media. He was born in 1881 in Málaga, Spain, and lived in Juan-les-Pins in the 1920s. He'd sleep late, take a swim in the sea, eat lunch on the beach with friends, and then work frantically from early afternoon until far into the night. In 1946, he continued this lifestyle and worked out of a studio in the medieval Château Grimaldi in Antibes, and from there he produced an amazing number of works. In all, Picasso produced more than 10,000 works of art over eighty years until his death in 1973.

Enlightened and inspired by this knowledge of art history, I walked over to a rack and selected four of the sharpest, most colourful postcards of Juan-les-Pins' sandy shores, and did so decisively, without having to spin the rack around more than twice.

10

Antibes:

Mega-yachts, Martinis, Millionaires, and Models

"*Bonsoir*, Mee-ster and Mee-ses Vancou-vair," Michel beamed as we approached the reception desk. "*Comment ça va?* 'ow was your day? *Très bon?* You 'ave much sun, yehz? Deed you go to Juan-les-Pins?" he asked without pausing for us to respond to each question.

"*Oui, très bon*. It was wonderful," we squeezed in, in duet, as we neared the top of the stairs.

"I 'ave, in your rum, poot some wine for—'ow you say?—your 'appiness 'ere at Hôtel Miramar," he shouted after us.

"*Merci beaucoup*, Michel. That's very kind of you."

A much-overlooked treat of staying at a hotel is returning to your room to find it clean and tidy. While we were away developing a suntan, swigging wine from a bottle, watching old men throw cannon balls, pulling on one-armed bandits, and reading about Picasso's many idiosyncrasies, the room, which we'd left in disarray, had been straightened, dusted, vacuumed, scrubbed, and polished. On the bed, clean sheets had been tucked in at the bottom and sides and folded back at the top exposing creaseless pillowslips, together with a perfectly positioned duvet. As a bonus, the staff had refilled the basket of soaps and shampoos, left the window slightly ajar, wrapped a "Sanitized" paper strip around the toilet seat, placed a wrapped chocolate on the pillows, and left the room smelling of flowers.

After stepping out of the shower, climbing over the bidet, and manoeuvring between the basin and toilet, I turned and caught a glimpse of my lily white rear end in the full-length mirror. After only one day soaking in the sun, my lobster pink back looked as if I had been sprayed with fluorescent pink paint—just as a boulder might be sprayed to prevent a sleepy-eyed bulldozer operator from driving into it during excavation. And I was quite disappointed that my skin showed no sign of turning bronze, *à la provençal* farmer or Coco Chanel client.

The evening beckoned and having discovered that all roads lead to the huge parking lot adjacent to the marina at Port Vauban Harbour, we drove back along the coast road to Antibes without glancing at our map. And, sure enough, as if on autopilot, we rolled through the parking lot entrance with the habitual ease of a local fisherman.

Instead of heading directly for the arched gateway of Porte Marine and beyond in search of a restaurant, we strolled the harbour walls and piers looking on in amazement at the many sleek, luxurious yachts tied up at them. Having no experience handling any type of watercraft, I couldn't begin to imagine the engineering and craftsmanship that must go into producing such works of beauty, performance, and luxury.

Port Vauban Harbour shelters some of the largest yachts in the world, and I doubt that their wealthy owners and crews would ever become complacent with the backdrop of Fort Carré and the snow-peaked Alps beyond. I read that the original port of Antibes was more of a sailors' retreat than a busy trading port, and the discovery of the Stone of Terpon—found in the harbour wall—with its phallic shape and inscription praising the physical rewards of love, suggests that brothels did a booming business.

Most of the yachts were berthed side by side with their stern facing the jetties. I assumed that such an orientation optimizes the harbour's berth capacity and makes it easier for boat owners, guests, and crew to step on and off board. Moreover, since the stern decks are open, curious onlookers can look in to the dining tables and chairs, dreaming and drooling over the built-in extravagances and expensive toys. From their strategic vantage point on these stern decks, the millionaires and their invited guests can look out upon the drooling dreamers while raising their martini glasses to toasts of never-ending financial success. The stern-to-jetty berthing also provides drooling dreamers an unobstructed view of the clever names that yacht owners have thought up and proudly display at the back of their floating status symbols. One English name, WAVES HELLO, was particularly imaginative—for an eight-year-old. Another, RICH BUT NOT FILTHY was blatantly boastful and NAUTICALLY NAUGHTY was nauseating. Below each name, in smaller letters, was the name of the port at which the boat was registered. Many of the ports were tax havens, a subtle reminder to drooling dreamers that many of these yacht owners have millions more stashed away elsewhere in U.S. cash, real estate, gold bars, and the best of Picasso's works of art.

As a child, I received a 5,000-piece jigsaw puzzle as a gift. The picture was of a harbour—similar to Port Vauban's—packed with yachts and sailboats. Many pieces contained a minuscule part of a sleek hull, a gleaming deck, a sheltered wheelhouse, a mast, a sail, a piece of rigging, or a chrome railing. Other than the straight-sided edge pieces, the ones that showed part of a flag were the easiest for me to identify and place into position. To those, I would add other pieces and build up the immediate surrounding picture until the puzzle was complete.

I believe it was this childhood pastime that initiated my interest in national flags, and so, as we strolled along, I took particular notice of the ones on the yachts and tried to recall the countries they represent. Many, of course, were the blue, white, and red vertical stripes of France; some were the green, white, and red vertical stripes of Italy. A few were flying the Union Jack of the United Kingdom and some flew the Stars and Stripes of the U.S.A. Many super-yachts were also flying the flags of tax havens: the Caymans, Bermuda, the Channel Islands, and so on. If Michel owned a boat, he would fly the French flag, and fluttering just below it the beige-and-green striped ensign of Hôtel Miramar. His boat would be named SOURIRE (smile). That one word would say it all.

Halfway along the row of bobbing fortunes, I caught sight of the unmistakable red-and-white flag of Canada, the Maple Leaf, fluttering atop a mast at the far end of the harbour. From that distance the flag would have covered a quarter of a piece of a jigsaw puzzle and yet it stood out from the kaleidoscopic scene like a lighthouse beam cutting the dark of night. Picking up our pace a little, ignoring other yachts, we headed towards it. On board were four smartly dressed young adults (two men and two women) having drinks at a table on its upper deck. We slowed our pace as we approached, and I was pleased to see a name that captured a dream of my own: SEEKING SUNSHINE. Not bad, I thought. Then I saw VANCOUVER in smaller letters below.

"Hi," I shouted. "We're from Vancouver," I continued, delighted at the coincidence.

"Hi. Is that right? D'ya wanna come aboard?" came the nonchalant reply from the older of the two men.

"That would be wonderful. Thank you," my wife replied.

"Yes please," I caught myself saying with the pleading inflection of a schoolboy accepting the offer of candy from a teacher. Before I knew it, we'd crossed the gangplank, boarded the craft, and were grabbing hold of the outstretched hands of the two young millionaire men as we stepped off the steep ladder onto the upper deck.

"We're having martinis. Would you care for one or would you prefer something else?" asked Hamilton Montgomery III, the older and more suntanned of the two men, who insisted we call him Monty.

"That would be wonderful," replied my wife, who was now sitting back comfortably with her legs crossed and her sunglasses perched fashionably above her forehead. She was smiling and making small talk with the two beautiful, tanned women—presumably, sought-after cover models for fashion magazines.

"Thank you very much indeed. A martini would be very nice," I slobbered with due reverence and humility. "So, how did you get here?" I asked, realizing the stupidity of my question the instant I'd blurted it out. I squirmed as I imagined one of them saying, "Oh yeah, we had the 500-ton yacht flown out of Vancouver to Nice airport. Then we had it trucked down here, where it was lowered into the water and tied up. We're taking it to the Seychelles next week provided there's a direct cargo flight available."

But instead the younger of the two wealthy adventurers, Richard Sanderson Jr, or Junior as he insisted we call him, explained: "We set off from Vancouver five months ago, brought her down the west coast via California, Mexico, Belize, Costa Rica, and Panama, through the canal and across the Caribbean to Puerto Rico. Then we made the long crossing of the Atlantic to the Canary Islands, and on to Gibraltar. For the past six weeks we've been making our way slowly along the northern coast of the Med, stopping at several Spanish and French ports, and now here we are in Antibes." He paused. "What about you? Done any sailing?" he asked cordially.

Not wanting to boast of my risky adventure peddling an enormous, white swan on a lifeguarded pond with my five-year-old niece as the boson, I responded with a modest, "Oh, just a little." Changing the subject, I began: "We've been away only a couple of days. We flew to Nice, rented a little Renault, and have a hotel room in Cap d'Antibes. We spent today on the beach at Juan-les-Pins, and this is our second evening visiting Antibes."

"Cool! That sounds *really* cool. Would you like another martini?" Monty asked.

Feeling much more relaxed around our new acquaintances, I began to settle into our luxurious surroundings. As the second martini—complete with two green olives on a swizzle stick—was placed on the table in front of me, I looked out over Port Vauban Harbour for the first time since boarding. Standing on the jetty, looking up at us sipping our martinis, were several tourists. I felt that I should shout to them that I too was a drooling dreamer unworthy of mingling with millionaires, but instead I enjoyed the pretence for a few seconds and then turned my attention back to our new friends. Judging by their laughter and chatter, the three women were getting along very well.

"Steve, where are you guys going for dinner?" asked Junior.

"We're not sure. Somewhere in the old town, I suppose."

"D'ya wanna tag along with us? We know a great place."

"Sure, that sounds like fun," I grinned. My wife smiled and nodded in agreement. Our new friends put away the bottles and glasses and battened down the hatches (or whatever it is that has to be done when leaving a yacht unoccupied), and then the six of us strolled off in the direction of Porte Marine and the narrow streets of old Antibes. Who could have guessed what would soon be revealed.

11

Antibes:

Fancy Names, Wrong Labels, and Cat-astrophes

We followed rue Aubernon to Cours Masséna, where we shuffled around the outer aisle of the busy covered food market that specializes in fruits, vegetables, and hand-stuffed sausages. Around us many small cafés catered to vendors and shoppers alike, and our conversation turned to the shop window displays, the many varieties of eateries, and the attractive flower-bedecked houses.

During the quiet moments while walking alongside Monty and Junior, with the three women chatting behind, I wondered about their names. Why had their parents named them so? Fleetingly, I imagined how they were addressed as babies—surely not, "Goochy, goo. Who's a cute little Hamilton Montgomery the Third?" For him, the nickname Monty was a good choice. It's suitable for a baby and a young boy; it's familiar enough for his adult friends and associates; and it conveys strength and authority when wheeling and dealing in the dog-eat-dog business world. With the future in mind, his parents had anticipated that his full name, Hamilton Montgomery III, would look good listed on the Board of Directors of any corporation.

My parents probably had enough of a challenge to agree upon Stephen. To think of a middle name, not to mention a suffixed mini-title, would have been unthought-of in their working-class circles. My name carries no clout, no authority, there's no suggestion of coming from well-bred, upper-class stock. I couldn't even boast of having letters after my name. The closest I came was when a professor told me that I might be accepted as a "licentiate" by the Institute of Mechanical Engineers. But I decided against his suggestion because I didn't like the way the suffix letters "Lic. ME." looked or sounded. I was seeking respect, not sniggers and ridicule.

We continued down several narrow, poorly lit streets until we came to the restaurant recommended by our new friends. The thought occurred to me that we might be headed to a millionaires' hideaway and a menu listing dishes at millionaires' prices. But as we entered the bistro, I was relieved to discover that it was charming and quite unpretentious. A sign announcing LOCAL HAND-STUFFED SAUSAGES as the evening's special was my initial inkling.

A waiter doubling as maître d' showed us to our table. Continuing to impress, Monty was fluent in French and helped us to interpret the menu. He ordered bread and a litre of red wine, and within minutes of being seated we were all sipping *vin de la maison* and biting into slices of baguette. From the bantering back and forth with Monty, I realized that our waiter had served our friends on previous occasions. Turning my attention from one to the other—like a spectator watching a game of tennis—I tried to understand what was being said, but failed miserably. As the waiter spoke, I found his animated gestures and facial expressions fascinating. How French, I thought. But then I wondered if, like Pierre at the bistro Chez Michel, he too had originated from somewhere between Wollongong and Burragorang.

"Monty, what size is the boat?" I enquired with genuine interest.

"Thirty-five metres or about 110 feet. Officially, it's ranked as a super-yacht, just five metres short of the minimum mega-yacht length," he replied. He followed that with a series of figures and letters, the word "horsepower," and a name that I believed was the manufacturer of the diesel engines.

"Wow!" I sighed. "What would a boat of that size cost?"

"Eighteen point five," was his nonchalant and succinct reply. I didn't think it necessary to ask for clarification. I simply assumed he had purposely omitted "million dollars" from his answer.

"Wow!" I sighed again.

"Yeah, but I tell ya, it's the running and maintenance costs that are exorbitant. You can figure almost a tenth of that, say, one point five a year to keep it operational."

"Wow!" I sighed again, thinking I've got to stop saying "Wow!"

"Something else to take into consideration is the rate at which they depreciate. It's unbelievable," added Monty with a shake of his head. "After a few years, a yacht may be worth only 50 per cent of its purchase price. Oh, and for a mega-yacht, you can figure on an initial outlay of a million bucks per metre. And with needing a crew of about twenty or more, you cannot begin to even imagine the operational costs," he concluded.

"Wow!" I mouthed, this time without making a sound. Then my curiosity, bolstered by the effects of the wine, got the better of me. "May I ask a personal question?"

"Fire away," he smiled and took a sip from his wine glass.

"How old are you, Monty?"

"Thirty-one," he answered, still smiling.

"So, how do you do it?" I hedged the question.

"How do I do what, Steve?"

"The boat, Monty, the boat," I blurted. "The eighteen point five million, the one point five every year, the expensive toys, the five months away from the office, how is it possible for a thirty-one-year-old to afford all that?" I continued, realizing that my tone might be revealing a slight inflection of envy.

"Steve, you've got it all wrong. I'm not the owner, I'm a yachtie," he beamed. "We're all yachties. We're four of a crew of ten. We were taken on in Vancouver and are along for a little paid adventure. We don't get paid much at all. And while on duty, which is most of the time, the work is demanding and boring. But it's times like this when we pull into port and the owner goes off for a few days that we're able to relax, grab some rays, and take in the local scenery," he explained.

Goodness! Never judge a book by its cover, I thought. Then Junior added, "Antibes is inundated with yachties. Many jump ship here in their quest to globetrot via the world's waterways. But, like Monty said, it doesn't pay well at all. Sure, the life of a yachtie sounds exciting, and at times it is, but no one gets rich doing it for a living."

"Interesting," I said, noticing that my tone had switched from utter amazement to sympathy. "What do you do when you're not crewing, when you're back in Vancouver?" I asked with increasing curiosity.

"I taught tennis during the day and worked as a waiter in the evening until this came up," answered Junior.

"And you, Monty?"

"Oh, I've done a bit of everything: painting, decorating, gardening, carpentry, and waiting on tables. I was looking for work up in Whistler so that I could ski during my free time, but then I heard of this great opportunity to crew and jumped at it."

"What about your families? Where are they? What do *they* think of you taking off like this?" I delved.

"My parents passed away a few years ago in a car crash. A drunk driver hit them head on," volunteered Monty. "I'm the only child. I have an aunt and uncle and several cousins living in Montreal. I get to see them once in a while. But that's it for family."

I looked at Junior. "I don't remember my father. He left us when I was a baby. My mother remarried and is living down in Louisiana with a guy she met on a cruise to Alaska. I don't care for him and he doesn't care for me. I have an older sister who lives in Calgary. She's married to a guy who sells pipe fittings to oil companies. He spends much of his time away from home and too much time in bars. I got to see them last Christmas, but he was drunk. He ruined the holidays for everyone," said Junior reflectively.

"I'm so sorry," I said, as I ruminated on how alcohol had impacted their lives. We fell quiet; it was one of those awkward, silent moments.

Noticing the change in our mood, my wife, who had been chatting and giggling like a schoolgirl with the other women, said, "Steve, Karen was just telling us about her Siamese cat, and it reminded me of when you took yours along with you to Italy. Tell them that story."

Feeling the pressure of having been pushed into the spotlight at centre stage, I told them about the unforgettable flight I'd taken many years ago on my way to Rome to start a long-term assignment. Before boarding, I'd fed Suki, my seal-point Siamese cat, a sedative and then placed her into a carry-on cage that fit under my seat. By about midnight, as we were halfway over the Atlantic, the effects of the pill wore off and Suki began to cry. With another pill at the ready, I pulled out the cage, opened its lid, and grabbed Suki by the scruff of her neck. Groggy and scared out of her mind, she frantically and instinctively clawed her way up my arm to higher ground: the top of my chair's headrest. Clinging on to it in terror, she stared and hissed at the woman sitting directly behind me. The unsuspecting woman, who'd been engrossed in the inflight movie, gave out a long, shrill scream and then shouted, "Where the hell did that come from?" Her scream startled awake her neighbours who, fearing the worst, thought they'd never see Saint Peter's Cathedral but that they were only moments away from meeting Saint Peter face-to-face.

Our seafaring friends were suitably amused, and for the next couple of hours we ate our delicious hand-stuffed sausages and laughed at their hijinks on the high seas. Once we'd finished with dessert and emptied our coffee cups, our waiter brought over the bill and placed it on the table between Monty and me. I picked it up, looked at the bottom line, and then glanced over at my wife who smiled approvingly as I handed over my credit card.

The evening air was still warm as we all strolled back to the parking lot to check on Twingo. Satisfied that it would be safe enough to leave overnight, we said goodbye to our new friends and returned to Porte Marine in search of a taxi to take us safely back to Hôtel Miramar. Considering Monty's and Junior's sad stories, one would think that, after a few drinks, taking a taxi back to the hotel was the sensible thing to do. Having said that, you'll understand why I began to second-guess my decision when our kamikaze driver, obviously under the influence, took the corners back to Hôtel Miramar on two wheels. By the time we'd said, *"Hôtel Miramar, s'il vous plaît,"* and looked up the French equivalent of "Slow down please before I soil my pants," we'd arrived back at the hotel.

12

Cannes:

Croissants, Poodles, and Promenades

Feeling anxious about having abandoned our car in Antibes, we decided to skip breakfast at the hotel and take a taxi to the parking lot, then drive to Cannes where we would sit in the sun at a café on boulevard de la Croisette—the most renowned promenade on the Riviera—and have a *petit déjeuner* of café au lait and croissants. While negotiating our way around the obstacle course of porcelain fixtures within the ablution space, we giggled like kids as we repeated the tongue twister: "Croissants on Croisette, croissants on Croisette."

"*Bonjour*, Mee-ster and Mee-ses Vancou-vair," came the familiar greeting as we exited Hôtel Miramar and stepped out into the sunshine. Michel was about to get into his car.

"*Bonjour*, Michel," we responded.

"Where ees your Renault? I 'ave not seen eet. Eet ees not 'ere, of that I am cer-tain," he went on.

"We left it in Antibes last night. We'll walk to the corner and get a taxi," I explained, cognizant of enunciating my words more slowly and louder than I would to an Anglophone.

"You moost go weez me. I go now to Antibes in my auto. You moost go weez me, *absolument*," he insisted, as he beckoned to us with one hand and opened a rear door with the other.

"*Merci beaucoup, Michel*," we answered in unison as we slid onto the back seat. "It's another beautiful day," I continued, experimenting no further with my French and keeping my English small-talk small.

"*Certainement! C'est magnifique.* Eet ees sunshine all day, every day. Eet ees glori-uz, *oui?*"

"Yes, today is glorious," I replied to his reflection in the rear-view mirror. "Are you going to Antibes for more food supplies?" I asked, doubting that he would understand the word "supplies."

"*Oui*, for bread and wine," he beamed.

It was still early and only a few joggers, dog walkers, and fishermen were out and about. A team of municipal workers had already raked clean the upper section of the beach, and the entire lower section had been washed and ironed smooth by the receding tide. The sand looked inviting, as if patiently awaiting the onslaught of fun-lovers. An hour or two later, the neatly groomed surface would be transformed into a mishmash of footprints, sandcastles, and imprints of every beach accessory imaginable.

Michel tooted his horn, and I looked up to see that we were approaching a roundabout. I made a mental note that he, too, took this precaution at TOUTES DIRECTIONS signs, as I checked the road for black streaks of rubber—evidence of last night's drag race back to the hotel with our inebriated taxi driver.

Before I knew it, we were in Antibes. Not knowing exactly where we were, we looked around to get our bearings. Michel pointed in the direction of a narrow passageway. "You moost go there. One 'undred metres, no more. Turn left and you 'ave Port Vauban. Eet ees where your auto ees, *oui?*" Michel smiled as we nodded our understanding of where to go. "I go 'ere," he said as he turned around and pointed to an old church. "Yehz, eet ees 'ere I go for my bread and wine—at mass." He giggled like a child telling his first joke. "*Au revoir*, 'ave a fantas-teek day," he said, then turned, walked up several stone steps to the huge wooden doors, waved back at us, smiled again, and then disappeared inside.

Crossing the deserted parking lot, I was pleased to see that Twingo was still there and that, despite the car's abandoned air, so too were its four wheels. But as we got closer, I noticed a piece of paper trapped under a wiper blade and suspected it was a parking ticket. I cursed under my breath, retrieved the paper, and read: "Thanks for dinner, eh! Leaving tomorrow, eh! Take care, eh! Have a great holiday, eh! Cheers, *Canadian Yachties.*" I smiled wryly. We turned to the jumble of masts at the far end of the harbour and spotted the Maple Leaf still fluttering in the breeze. Without a word, we set off for SEEKING SUNSHINE. Unfortunately, there was no sign of life aboard the yacht. The gangplank had been retracted and the doors were shut. There was no sound of music, and no aroma of coffee brewing or of bacon frying. I shouted several times, but no one was home. Obviously our Canadian friends had got an early start to the day—probably shopping for supplies in preparation for the next leg of their voyage. Perhaps they were at the market buying bags of fruits, vegetables, and hand-stuffed sausages. Or perhaps they too were at church. Wondering if we'd ever see them again, we wrote them a note. "Don't hit any rocks, eh! Take care, eh! See you in Vancouver, eh! Cheers, *Drooling Dreamers.*"

Our drive west along the coast road to Cannes was very pleasant and free of drivers qualifying for the Monaco Grand Prix. On the way we stopped briefly in Golfe-Juan. We'd read that Golfe-Juan is popular with the locals because the beach is free—free of pay-as-you-lay establishments. We parked Twingo and strolled down to the attractive marina where we came upon a brass plaque that commemorates the spot where Napoleon returned to France on March 1, 1815, after his exile on the Isle of Elba.

As we turned onto the beautiful, palm-lined boulevard de la Croisette, Cannes looked prosperous with its luxurious hotels; upscale shops; manicured lawns; semi-tropical gardens; high-end, pay-as-you-lay beach establishments; and an attractive harbour filled with sleek, gleaming yachts. As we parked—between a Rolls-Royce and a full-size Mercedes—in front of an outdoor café, common sense forewarned me to expect a large bill for croissants on Croisette.

Nothing in life is perfect, not even the picture of us sipping café au lait in the sunshine on boulevard de la Croisette looking out between palms and over flower beds at the beautiful bay, Golfe de la Napoule. Sitting at the table to our left was a wiry old woman. Attached to a leash and sitting on the ground between us was her wiry, old dog—a white poodle. Madame was petite and sun-wrinkled, and was wearing a ring on each finger, several bracelets on each wrist, dangly earrings on both lobes, and a string of pearls around her neck.

Madame, or some other vision-impaired person, had applied an overdose of rouge to her cheeks, bright red lipstick beyond the perimeter of her lips, and two black-arched lines to her forehead—half an inch above where her eyebrows used to be before havoc was unleashed with a pair of tweezers. Even though it was warm in the shade of our umbrellas, she wore a black hat that had a barely visible black veil hanging down from its brim, a fox-fur stole around her shoulders, a long-sleeved black silk blouse, a side-slit black skirt, a pair of black fishnet pantyhose (or thigh-high stockings—I didn't ask), and a pair of high-heeled black suede shoes. My guess at her bathroom-scale weight would have the pointer indicating no higher than forty kilograms (ninety pounds), but her street weight—taking into account her winter clothes, her display-case load of jewellery, and her dead fox—would be twice that. If she were to trip and fall into the harbour, she would sink to the seabed quicker than a mega-yacht's anchor. And to quote Michel: "Of that I am cer-tain."

It wasn't her distinctive apparel that ruined the picture—it was the white poodle. The dog would not stop yapping. Madame, apparently oblivious or stone deaf, sipped from her cup and nibbled on her croissant without so much as registering a frown, or giving a gentle tug on the dog's leash. Meanwhile, Noodle the Poodle—a pink ribbon tied in a bow on her head, shaved bald areas over most of her body, and fluffed-up pompoms at her feet and the tip of her tail—yapped on incessantly. It yapped at people, cars, and dogs passing by, and for no other apparent reason. Driven to the verge of force-feeding the poodle a shoe sandwich, I threw her a piece of croissant without Madame (or the dead fox) seeing the sneaky move. Noodle would be silent for only a moment, but would start yapping again until I broke off another tidbit and threw it her way. And so it went until Madame finished her breakfast, got up from her table, and set off walking towards the harbour, dragging the bitch behind.

Unperturbed, my wife had been reading our guidebook. And as I sipped on another café au lait, she shared what she'd learned. Cannes was a simple fishing port until 1834 when Lord Brougham and his sick daughter, Eleanor, stopped over on a get-away-from-it-all-and-recover holiday. Brougham, who was the Lord Chancellor of England, not only detested the miserable English winter weather but was also burned out from leading the movement to abolish slavery. He was so enamoured by the climate and beauty of the area, he had a villa built and returned to it every winter. News of this spread among his peers and it wasn't long before escaping the winter became fashionable for the English nobility, and, eventually, Cannes became famous.

And it was Brougham who was responsible for creating the boulevard de la Croisette, now a promenade for the fashion-conscious masses to saunter and strut along. Poseurs galore flaunt their fur coats and dead foxes in tropical weather; curvy bodies in colourful, skin-tight athletic gear whiz by on in-line skates while talking on their cell phones; young men lean against late-model Italian sports cars; and fashionable young women wear sunglasses at night—without the need of white canes.

Contrasting dramatically to the fishing port of 1834, Cannes today is both a tourist resort and a convention town, and it's particularly famous for its annual film festival. It appeals to those with expensive tastes and large bank balances, and to those who need to escape miserable weather and develop a suntan. It's a place where millionaires have been heard to "tut tut" over their morning champagne and freshly squeezed orange juice after reading that there are now only twenty compact cars to every Rolls-Royce. Still, as Lord Brougham understood, Cannes is a great place to pass the winter, with or without a sick daughter. But do what you can to avoid the poodles and the noodles on boulevard de la Croisette.

13

Cannes:

Wedding Cake, Cleavage, and Red Carpets

We strolled wide-eyed along the boulevard de la Croisette in search of more ostentatious affluence in the form of the InterContinental Carlton Hotel, which we'd read about after our tense *petit déjeuner* with Noodle the tense poodle. The Carlton is the oldest and most famous of the Riviera's seafront palace-hotels and its front elevation has been emblematic of Cannes since its doors first opened. It has a terrace-level brasserie where high-society members and impostors go to see and be seen. But of more interest to *this* impostor were the building's main neoclassic architectural features—great examples of Belle-Époque craftsmanship and extravagance—which made it resemble a wedding cake with a pair of huge breasts on its roof pointing skyward.

It all began with a love story, then a love triangle. It may end in a Hollywood movie. I interpreted the essence of the screenplay this way. Once upon a time in the early 1900s, Henri Ruhl, an accomplished builder, and Charles Delmas, an accomplished architect, decided to design and build an all-white palace-hotel primarily to receive royalty and wealthy guests from all over Europe. Now, while Henri and Charles were staying in Nice, with their shirt sleeves rolled up and their noses to the drawing board, Henri fell in love with a local actress and courtesan—the half-gypsy, Caroline Otero. As any lovesick man would do, he grovelled on his hands and knees, begging and pleading with her to leave her high-society friends and her lifestyle in Monte-Carlo and

---

Nice and shack up with him in Cannes. Alas, he was unable to persuade her and so they split. Rejected and dejected, Henri channelled his energy, creativity, testosterone, and investors' money into completing the construction of the hotel. Now, what Henri didn't realize was that Charles had also fallen in love with Caroline, and he too had begged and pleaded with her to leave Monaco and Nice and shack up with *him* in Cannes. But alas, he too was unable to persuade her. Rejected and dejected, Charles channelled all his energy into revising the roof design to incorporate Caroline's most memorable feature, the voluptuous twin cupolas with nipple-globes atop. And there you have it, the premise for the screenplay of an epic that could rival *Gone with the Wind*.

Leaving the shadows of the palms, we crossed the boulevard to the seafront promenade. As we sauntered along, I noticed that each private pay-as-you-lay establishment displayed a rating sign beside its name. Unlike the star symbols used to rate hotels or the red-chilli-pepper symbols used to rate spicy dishes, these establishments were rated with lifebuoys. Apparently, four lifebuoys indicate the best quality and most expensive pay-as-you-lay services.

Giving this more thought, I supposed that people who bathe at one-lifebuoy establishments do so in the hope that one day, when their financial advisors actually give them some worthwhile advice for better returns on their investments, they will move up to two-lifebuoy establishments. People who bathe at two-lifebuoy establishments are probably waiting for an inheritance to be dead sure of being able to afford the move up to a three-lifebuoy establishment. People who bathe at three-lifebuoy establishments are trusting that their first nomination at the Cannes Film Festival will bring a starring role and heaps more money, thereby enabling them to afford to mingle with other rich and famous four-lifebuoy bathers.

But then I began to question the appropriateness of the symbol. As a lifebuoy would be thrown to someone to help prevent them from drowning, are we to presume that the rich and famous, who roll off their sun lounges and bounce off the jetty into the sea, would be thrown four lifebuoys? Or are the signs a bit more subtle? Perhaps a one-lifebuoy rating is indicative of those closest to drowning in debt. So, wouldn't the outline of a bottle of sunscreen be more appropriate than that of a lifebuoy? Or how about simply displaying one to four dollar ($) or euro (€) symbols? Or would that be considered inappropriate because it's too—how should I put it?—appropriate?

Viewing the front of the Carlton from the promenade, we understood why it was likened to a wedding cake. Not that it was the traditional multi-tiered, cylindrical shape; rather, it was oblong. Only seven floors high but wider than the length of a football field, it stands symmetrical about its central entranceway and, despite rumours of a planned change to its exterior colour scheme, is painted entirely in white. Its façade encompasses a mass of reliefs and evenly spaced, tall and narrow French doors that open out onto small balconies with ornate wrought-iron railings. And, yes, if you squint, all the architectural features look like intricately piped icing on the sides of a wedding cake. And on the roof, at either end of the main oblong section of the hotel, a rotunda supports a domed cupola—together representing Caroline Otero's breasts. But as the cupolas are hundreds of feet apart, it makes for one very disappointing cleavage.

After observing the four-lifebuoy rating of the Carlton's private beach, we took a close look at the lunch menu in the glass case by its entranceway. I focused specifically on the number of euros tagged on to the end of each exotically described dish, and the figures suggested that an extra zero had been added by mistake.

The beach and the hotel's wooden jetty were covered in a row of blue-and-white umbrellas and many bright yellow chaise lounges and mattresses. Considering the four-lifebuoy admission price, I was surprised to see how many people were already settling into position with Carlton monogrammed towels, trendy fashion magazines, cell phones, cigarettes and cigars, fancy drinks, and designer sunglasses and swimwear. Not that the women were wearing much in the way of swimwear, as the Carlton beach is a T.O.B. And there was certainly no need for me to strain my eyes to notice that each of the many pairs of exposed, skyward-pointing cupolas presented more attractive cleavages than the one of the hotel's roofline.

Accepting that we would barely qualify as one-lifebuoy bathers, we decided not to cross back over the boulevard, enter the hotel, and attempt to impersonate high-society members on the terrace-level brasserie. Besides, dressed in shorts and T-shirts, we knew that our true one-champagne-glass rating would be spotted immediately, and deny us entry. Instead, with plans of buying another picnic lunch, we walked on towards the port and the Palais des Festivals.

Being avid moviegoers, we were interested in seeing The Bunker, the largest and most famous of the twelve theatres used during the Cannes Film Festival in May each year. The building is a massive concrete structure that seats 2,400. Surrounding the building is Allée des Étoiles (Stars' Alley), a concrete sidewalk with the autographed handprints of over 300 stars set into small clay tiles. Several of the celebrity squares had been the recipients of dog poop, and I wondered if the desecrating canines had left their droppings behind indiscriminately or as a critique of the stars' most recent performances. Running up a flight of concrete stairs and in through the entrance to the foyer was a red carpet which, I believed, had been deliberately left in place to help visitors imagine the "action" during the ten-day spectacle.

Most of the "action" during the festival is performed by female stars (and females accompanying male stars). To meet the demand for titillating photographs of exposed skin and cleavage demanded by entertainment-crazed readers and TV viewers around the world, the paparazzi focus their telescopic lenses specifically on what these women are wearing—and not wearing—as they slowly ascend the red-carpeted stairs. As critical as I may sound, if it's on TV, I usually remain tuned in long enough to check out which nominee for Best Supporting Actress has been blessed with the best, and what, if anything, is supporting them.

Apparently, Cannes' tourist population triples to 70,000 visitors during the festival. Of those, 7,000 are names in the business, many of whom have attained four-lifebuoy ratings and four-champagne-glass status and, therefore, qualify to stay at the Carlton or one of the other three seafront palace-hotels. And more than 3,000 are journalists and paparazzi and, of those who work for the smaller newspapers and magazines, many stay at the one-star hotels in the seedier section of town by the railway station. To impress the crowds of visitors and TV audiences around the world, Cannes ensures it is looking its best each May. Its beaches are raked—even disinfected—daily, and gardeners galore trim the palms, mow the lawns, and tend to the magnificent floral arrangements that require in excess of 400,000 plants each year.

If I were the mayor of Cannes sitting behind a Louis XIV desk in the Hôtel de Ville, I would impose a ten-day bylaw during the festival that prohibits yappy little dogs from yapping, and another bylaw that demands that dog owners carry a scoop for poop clean-up. Harsh as it may seem, anyone caught contravening my laws wouldn't be allowed outdoors wearing jewellery, make-up, or furs for twelve months.

Standing in front of The Bunker, we referred to our guidebook. It informed us that the festival is also known for its outlandish behaviour, including over-the-top displays of affluence, like hiring an entire circus to help publicize *Around the World in 80 Days* and having guests smash over 5,000 champagne glasses at a party given by the Greeks to promote *Never on Sunday*.

I reflected on those extravagances and how they contrasted to my impoverished start in life. Anyone walking by our two-up-two-down row house on a working-class street in England (it was condemned by the local council to be demolished twenty years before we moved in) could see that ours was not a family of sound financial means. In those days, if my behaviour was outrageous, I was chastised—dare I say, even spanked. If I boasted, I was brought down a peg or two. The highlight of my entertainment was a Saturday matinée at the movies. And once a year, my parents would take me to see an epic—like *Around the World in 80 Days*.

Other than that, my entertainment was kicking an old plastic soccer ball around the streets with neighbourhood kids or playing self-created word games with my sisters. A circus was something I only read about in books. Lavish was having a lamb chop and three veggies for dinner. If I left a scrap of food on my plate, I was reminded of the children dying of starvation in Africa. If I broke a cup or a plate while washing the dishes, I was reprimanded and unnecessarily informed that money doesn't grow on trees. In one corner of our living room was a wall cabinet that displayed tacky ornaments and souvenirs from occasional trips to the seaside. Also on display were two champagne glasses— Christmas gifts to my parents—used only on New Year's Eve to drink a toast to continued blessings throughout the coming year. My parents worked hard to provide for us, they encouraged us, sacrificed for us, disciplined us, and guided us as best they could. In short, they loved us.

Feeling a little guilty in knowing how much my cup now overflows, I suggested we walk to Le Suquet—the oldest part of town—and to the lookout point at the top of the hill for a picnic of champagne and lamb chops. Understandably, my wife frowned at the suggested picnic items as we strolled away, leaving my profound thoughts to evaporate into the hot air that enveloped the vacant grey bunker and the empty red carpet. My next thought was about lunch, and my hope was that it be free of yapping poodles.

14

Le Suquet:

George, Jack, Casanova, Michael, and Zorro

Described as an old, picturesque hillside town of steep and narrow cobbled streets and passageways, Le Suquet is just a stone's throw from the four-lifebuoy-rated glitz and glamour of Cannes' seafront. As we strolled along rue St-Antoine, I nodded good morning to an old man sitting smoking a pipe beside a beautifully crafted wooden door set into Gothic stonework. He smiled at us and raised his glass of wine. Farther along, a woman wearing a headscarf and an apron was sweeping dust from her doorstep with a straw broom. We wandered into an alley shaded by criss-crossing clotheslines hung with underwear, shirts and floral bed sheets flapping in the breeze. I photographed window boxes bursting with geraniums and brilliant red bougainvillea vines climbing sun-drenched façades, trellises, and stone archways.

Le Suquet has its fair share of small shops offering local goods, craftworks, and souvenirs beautifully displayed in their windows enticing soon-to-be-departing tourists to enter, peruse, select, and buy. Also, there are plenty of bistros and small restaurants. Several—all distinguished by artistically arranged table linens, shade umbrellas, and the prospect of dining *al fresco*—lure customers to their tables with a specific theme. Famous movies seems to be the most popular.

"George, look at that place over there, it's called *Out of Africa.* Doesn't it look nice, George? Look at that one over there. It's called *Barbarella.* Look at those lovely table settings. Let's sit outside and eat at that one, George."

Although we had every intention of buying picnic food, it was the smell of garlic cooking in oil that lured us past a small grocery store and up a steep and narrow side alley to its source: a small exhaust vent in the front wall of a charming little eatery, Bistro Casanova.

The waiter, who came to greet us at the display menu (mounted upon an easel in the alley), beckoned us into the shade of an umbrella in a cunning attempt to get us to commit to eating there. On seeing my victory sign of two raised fingers, he grasped that not only would we require a table for two but also help with our French. Our tall, dark, and handsome waiter smiled, showed us to a table, and helped my wife with the final adjustment of her chair. Using the tips of his thumb and first finger, he plucked her folded linen napkin from an empty water glass and shook it open with a flick of his wrist—like a magician unveiling a silk scarf before making it disappear into thin air—then spread it over her lap and fussed with its edges until he was happy that it was perfectly positioned. Thankfully, Casanova stopped short of tucking one corner of it into her waistband. He left me to fend for myself—not that I've ever been so weak from hunger that I've needed help unfolding a napkin. With raised eyebrows and wearing a smarmy smile, Casanova rushed away stroking his black moustache with two short swipes of his right index finger—just like a villain in an old silent movie. In an instant, he returned with a menu. "*Voilà! Madame, le menu en anglais,*" he said, and then, turning to me, added the translation: "The menu, eet ees een Eeng-leesh."

I would never have guessed.

As we sipped on chilled rosé wine and nibbled on bread sticks, waiting for our *salade Niçoise* to be served, we watched people on the street below. The local women were slim and petite, typical of the women we'd seen since arriving on the Riviera. In stark contrast, the typical North American tourist was overweight. And, dressed in a floppy broad-brim hat and a bright, tight-fitting top and shorts, and carrying a large fanny pack and drowning in photographic equipment, they could be spotted and heard a mile away.

"Hey Jack, won't ya jus' look at that priddy store. Ain't that tha cutest store ya ever did see? Whaddya think? Should I take a photo or are you going to shoot some video? Look at that cute vase in tha window. Hey, they only want 5,000 euros for it. What's that in dollars, Jack? That would look great by the pool. We could get them to ship it. Hey, look at those clothes hanging up there in that alley. Ain't they got dryers? But ain't that cute, Jack?"

Generally, North Americans accumulate things to excess: body mass, baggage, bank balances, and vocal expressions, but when it comes to excess in fashion, Europeans have us beat. From our three-square-metre observation deck at Bistro Casanova, we were able to zoom in on a young couple that was strolling along hand in hand speaking Italian. Naturally, I first noticed the tall, slim, young woman. Her purple hair had been gelled into a single row of extraordinarily long spikes that fanned out from her skull. Her platform-soled, black, leather boots ended just short of her kneecaps, and her short, black leather skirt ended just short of indecency. Her white bustier was strapless, ribbed, elasticized, and under-wired, and yet there was so little to it. Very feminine and very sexy, it covered some of her middle and pushed up her top—a great engineering marvel and an uplifting experience for both wearer and beholder.

Unlike most young women, her skin was unblemished, like white porcelain. A sparkling stone attached to a ring speared her navel. Barely protruding above her belt was the top of a tattoo. I suspected that her make-up had been applied by an artist—the struggling, starving type—who loved Picasso's work. Her lips and fingernails were black, and her black eye shadow covered such an extensive area that she resembled a large raccoon, but I could only assume that she was on her way to a fancy dress party as Futuristic Zorro. One nostril displayed a sparkling stone similar to the one she had pinned to her navel, and one ear had so many rings dangling from it that had a breeze picked up, they would have sounded like wind chimes.

The guy was handsome and reminded me of Michael J. Fox. He

wore a lightweight, stone-grey suit and a white shirt unbuttoned to his navel to reveal a deep golden suntan. Oddly, he was barefooted and, just like Michael J. Fox, he was short. So short, in fact, that he would have to stand on his tiptoes for his eyes to come level with the top of Futuristic Zorro's bustier and its voluptuous contents. I considered his shortcoming a dreadful blow of fate. He was carrying a small plastic bottle with a spray nozzle, and at about every tenth stride he would point the nozzle square at his face, pull the trigger, and spray himself— I assumed with water to cool down. Considering the blazing sunshine and hot cobblestones, and the possibility of stepping in dog poop, I was surprised he didn't direct the spray at his feet.

By the time we'd finished our *hors d'oeuvres* it was plain to see, from the giggles and outbursts of laughter from the English women at neighbouring tables, that Casanova's flirtatiousness and wit were being well received. Then, when Casanova came to clear away our plates, my wife asked him innocently, "What is the catch of the day?" In the absence of a drum roll, but with perfect timing and absolute predictability, he answered, "Eet ees me, of course," and beamed triumphantly. Then he added unnecessarily, "*I* am the catch of the day."

"So go cook yourself!" I thought. Had he replied, "Swordfish," I fantasized him tripping on his way out of the kitchen and skewering himself, harakiri-style. Clearly I needed to lighten up before his stand-up routine triggered a serious bout of indigestion.

Satisfied with our delicious meal, especially the *salade Niçoise,* we paid the bill and left Bistro Casanova, our waiter, and the tables of English women buzzing with the possibility of a torrid holiday romance. Continuing up the cobbled slopes, we eventually came to place de la Castre at the top of Le Suquet's hill—identified on our map as Mont Chevalier. From that lookout point we had wonderful views along the shore to the east and west, inland to La Californie, and out from the shore at the Îles de Lérins to the south. Cannes seafront looked resplendent and prosperous; its golden beaches glistened and the azure sea sparkled under the bright sun and clear, blue skies.

Atop Le Suquet's hill were several interesting buildings, including the historic Château de Cannes, with its imposing 11th-century square tower, Tour Sarrasine; the 12th-century Chapelle Ste-Anne; and the 17th-century Notre-Dame d'Espérance church.

Like most females, my wife loves to attend or watch weddings on TV. So when she noticed rose petals scattered about the front steps of Notre-Dame d'Espérance, she scanned the area in the hope of seeing newlyweds having their photographs taken. In the absence of ringing bells, wedding guests, or ribbon-decorated cars, she concluded that the trail had grown cold. Somewhat disappointed, she insisted we enter the church to see if vases of flowers remained or if candles had been left burning. Had that been the case, she would have stayed for a while and relived the highlights of our wedding day over and over. I would have taken a nap.

Stepping out of the sunshine into the shade of the church was like stepping out of a sauna into an igloo—not that I've ever done that or ever will. After adjusting to the coolness and lack of light, we slowly made our way to the main altar and sat down in the first row of old wooden pews. There were no bouquets of flowers and, as far as I was aware, no other people. The only sounds were roof beams creaking periodically and what sounded to me like a boiler's relief valve letting out a little steam every ten seconds or so. After reflecting upon how exciting it was to be on holiday and how we had been blessed with a wonderful marriage and a bountiful life in Canada, we whispered a simple prayer of thanksgiving and then got up to leave. As we turned to walk back up the central aisle, I caught a glimpse of the outline of someone in the shadows kneeling in prayer. It was the unmistakable profile of Futuristic Zorro's equally spaced spokes of purple hair. And though I couldn't see her footloose-and-fancy-free companion, I knew he was there because what I thought to be a hiss of steam every ten seconds was now identifiable as the Michael J. Fox look-alike spraying himself square in the face.

15

Cannes:

Markets, Boutiques, and a Plan of Escape

At the bottom of Le Suquet's hill, we strolled through the busy covered market at rue du Marché Forville. Although the morning rush was long since over, there was still plenty of commotion about the place, which was exhilarating but at times almost deafening. Especially loud were the vendors shouting to the no-time-to-waste, looking-for-a-bargain, last-minute shoppers. Local fishermen and their wives broadcasting their pre-dawn catch were noticeably louder than the local farmers and their wives advertising their morning-fresh produce. And like most markets, it was a jumbled mass of colours, smells, noises, and frenzied movement. Organized chaos best described the higgledy-piggledy arrangement of goods, produce, boxes, sacks, cartons, tables, and stalls. Bruised fruit, vegetable leaves, crustacean shells, toothpicks, wrappings, straw, and other packing stuff lay around on the floor with the usual paper coffee cups and cigarette butts. Having taken several artsy photographs, consumed several free samples, and gesticulated our way out of purchasing a five-litre jar of olives, a twelve-inch wheel of Banon cheese, and a ten-kilogram carton of assorted shellfish, we left the market and turned onto rue Meynadier.

I don't really enjoy shopping, but I did enjoy looking at the mouth-watering displays in the many fine-food shops and checking out the fashions in several of the trendy boutiques. I also liked that rue Meynadier was a pedestrian thoroughfare and crossing from one side of the street to the other was stress-free. Cognizant of our vacation budget, I breathed a sigh of relief as we left rue Meynadier without having purchased a single item. However, as we turned onto rue d'Antibes, I braced myself for the high-end shops and the accompanying high-end prices. Set back two blocks behind boulevard de la Croisette and running almost parallel to it, rue d'Antibes appeals to any fashion-conscious woman with credit left on her (or her husband's) credit cards. And as we strolled along, I wondered if our inexpensive window-shopping experience would evolve to the feeling-the-material stage, then to the holding-a-dress-up-in-front-of-a-mirror stage, and finally to the full-blown, spending-spree stage. Given that we were probably one of the few couples on the street that doesn't have a Swiss bank account, a villa in the hills, a Picasso on our walls, a large stake in an Arabian oil field, or even a large steak in our freezer at home, I sensed it was time to have a plan of escape. It would have to be cunning and devious, yet subtle enough to be believable—a plan that only an experienced husband could dream up. I had several such plans ready to put into operation.

Halfway along rue d'Antibes, the inevitable happened. We were in a fancy swimwear boutique when I espied my wife holding up a tiny bikini in front of a full-length mirror. I walked over and feigned a few words of enthusiasm. As the seventeen-square-centimetre, two-piece garment—one of my neckties could be made into several such sets—was being dangled in front of the appropriate but much larger areas of her body, I caught a glimpse of the price tag. After a short gasp for air, I somehow managed to produce a smile. "Wow! That's a nice bikini," I spluttered without a hint of a quaver in my voice.

"Do you think that the horizontal stripes will make me look—?"

"Not at all, honey," I interrupted "Are you going to try it on?" I bluffed, fully aware of the gamble.

"I'm sorry, I'd really love to, but I need to go to the bathroom— real bad!"

Bingo! I couldn't have come up with a better line myself, and then made a mental note of it for future use. We left the store rapidly (with credit cards still slumbering in my pouch) and I suggested that she go into one of the nearby restaurants or hotels to use their facilities. Considering her anguished expression and increase in pace, I thought my suggestion a good one.

"No! I need to go back to our room at the hotel, right now!"

"But that's several miles away," I countered.

"I don't care! I am *not* going to use a strange bathroom."

"But we've only had the room at the hotel for a few days. Doesn't the bathroom *there* still seem strange to you?" I reasoned.

Over the years, I've learned that there are times when it's best to say nothing and just go along with my wife. Without speaking a word, we raced back to boulevard de la Croisette, hopped into Twingo, and sped off along the coast to Cap d'Antibes, Hôtel Miramar, and her most familiar of Riviera toilets.

We spent the late afternoon and early evening relaxing on the hotel's rear patio. With the soothing sound of the fountain in the background, we read our books and sipped on the wine that Michel had generously left in our room and that we'd chilled in a "guest-only" refrigerator at the bar next to the dining room. A glass display case held an assortment of plastic-wrapped sandwiches, cheese platters, and dips that had been prepared specifically for guests who wanted to stay on the property and have a light dinner. Guests were to write down what they'd taken in the open account book lying beside the case.

Obviously, this kind of honour system relies on trust. After making our selection, I wondered if I might have overcompensated by not only recording the sandwiches but also the olives, lemon wedges, and bread sticks. And as I did, I wondered if those would appear on our bill. Not that I'm so frugal, just curious. I imagined advising our friends back home how best to estimate a conservative budget for a similar trip to the French Riviera. "Avoid five-star hotels, four-lifebuoy beaches, four-champagne-glass brasseries, casinos, and high-end boutiques. Count on at least double the price for gasoline and throw in a huge allowance for highway tolls and cafés au lait. However, in our case, we blew our budget on olives, lemon wedges, and bread sticks at a little hotel in Cap d'Antibes."

After dinner, we discussed our plans for the coming days. Three nights had flown by and unfortunately it was time to move on to another base camp, as Hôtel Miramar was fully booked for the rest of the summer. We were sad at the thought of leaving. Our room, the hotel's location, its staff, and especially its smiling proprietor had been a wonderful start to our vacation, and we were going to miss them—of that we were cer-tain.

Part Two

16

Cap d'Antibes:

A Change of Hotels and Stripes

"And so, Mee-ster and Mee-ses Vancou-vair. Eet ees terr-ee-bla you 'ave to go today. I 'ope your stay at Hôtel Miramar was satis-fi-eeng. I 'ope you 'ave a fantas-teek voyage from 'ere," Michel rambled as he presented the bill. (A quick glance revealed we had not been charged for the olives, lemons, and bread sticks.) We thanked him, then he insisted on carrying our bags to the car, where he gave us a hug and wished us *bon voyage*.

Not having the faintest idea where we were going to spend the night, we set off, turned onto boulevard Kennedy, and almost immediately came across Hôtel Beau-Site. Its light cream stucco walls, lilac window shutters, and terra cotta roof tiles gave the three-floor building splendid curb appeal. I stopped Twingo and read the sign beside the black wrought-iron gate. Confident that we would qualify as three-star guests, we drove onto the gravel forecourt, parked, and followed the sign to *Réception*, which faced a large, crazy-paved patio furnished with tables and chairs and yellow-and-light cream striped umbrellas. We smiled at each other at the sight of a kidney-shaped swimming pool beyond the patio. Its deck accommodated a dozen or so white sun lounges and on each was a yellow-and-light cream striped mattress.

On entering the small but well-appointed lobby, we were impressed by the hotel's décor. The designer had, for the most part, succeeded in achieving an airy, Provençal summertime mood. But I thought that the old-fashioned black-and-white floor tiles set in checkerboard pattern clashed severely. I could only presume that the original designer of yesteryear was an avid chess player before being sent to the guillotine.

A bellboy, dressed in a mauve uniform with yellow trim, stood to attention on a black tile to the left of *Recéption*. He looked rather like a chess piece: a pawn waiting to be moved to another square or to be knocked clear off the floor by an aggressive queen. Had we been in Vancouver, I would have lifted him up and placed him in front of the similarly uniformed waiter standing to attention on a white square in the dining room, and shouted, "Checkmate!" But no, we were on the French Riviera and this kind of behaviour was unbecoming a guest of a three-star hotel.

Our reception at *Réception* was mixed. The refined middle-aged man behind the counter greeted us with a smile and fluent English and introduced himself as André, the manager. He then introduced Jacques, the assistant manager, a younger man who'd been busying himself at a desk behind the counter. Jacques greeted us quite formally and without a smile. Perhaps he felt that we fell short of the hotel's three-star rating.

I told André the Man-ager that we were looking for a double room. He smiled and responded, "*Oui, Monsieur.* Yehz we 'ave. And for 'ow many nights, *s'il vous plaît?*" Then Jacques the Ass-istant muttered something in French that led André the Man to say, "Er, I am sor-ree, we 'ave only one *chambre.* Would you like to see eet? You can 'ave eet at a spe-ci-al price."

The rate quoted was lower than the one displayed at the front of the hotel, and I was immediately suspicious of the offer. However, with André the Man acting as our guide, we agreed to look at the room. Meanwhile, Jacques the Ass moved into position at the front desk— like a first mate substituting for a captain stepping away from the bridge of his ship.

The room was large, nicely furnished, and decorated Provençal-style in more light cream, yellow, and lilac. I opened the French doors and stepped out onto a small balcony that looked out over the swimming pool. Like our room at Hôtel Miramar, this one too received the morning sun. But unlike Hôtel Miramar, the drapes and bedcover were striped in yellow and lilac. When André the Man opened the bathroom door, we almost jumped for joy at its spaciousness. Not only could we go about our ablutions without elbowing each other, there was no chance we'd get trapped in, on, or between fixtures. The walls, fixtures, and tiles were light cream, and the towels, bathmat, and shower curtain were, as you would expect, striped in yellow and lilac.

We couldn't find anything wrong with the room. It was perfect. So then, what was the catch? My wife looked at André, smiled and said, "This is fine. Thank you. We'll take it."

André the Man phoned down to Jacques the Ass who instructed Pawn the Bellboy to move from his black square and meet me at our car to help carry our luggage. With registration card completed and bags unpacked, we changed into our swimwear and headed straight for the pool. Stopping at the reception desk, I asked Jacques for poolside towels. He retrieved two from a cupboard and then handed them to us without speaking a word. He looked forlorn. I thanked him, but he'd returned to his paperwork. Now isn't that interesting? Here was an employee working on the front lines of a service industry, probably trained in all aspects of hotel management, and yet he hadn't grasped the fundamental meaning of hospitality. There had to be a reason, one that my wife would surely uncover. It would just be a matter of time.

After a refreshing dip in the pool, we settled onto our towels on the comfy sun lounges, applied a liberal coating of factor-15 sunscreen, put on our sunglasses, adjusted our sun visors, and began reading to the sounds of chirping birds and rustling palm fronds. After reading a page or two, I looked at my watch and realized that only an hour earlier we were having breakfast at Hôtel Miramar. Then, I thought of Michel greeting new arrivals with smiles, hugs, and kisses. "What a difference attitude makes," I muttered under my breath before blocking out the "special rate," Jacques the Ass, and the mystery behind his sullenness.

17

Cap d'Antibes:

Poolside Acquaintances

A splash of cold water woke me up, followed immediately by the shrill scream of a hysterical young child. As I came to my senses, I realized that I'd drifted off to sleep by the pool. My book lay flat on my lap, I was still gripping it with both hands, and the rest of my body was exactly where I'd left it—propped up against a comfy sun lounge. Stirring from my brief state of rigor mortis, I focused on the noisy culprit: a little girl swimming away from me, screaming in French at her mother and father who had set up camp on the other side of the pool and were paying her attention with their applause, smiles, and words of encouragement. There was no sign of any other siblings around, so I assumed that their water-winged, blonde-haired, chubby-cheeked cherub was their only child—a spoiled brat, no doubt.

The brat was now out of the water and wrapped in the arms of her father, who was a big man. He was not quite twice my size. His thighs were like tree trunks. A tattoo covered both biceps and ran over his shoulders, terminating at his neck. I couldn't make out the design, but, judging by the amount of skin it covered, it could have been a roadmap of the entire state of California. Hung around his neck was a heavy gold chain, and hanging from it was a large cross. His hairy chest spanned into the next time zone. Had he stood up, we would have been eclipsed in shadow. His long brown hair was tied back in a ponytail and dark whiskers covered his face. A long, well-healed scar on his left cheek and a poorly set broken nose were the finishing touches to his don't-mess-with-me-and-my-gal image. My goodness! What had three-star-conscious Jacques the Ass been thinking when he checked in the pony-tailed mountain of muscle, an honorary Hells Angel?

Muscle Mountain's thirty-something wife was beautiful—a pin-up model, a Playboy Bunny perhaps. She was tall, blonde, and suntanned. Her mascara, nail polish, and lipstick covered more of her body than her bikini did. I glanced quickly over the top of my book as the Playmate of the Year stood up and noticed she was wearing high-heeled sandals. And although there was a bounce in her stride as she walked over to the steps at the shallow end of the pool, that's where the bouncing stopped. There was an abnormal amount of solidarity to her top-heaviness. Clearly there had been surgery; clearly there had been enhancement. Expecting the vision to dip her toe into the water, I was surprised when she knelt down at the end of the pool, leaned forward (revealing a thong-style bikini bottom, but neither tattoos nor body piercings), reached down, and placed her cupped hands beneath its surface. Just as I was thinking that this image gave new meaning to Silicon Valley, my wife asked, "Don't you think she's beautiful?"

Pretending to read my book, I answered casually, "Who, darling? Oh *her*. Yes, I guess she's sort of attractive, if you like that kind of look." Then I added, "You're much prettier, darling."

Playmate strode elegantly back to her sun lounge and the protection of Muscle Mountain.

"Do you think they're real?" whispered my wife.

"Do I think *what* are real?" I answered, pretending I hadn't a clue what she was talking about.

"Her *boobs*. Do you think she's had a boob job?" she pressed.

"Oh, I don't know. I never really give these things any thought," I lied. Then I added: "It's amazing what lengths some women will go to, to look as good as you, honey."

☼

Ooh-la-la Land

I returned to my reading but as much as I tried to concentrate, I found myself eavesdropping on the conversation of a portly older English couple that was sitting to my right. Both were dressed in Marks & Spencer summer attire that exposed very little of their flabby, white skin. The husband, whom I pictured as a World War II navy type—an Able Seaman—was probably wishing that the war had never ended and that he'd never set foot on dry land again. He was reading the sports page of the *Daily Mail*. The headline read "France Is Out!" and every French soccer fan already knew that yesterday's loss had brought an end to their team's chances of winning the FIFA World Cup. Able was either catching up on the news from back home or he was deliberately reminding the Frenchmen around the pool that France, like England, had been eliminated from the tournament. There has never been much love lost between the English and the French, especially among their soccer fans, and considering his proximity to Muscle Mountain, I believed Able's safety was in jeopardy. Furthermore, he really pushed his luck when he lowered his newspaper to ogle Playmate as she walked by. Able was in his seventies, bald on top, grey at the sides, and sported a pencil-thin grey moustache. His flabby jowls, flushed cheeks, purple nose, and bloodshot eyes were evidence of his poor health, and I worried that Playmate's two-minute poolside cool-down routine had potentially been life-threatening.

Able's wife had been reading *People* magazine, and I took an instant dislike to the annoying way she licked her thumb with a loud slurp when turning each page. Equally annoying were her brief commentaries on people in the photographs: TV celebrities, movie stars, and members of the British Royal Family. She spoke as if her comments were of interest to her husband and both of them knew the famous people personally. "Good gracious! I see Princess Anne has put on a bit of weight. She should go to Weight Watchers. They've done wonders for Fergie, yer know?" she remarked after licking her thumb and turning the page. "Well, would yer look at that? Tom Cruise is with another woman. We've not seen much of Tom in a while, 'ave we?" She licked her thumb and turned the page. "Guess who's on the arm of

Leonardo DiCaprio? It's that girl, the one who plays a nurse on that show we watch after Match of the Day on BBC. Yer know the one, she falls in luv with that one-armed brain surgeon. Oh, what's her name? Yer know who I mean, don't yer?"

While listening to her annoying thumb-licking slurps and running commentary, I'd spotted the gleaming brass handle of an attractive walking cane that hung from the back of her chair. I had also noticed that her ankles were swollen and her calves were patterned with varicose veins. I suspected she was unable to walk without her cane, and probably unable to swim in the pool, and that reading the fluff in *People* magazine was one of her few remaining pleasures in life—that and hen-pecking her husband.

Able had brought down a tuna sandwich to the pool and he was chewing on it as he read his newspaper.

"Look, a pussycat!" spluttered Cane, pointing to a black cat on the pool deck as if she'd just spotted a leopard on safari. "What a pretty little pussycat."

There was no response from Able, who continued to annoy the French soccer fans around the pool with his sports page held high, like a mini-billboard, reminding them that "France Is Out!"

"Look! It's coming closer. It wants a bit of yer sandwich. Give 'im a bit of yer sandwich," she commanded.

"No, don't want to," came the reply from behind the newspaper.

"Give 'im a bit of yer sandwich!"

"No. Don't want to."

"Give 'im a bloody bit of yer sandwich!" she insisted.

Again, there was no response from Able, as the black cat sat at his feet waiting for a handout.

"Yer bloody daft, you are!" Cane blurted. Then, with the lightning speed and dexterity of a swashbuckler, she reached for her cane, swung it behind the newspaper, and jabbed free what was left of Able's tuna sandwich into the waiting claws of Felix.

Appreciative of the tasty snack, Felix slunk up to its swashbuckling provider and affectionately rubbed up against her varicose veins in the hope of a second feeding. Not caring for the cat's close encounter with her calves, she yelled, "Go away. I said, 'Go away!' Shoo! For goodness sake, get this thing away from me. Shoo!" But Able just smiled. Then, resorting to her swashbuckling ways, she hooked Felix with the cane's shiny brass handle and, in one smooth motion, flicked the cat into the bordering hedge. "Fat lot of use you were," she scowled in the direction of the newspaper.

By then we'd had enough—of the sun and of our fellow guests. We packed up and set off to our room. As we passed by the sports page and the varicose veins, I was surprised to receive a pleasant smile and a cordial, "Hello," from both Cane and Able. Even more surprising as we passed Muscle Mountain, he turned to me, smiling apologetically and said softly: "*Monsieur*, we are so sor-ree for our leetle girl deed splash and take you from your sleep. She ees so 'appy een *la piscine*. She lurves the water, *absolument*," Playmate nodded and smiled in agreement, as their daughter shyly pressed up against her mother's lovely long tanned legs.

"That's no problem. I'm glad she woke me up actually," I half-lied, picturing my fifteen-minute head-back, mouth-wide-open snooze.

And so began our poolside acquaintance with Cane and Able, Muscle Mountain, Playmate, and their chubby-cheeked cherub.

18

Biot:

BS and BS Bingo

After a refreshing shower and change of clothes, we headed downstairs to the checkerboard floor where, like a white bishop on black squares, I took a diagonal path over to the reception desk. Ready to explore beyond the busy beachfronts, I asked André the Man to recommend an interesting inland town where we could have lunch and spend the rest of the afternoon seeing the sights.

"Biot. Go to Chez Odile in Biot. A *village perché* full of blown-up glass. From Antibes, go 11 novembre to N98 to D4, under N7 and over A8, and you weel be in Biot," he explained enthusiastically.

"I'm sorry, would you mind repeating that a little slower, but first, please pass me the enigma code-breaking machine," I thought, as I stared back at him with mouth agape.

With the name Biot etched in my brain, a complimentary map in hand, and a guidebook in our bag, we stepped off the chessboard and outside into the blazing sunshine. I had parked Twingo in the sun and was instantly hit with a blast of superheated steam when I opened my door. As I waited for the car to cool down, I scanned the forecourt for Muscle Mountain's Harley-Davidson combination, but there were only cars, and those were parked in the shade of trees. I made a mental note to park in the shade in future.

One car was a Jaguar XJ12 convertible in immaculate condition. Its recently polished, unscratched British Racing Green body gleamed. Its soft-top was retracted and revealed tan leather upholstery and varnished wooden trim. It had British licence plates; the steering wheel was on the right. Attached to a chrome bar above its front bumper were three badges: AA, RAC, and GB. I recalled that AA stands for Automobile Association, not Alcoholics Anonymous; RAC for Royal Automobile Club, not Rust Ain't Curable; and GB for Great Britain, not Grumbling Boozers. A wheelchair sticker was in the bottom left-hand corner of the windscreen. Obviously this was Cane's car.

There was a white 740 BMW with French licence plates and a child's seat in the back. This was most likely Muscle Mountain's car. I looked for more clues—a violin case, a wooden-handled cheese wire, a Playboy Bunny bumper sticker—but I found nothing other than a chrome badge in the shape of a fish above the rear bumper.

Driving out through the rear gate, I saw Jacques the Ass standing in the shade watering a flower bed. He held a hose in his left hand, and I couldn't help but think that he resembled a large garden statue with a fountain spraying forth from its pelvic region. I rolled down my window, waved to him, and shouted, *"Au revoir."* He didn't smile, didn't speak, and didn't wave; he just flicked the nozzle of the hose, shooting the spray up and down a couple of times. "Hey, I think Jacques is warming up to us," I remarked as we sped off hoping to navigate our way to Biot in search of Chez Odile and blown-up glass.

In stark contrast to the beauty of Cap d'Antibes, the drive northeast to Biot took us through an unattractive industrial area, which the bumper-to-bumper traffic did nothing to conceal. But not long after crossing over the A8, Biot appeared, sitting impressively on a hilltop, just like a scene on a French Riviera postcard.

We parked Twingo at the foot of the hill, climbed the cobblestone ramp, and entered the ancient walled village through the 16th-century Porte des Tines. Following the hordes along rue St-Sebastian—a street lined with potteries, glass shops, and cafés—we stepped into a tourist information office, picked up a local map and a Biot tourist leaflet, and asked for directions to Chez Odile on chemin des Bachettes. Seemingly tired of assisting throngs of tourists, the middle-aged woman behind the counter glared at me as if I were a half-wit, and then marked the map. "You are 'ere. Chemin des Bachettes ees 'ere and Chez Odile ees 'ere," she said, as if I'd lived in the small town all my life. Granted, her two scribbled circles almost overlapped each other, we were so close. "You under-stand, yehz?" she asked, then sucked on her teeth, adjusted her bra strap, rolled her eyes, and muttered something in French. Clearly, she thought I was a directionally challenged idiot who would get lost in a bathtub.

We began to appreciate André the Man's recommendation as soon as we were seated on Chez Odile's attractive terrace and inhaled the divine aromas coming from the kitchen. A glance at the menu revealed a limited selection of dishes. A longer look at our phrasebook revealed that one of them was stuffed rabbit, which reminded me of the first (and last) time I ordered one of its cousins: Jugged Hare.

Several years after immigrating to Canada, I returned to my home town in England as "Local boy made good in North America," and I thought I would impress my family by treating them to lunch at a fancy restaurant in the countryside. Sitting at the head of the table, I ordered Jugged Hare, not that I had a clue what would be served, but more to show off that I'd become a man of the world. While we were eating our salads and soups, we became engulfed in a putrid smell—a combination of body odour and burning tires. Concerned, I beckoned the maître d' to our table and, whispering in his ear, asked if there was a fire on the premises. "Oh, no sir," he replied, "That's your Jugged Hare cooking. Indeed, 'tis a little gamey. But, if I might add, it's an excellent choice, sir."

Recalling each wretched or, much more accurately, retch-inducing mouthful of Jugged Hare and thinking that Chez Odile—a family-run bistro—might be serving up its pet as *Stuffed Fluffy à la provençale*, I selected bouillabaisse. Not that I could pronounce it or knew what it was, I simply pointed to it on the menu, then hoped for the best. As it turned out, it was a delicious fish stew of squid, cod, conger, octopus, mussels, and shrimps.

Ooh-la-la Land

One of the things I admire about the French is their love of food and the time they spend loving it. Lunch is never a quick tuna sandwich and a Pepsi while sitting in front of a computer complaining to a co-worker in the next cubicle about unrealistic deadlines and a boss who just doesn't understand. The French excel at minimizing their workday by extending their lunch break. They don't go to lunch to talk about work but to forget about it. They focus on the food, the wine, the ambience, and on relaxing. Only a pretty young woman walking by would distract a Frenchman from his lunch. And only a handsome young man walking by (or, perhaps, an old, wealthy one shuffling by) would distract a Frenchwoman from hers.

Talking of distractions, I couldn't avoid overhearing the conversation between two American businessmen at a nearby table. What they were doing in a *village perché* in the south of France, I'll never know. Their jarring New York accents irritated me somewhat, but it was their shop talk that annoyed me the most.

"The CEO has the wrong mindset. He's gotta start to think outside the box, revisit his approach, touch base with suppliers, become more client-focused, and more proactive. He has to identify the best practice, empower his subordinates, and get a techie to increase the bandwidth. If not, he'll be out of the loop. Let's face it, he has the leverage and knowledge base to make the game plan work, and if he plays hardball at each benchmark, does a gap analysis, and finds a strategic fit, then the synergy will give the fast-track aspect a value-added component that will realize a total-quality, results-driven, win-win situation that is bound to affect the bottom line."

Their jargon brought to mind the "Bullshit Bingo" card that once circulated our office. And as the BS continued to waft across from the dynamic duo from Manhattan, it was impossible to concentrate on what my wife was reading to me from our guidebook:

"For centuries, potters worked the fine yellow clay of the area in the production of huge oil and wine containers. This has been replaced by the glassware and terra cotta ceramic industries..."

"I'm in the process of upgradin'. I figure if I throw some money at a P4 3.06-gigahertz 533fsb CPU with a 10-gig Ultra 2 motherboard and an 8-gig Powerdata USB drive, I'll be able to provide the CFO with amazin' graphics. And I'll be able to download *Shrek* for the kids."

"*The narrow cobbled streets of this medieval village, especially the quaint arcaded quarter, are very charming. Many shops sell locally made handcrafts and blown glass...*"

"I lost a bundle when the tech bubble burst. My broker pushed Nortel as a strong buy at fifty. Many bought on margin, took their profits, and are now on the sidelines sitting on cash."

"*In the centre is place aux Arcades... once a Roman town... the 15th-century church... on rue de la Vieille Boucherie there is an old butcher's shop with metal meat racks hanging in the street outside.*"

"Man, that fish soup just didn't do it for me. D'ya see what I'm sayin'? I could go for a cheeseburger and a Budweiser right now. What should I leave as a tip? D'ya think 20 per cent should do it?"

"*The Musée national Fernand-Léger contains 360 works from the artist Fernand Léger... the massive colourful mosaic decorating its façade are worth seeing.*"

"Are ya goin' to the casino tonight or just chillin'? I gotta check out them chicks dancin' around in nothin' but high heels and G-strings. Wouldn't mind bumpin' one o' them up the boulevard. D'ya see what I'm sayin'? So, if ya cool, dude, let's split."

"*At La Verrerie de Biot, you can watch glassblowers creating artistic, high-quality bubble-glass containers and ornaments...*"

As the Mad Hatters from Manhattan got up to leave, I was tempted to interrupt my wife and catch their attention: "Hi. We're from Canada where many are tired after spending the winter digging out from knee-deep snow, just as you must be tired from digging out of knee-deep bullshit. May I suggest that the next time you're in a restaurant you order Jugged Hare, as I'm certain it would suit your conversation?"

As they passed by, they nodded at me and said, "How's it goin'?"

"Fine, thanks," I said. And then they were gone.

Bullshit Bingo

Do you keep falling asleep in meetings and seminars?
What about those long, boring conference calls?
Now here's a way to change all that.

How to play:
Check off the appropriate square when you hear any of the following
words during a meeting, seminar, or conference call.
If you check off five squares horizontally, vertically, or diagonally,
then stand up and shout out **BULLSHIT!**

Value Added	Proactive	Win-Win Situation	Think Outside The Box	Game Plan
Fast Track	Synergy	Strategic Fit	Gap Analysis	Revisit
Best Practice	Bottom Line	Band-Width	Hardball	Touch Base
Out of the Loop	Bench-mark	Client-Focused	Mindset	Ball Park
Results-Driven	Empower	Knowledge Base	Total Quality	Leverage

Testimonials from satisfied players at an engineering consulting company:

"I'd only been in the meeting for five minutes when I won." – Jack W.

"My attention span at meetings has improved dramatically." – Susan M.

"What a blast! Meetings will never be the same after that first win." – Bill R.

"The atmosphere was intense as four of us waited to check off the fifth box – Lil. T

"He was stunned, as two of us shouted "Bullshit!" for the third time in an hour." – Ben G.

19

Biot:

Blown Glass and a Bedside Table Light

After sauntering around the ancient streets of Biot, photographing medieval architecture and stepping into shops to admire the beautiful glass art, my wife began to zero in on a potential souvenir. As much as she loved the huge vase (that would need a shipping crate as large as our living room), I managed to convince her that the small blown-glass Santa Claus with a small, red, tube-shaped twinkling light bulb embedded just below its fat belly would be more practical to carry home, would look lovely on the Christmas tree, and, until then, could serve as a bedside table light back at our hotel.

Returning through the ancient walls of the Vieille Ville and down the cobbled ramp to the bottom of the hill, we agreed that a tour of Biot wouldn't be complete without a tour of a glassworks. La Verrerie de Biot was the obvious choice, as it stood right before us. My wife knows that I'm not normally interested in such things, which is why she was thrilled that I shared her enthusiasm. So much so, in fact, that she skipped on ahead towards the entranceway like an excited young girl. Although I shared her enthusiasm, I was so desperate to use a toilet that had I skipped along with her, I would have had to spend the next ten minutes drying off in front of a glassblower's furnace.

We found the glassblowing process fascinating and marvelled at the beauty of the finished products. La Verrerie de Biot became famous for producing "bubble" glass, which is produced by taking a glob of molten glass (on the end of a steel rod) from the furnace's reservoir, placing it into a fine stream of chemical-powder dispensed from a hopper by way of a small auger, and once the entire surface of the glob has received a fine dusting of powder, dipping it back into the furnace's holding tank for another layer of molten glass. As the glass cools, a chemical reaction takes place between the particles of powder and the glass, and *"Voilà!"* tiny bubbles are created within the glass which gives the finished product an attractive and unique appearance.

In the open-plan workshop, halle Eloi-Monod, nine men work in three teams of three—each member completing a single stage of a three-step process—to produce wine glasses, vases, and water jugs. The men we saw wore no special fireproof clothing or goggles, but rather regular summer shorts, T-shirts, and open-toed sandals—the less combustible the clothing, the better. Apparently, wearing additional protective clothing is uncomfortable, inhibits movement, and saps the glassblowers' energy—to the detriment of their safety, the quality of the finished products, and their production targets. And, we were told, that it was proven many years ago that wearing long cotton pants and long-sleeved shirts is a much greater hazard—the slightest contact with molten glass ignites them immediately.

Shuffling through the halle Eloi-Monod, we sidled up to a small group of tourists watching a demonstration of the basic art of glassblowing. At the end of the demonstration, the glassblower addressed the group in French. Most people giggled, and then a young man stepped forward—a volunteer, I realized. Once he'd been outfitted with goggles, fireproof apron, and steel-toed boots, he did exactly as the glassblower instructed. He manoeuvred the molten glob of glass just like an expert. He blew, rolled, inspected, blew, and rolled again. Gradually, a long-necked vase began to form, to the applause of our group. Unfortunately, he stopped rolling at one point when he shouldn't have, then blew when he should have been rolling. The large bulbous bottom half dimpled and the long neck collapsed in an arc to one side. The whole mass solidified into a shape not unlike a huge, crystal-clear, limp genitalia.

"Oooha! What a dreadful pity," commented a Cockney woman standing next to her husband. "He was goin' at it so well, and then all ov a sudden it went soft on 'im. Maybe they'll giv' 'im anuvver go in a minute," she said in all seriousness.

"Nah. There's no bladdy way. He needs more time to recover; besides, the young kid 'as no experience. You 'ave to know what yer doin', where to move yer 'ands, and when to blow," the husband said.

Stepping onto the crazy-paved patio back at Hôtel Beau-Site, I noticed Cane and Able were strategically positioned to scrutinize people coming and going. Cane was looking over the top of a *Hello!* magazine with a smiling Catherine Zeta-Jones on the front cover. Able, who was sitting at the same table but out of reach of his wife's swashbuckling weapon, looked up from *The Perfect Murder*—a murder-mystery not a "how-to" book—and asked, "Had a nice day, 'ave yer then?"

"Wonderful. Thank you," my wife replied. "And you?"

"Marvellous. Thank you. I stayed by the pool, but the Misses shot over to Monaco," he answered, his blood-shot eyes twinkling as he recalled treasured time without his wife and poolside thong routines. I imagined his wife in her open-top Jaguar XJ12 hurtling along the spectacular Grande Corniche coastal road, her cane handle gleaming in the sunshine. Taking that route, she'd have been thinking of Princess Grace's fatal car accident back in 1982, and the years of tabloid gossip surrounding her and her family. Finally, I pictured her skidding to a halt at a handicapped parking space in front of the world-famous casino and then looking around expectantly for famous people.

"Yes, I took a forty-five-minute guided tour of the Palais Princier," volunteered Cane. "Monaco's royal family is so very wealthy, you know," she continued. "They must 'ave everything. And I tell you this much," she confided in a hushed, secretive whisper, "I wouldn't 'ave a clue what to buy them for Christmas."

"How about a year's subscription to *People* magazine?" I was about to suggest, before my wife tugged me away, smiled, and wished them both a pleasant evening.

Ooh-la-la Land

By ten o'clock, the patio was crowded, much wine had been consumed, and the whispered conversations had built to a crescendo of loud, inebriated chatter and giggles. Jacques the Ass attended the patio bar; his sad face giving new meaning to "Happy Hour." On duty at a three-star French Riviera hotel was not the time or place to let his hair down—not that he had much left to let down. No, his mission was to serve the guests professionally and to frown on anyone who may cause the hotel to slip to a two-star rating.

As engrossed as I was in the story, a sudden quietness made me look up from my book. It was as if a lifeguard had blown a whistle and everyone had fallen silent, awaiting instructions to evacuate the pool or to start dredging it for a child who was last seen jumping into the deep end with deflated water wings. Even the cicadas went quiet. Then, striding elegantly past Cane and Able's table came Playmate. Wearing her hair in a French twist, perfectly applied make-up, a modicum of sparkling jewellery, and a short, white chiffon outfit—best described as a dressless evening strap—she made her way over to the corner table. Following in her wake was a fragrance so divine that of all the men sitting close enough to inhale it, none noticed or even cared that following in her footsteps was her larger-than-life husband, Muscle Mountain. And if it weren't for the cutlery rattling on the tables, it was doubtful whether anyone, male or female, would have noticed him.

Minutes passed before all of us, rapturous gawkers, picked up where we'd left off. Judging by Able's bulging eyeballs, I thought that perhaps his electronic pacemaker was short-circuiting. And after my own cataleptic moment, I continued to read.

"Did you see what she was wearing?" my wife whispered.

Here we go again, I thought, "Who, darling?" I faked, wiping drool from my mouth.

"That beautiful woman—you know, the woman with the *boobs*. The mother of that little girl who splashed you at the pool."

Knowing that I would be able to recall the vision in chiffon at any moment for the rest of my life, I continued my pretence. "Where is she?" I asked, turning my head, avoiding looking at the corner table.

"Over there, in the corner."

"Oh *her*. Yes, now I remember. Sorry, what was your question?" I feigned, thinking that she should have asked, "Did you see what she *wasn't* wearing?"

"Those are Manolo Blahnik's sandals," she squealed, as if she'd just discovered we'd won a seven-figure lottery.

"Is that right?" I replied, not even realizing that Playmate was wearing anything on her feet. "How do you know?" I asked, not knowing who Manolo Blahnik was or why he'd loaned her his sandals.

"Believe me, I just know it," she said. "They look so good on her. I look so frumpy in my sandals," she complained.

"No, you don't. Your sandals look good on you," I consoled her, remembering her thick, all-terrain soles on the cobblestone ramp that led to the old walled town of Biot. "Besides, you can always buy a pair of those Barry Manilow's when we get home," I suggested, not having any idea of the outlandish price of a pair of Manolo Blahniks.

"Thanks for being so thoughtful." She kissed me on the cheek.

It was a little after eleven when we returned to our room. I opened the door and flicked on the light. And although it was not the appropriate time of year, it was the appropriate time of day to have the bed illuminated by a twinkling, turned-on Santa.

20

Between Cannes and Saint-Raphaël:

A Psychologist Would Be Impressed

A lone mosquito, whose sole purpose in life was to circle the air space directly above my head during the pre-dawn hours, was good reason to get up early and set off for a day of touring more of the Côte d'Azur, west of Cannes. My first reaction to Mozzie smart-bombing my eardrums had been to retreat beneath the yellow-and-lilac striped bed sheets, but I almost suffocated once I'd ensured that there were no openings larger than a mosquito's wingspan. I resurfaced, gasping for air and committed to confronting the enemy in arm-to-arm combat. My initial surface-to-air assault—blindly flailing my arms about in the dark—proved ineffective, and so I mobilized an air-to-air attack that employed my night-vision bifocal glasses and a rolled-up fashion magazine. Having reconnoitred the walls and ceiling and identified the tiny black-winged threat above the door frame, I advanced to a higher strategic position: atop a three-legged, pie-crust table that put me at the right altitude and within striking range. A flick of my wrist propelled my weapon on target—a direct hit. The whack of the impact awoke my wife who propped herself up on one elbow and stared blurry-eyed at the life-sized, nude figurine atop the table by the door and asked: "What the heck are you doing?"

With neat adrenaline pumping through my veins, I triumphantly explained why I was tottering atop a three-legged table wearing only my bifocals and holding a rolled-up *Chatelaine*. To corroborate my debriefing report, I pointed victoriously at the motionless black dot above the door frame. My wife was not impressed. Respectful of my stealthy opponent, I went to remove it from the wall with the intention of giving it a decent burial: flushing it down the toilet. When I was about to scrape it off the wall, a closer look revealed that I'd whacked a protruding nail head. "Blast!" I cursed, realizing that Mozzie was still out there, flying under the radar, continuing to assess my firepower and strike capabilities. Mozzie was not impressed.

Only André the Man was around as we passed *Réception* on our way out to the brilliant sunshine, blue skies, twittering birds, and dew-fresh fragrances of flowers and pine trees. Not even Pawn the Bellboy had reported for work yet; his black tile lay unoccupied. *"Bonjour, Madame et Monsieur. 'ow are you thiz mor-neeng?"* greeted André the Man.

"Bonjour. Très bien, merci. Et vous?" I replied. *"Comment-allez vous?"* I added, keen to practice a little of what I'd learned from "Lesson 7: Hello" in our phrasebook. But after experimenting a little, I realized that I'd failed to roll my r's, pull a pouting expression, and make hand gestures *à la française*. Ecstatic that I'd spoken to him *en français*, André the Man fired back fifteen sentences, pulled all sorts of facial expressions, rolled his r's, and gesticulated so wildly that I thought the hotel could save on electricity costs by turning off the ceiling fan. At each pause between sentences, I nodded, smiled, and muttered *oui*, as if I knew what he was talking about. For all I knew, he could have been asking me if I was a terrorist or if I knew that my fly was open. But he continued to talk, smile, shrug his shoulders, and wave his arms about, so I concluded that he believed that I understood more French than I actually did. At the end of his final sentence, he punctuated it by simultaneously raising both eyebrows, shrugging his shoulders, showing me the palms of his hands, and blowing a soft, wet raspberry between pursed lips. Rather than close off with just another *oui*, I tried to mimic his final combination of gesticulations, but my wet raspberry shot forth spittle that hit the bell on the front desk. *Ding!* André the Man was not impressed.

Ooh-la-la Land

☼

We took the usual scenic coastal route through Juan-les-Pins towards Cannes, stopping briefly in Golfe-Juan for cafés au lait and chocolate croissants at a charming little beachside café that was perched above the shallow surf on a wooden pier. From Cannes, we kept on the scenic coastal road D559—the Corniche de l'Estérel—with the intention of heading straight to Fréjus, an estimated one-hour, leisurely drive. Buzzing on caffeine, we pioneered westwards, navigating the twists and turns of the scenic route. With one eye on the road, one eye on the beautiful scenery, and only one ear listening to our favourite music, we were happy to be exploring the coast. But we felt restricted in our movements and were especially careful not to make any sudden head movements. Why? I will explain.

Captain Good-Looking had advised my wife that the car came equipped with a CD player. "And thiz ees for your mu-zeek. We, at Renault, try always to pleaz," he'd said, flashing his teeth. Then, pointing to a knob on the side of her seat, he'd said, "Eef you pull thiz, your chair back weel go 'orizon-tal. I weel try for you. Yehz?"

"That's really not necessary," I'd blurted, as my wife suddenly shot back into a fully reclined position, looking up helplessly at the sun roof. "Hey! Cut that out!" I'd been about to say, as Captain Good-Looking continued.

"Pull eet again and eet comes up vertee-cal," he'd said as my wife reappeared upright beside me just as suddenly as she'd vanished. I was not impressed.

But I digress. Although I was happy that Renault had provided us with a CD player, Twingo had no socket to accept the plug for my iPod. In preparation for our trip, I'd spent hours downloading our favourite music. So, as a work-around, we placed the iPod in a coffee-cup holder between our seats and then shared the two earpieces—one screwed into my right ear, the other screwed into my wife's left ear. The monophonic compromise was better than nothing; at least we could hear our favourite music. That is, until I took a quick look over my left shoulder to check my blind spot. My sudden movement pulled tight our common earphone wire, yanking my wife's earpiece right out of her ear—like a cork from a wine bottle. She screamed in pain. My wife was not impressed.

A delightful surprise of driving the Corniche de l'Estérel from Cannes to St-Raphaël was coming across the pretty little towns, most with a backdrop of red rocks and plane trees. At the first of these towns, La Napoule-Plage, we counted three fine-sand beaches and walked around the 15th-century castle that overlooks the small harbour. We read that the castle was partly destroyed in the 18th century. However, thanks to the rich American philanthropist Henry Clews Jr, it was restored in the 1920s. Apparently, Henry was a sculptor, although not a good one, and his work displayed in the castle has been described as possessing a breathtaking lack of talent, which is why his talented peers nicknamed him Clueless Clews. Henry would not have been impressed.

A little farther along the coast, we came upon Théoule-sur-Mer where we parked Twingo and set off on a stroll. We started at the main street, avenue Charles Dahon, which has just the right number of cafés, gift shops, and restaurants to live up to its description as a small seaside resort. Apparently, it is steeped in history and you can visit the Château des Mineurs, a hard-to-miss battlemented castle that used to be an 18th-century soap factory. The village also has a pleasant old harbour and a beautiful sandy beach with clear, shallow water that's ideal for children to swim and play in safely. Having made that assessment, we were alarmed by the screams of a little girl who went running by with a small octopus clinging to her back, its tentacles reaching up over her shoulders. Her screams faded as she turned the corner around the rocky promontory and disappeared from sight. She was not impressed.

The sight of the Massif de l'Estérel's rugged, red volcanic rock was strikingly attractive and impossible to miss along that stretch of the D559. Growing hither and thither in the rock's cracks and crevices were clumps of gorse and scrub pine that softened the ruggedness and added finishing touches to the beautiful landscape that attracts artists from around the world. We stopped several times at lay-bys to view the red rocks and the lovely bays. A couple of times we asked like-minded tourists if they would take a photo of us posing in the foreground— using *our* camera, of course—and most accommodated our request. Some of those who spoke English asked us to reciprocate, after which a short conversation would ensue. The Brits were the most inquisitive, almost annoyingly so. "Where are you staying? Have you been to Cannes? Is that a digital camera? You don't get weather like this back home. Have you been to a casino? Aren't the French crazy drivers? Where are you from? I have an uncle who lives in Vancouver, you might know him: Paul Clanger. Does the name ring a bell?"

After stopping briefly at Port-La-Galère, Miramar, Le Trayas, Anthéor, Agay, and Boulouris, we had trouble recalling details of each. All were small and picturesque resort towns. All had a sandy beach and an attractive leisure harbour, and all offered a quiet stay in a small hotel or a cliffside villa. And we agreed that, should we ever return to the French Riviera, we'd stay at one of these jewels on the D559 necklace that links Cannes to St-Raphaël. We were so impressed.

Although I'd apologized to my wife for the sudden uncorking of her iPod earpiece, her reluctance to converse with me was proof enough that I was still in the doghouse. For the rest of the drive to St-Raphaël she remained silent, looking out of her window. With my left side feeling the warmth of the sun's rays and my right side feeling the frostiness of my wife's "cold shoulder," we drove into the outskirts of St-Raphaël. My suggestion of a picnic lunch seemed to warm the atmosphere a little, and before it had a chance to cool down again, I followed that ice-breaker by telling her that I thought her shorts and top contrasted well against her developing tan. Within seconds the frostiness thawed and the atmosphere returned to bright, sunny periods. A psychologist would be impressed.

21

Saint-Raphaël:

Golf but no Ruins; Popeye but no Seizures

We ate our picnic in a shaded park that looked out over a huge yacht harbour and convention centre. After wiping the bread crumbs and rosé wine droplets off our plastic tablecloth, we unrolled our beach mats and lay down to digest lunch in the warmth of the sun. Its rays penetrated the foliage of the trees and threw a mottled pattern over our bodies, the lawns, and the bordering flower beds. Lying square to my wife with my head propped up against her waist, I read aloud from our guidebook:

"*St-Raphaël is less popular than Fréjus—its neighbour to the west—and has less to offer tourists who are usually more interested in bathing on a beach than bathing in history. Although it was once a Roman settlement, for in-your-face, wide-angle, photographic evidence of Roman ruins you are better to visit Fréjus.... St-Raphaël is the underdog of the two vacation towns. It has an excellent sandy beach, a casino or two, and a long boardwalk that turns into a paradise for strolling families and flirting teenagers.... St-Raphaël should be avoided if you're looking for a quiet seaside resort, but for those who cannot afford to stay at the hotels in St-Tropez or Fréjus, it offers a selection of cheaper accommodation.*"

The last sentence read: "*St-Raphaël has five golf courses.*"

Now *that* is noteworthy, I thought, as I started to recall every stroke of my best round a couple of years ago at Northlands Golf Club in North Vancouver. Who cares if St-Raphaël hasn't got as many Roman ruins as Fréjus, when there are five golf courses nearby—all within a 3-wood and a pitching wedge distance? Who cares if Napoleon landed here on his triumphant return from Egypt in 1799, and then later, in 1814, cast off from here for Elba in disgrace? And who cares that the Allied forces landed here, in August 1944, to start part of their final offensive against the Germans, when I could be investigating which of the five golf courses is the most difficult and which is the prettiest?

Even though these facts were, no doubt, irrefutably accurate, and the town's historical events had been of monumental significance and created great excitement in their day, nothing can compare with the thrill of sinking a right-to-left, severe-breaking, ten-metre downhill putt for a birdie.

Not far from our picnic spot, boulevard du Général de Gaulle runs into promenade du Président René Coty. Both streets are lined with early 20th-century hotels and modern apartment buildings, most of which were in need of a fresh coat of paint. I thought the grandest thing about the streets was their names; only in France would you see such lengthy and patriotic ones. The street that runs by both the Continental and Excelsior Hotels has three names: promenade du Président René Coty, boulevard de la Libération, and promenade de Lattre de Tassigny. I don't believe we have such grand and patriotic street names in Canada, but I can imagine it. "Yeah, just continue along Prime Minister Stephen Harper Avenue, turn left at Royal Canadian Mounted Police Boulevard, then turn right at Ice Hockey Champions of the World Street."

Many North American towns have simply named their streets numerically, counting off consecutively from the main street that runs north-south or east-west, often for several hundred miles. And to an unfamiliar ear, receiving directions may sound like a test for a Boy Scout or a Girl Guide when trying to attain their Navigator badge. "Go east on 17th West, under the Highway 89 overpass to Main, hang a right and head north for two-and-a-half hours, and you'll find the 7-11 convenience store on the southeast corner of the Arctic Circle Bypass. You can't miss it. It's at 13,556."

Stephen Foey

At the far end of promenade du Président René Coty (but not beyond the "out of bounds" markers), just in front of the 19th-century Vieux Port, stands the Grand Casino, partially obscuring the view of the domed 19th-century church, Notre-Dame-de-Victoire-de-Lepante. And clashing with the church's dramatic architecture and countless ornate stone details is a relatively modern, white-and-flamingo-pink apartment building. What were the officials in the city planning department thinking when they approved the plans for this rectilinear eyesore, especially so close to a magnificent church? They were clearly "out to lunch"—or downing a beer at the nineteenth hole—when they made *that* decision.

The most popular seafront attraction for children, after the sandy beach, of course, is St-Raphaël's famous fairground ride. It's a reproduction of an 18th-century carousel and has been in operation since the early 1900s, the sight and sounds of which must bring back childhood memories for thousands of adults over many decades. Several of the younger children on the merry-go-round rocking horses were screaming and crying as they hung on for dear life. What they first thought was going to be so much fun, turned out to be a never-ending cycle of ups and downs and fear and monotony—an introduction to what, perhaps, awaits them in adulthood.

In between sips of café au lait on a patio of a quayside café at the attractive 19th-century Vieux Port, I focused my telephoto lens on an old fisherman who was sitting on a wooden box repairing his nets. His leathery, craggy, tanned face reflected his years exposed to the elements at sea. I imagined him standing on deck, hauling in nets while facing gale-force winds, and braving icy-cold spray as waves crashed over the boat's bow in heavy seas. He sported a well-worn captain's hat, a navy blue T-shirt, and a pair of baggy black pants tucked into his black knee-high waders. To his left were a few net-mending implements, a roll of fine nylon line, a leather tobacco pouch, and a small glass that I presumed held a tot of rum. As he threaded the fine line, tied knots, and inspected his work, he sucked on a clay pipe, which didn't appear to be lit.

As the fisherman concentrated on his work, his green eyes sparkled, radiating a calm contentedness that gave me the impression that he was happy just to be alive. As I shot several frames of him, I realized that I was photographing a real, live Popeye. Zooming in on his biceps, I half expected to see a tattoo of an anchor, or a heart with an arrow through it and "Olive Oyl" written below. Occasionally he stopped to scratch his whiskered jaw, sip his rum, or sneak a peek at the bow of a pretty woman coming into view on his port side, and then at her aft, as she glided by on his starboard side—evidence that there was plenty more life left in the old seadog.

As he sucked on his pipe, he was able, somehow, to whistle out of the other side at the same time. Being somewhat of an accomplished whistler myself, I tried to perform this feat—using a teaspoon in place of a clay pipe. Alas, my attempts were unsuccessful. Even though I managed to keep the teaspoon from falling from between my lips, it toggled up and down uncontrollably when I tried to whistle, producing only a short rush of air and a flurry of expanding bubbles of saliva that burst and formed a rivulet down the side of my chin. Looking up from her magazine and suspecting that I was having a seizure, my wife asked semi-hysterically, "Honey! Are you okay?"

"Yes, darling, I'm fine," I answered, as I removed the spoon from my mouth and wiped my chin.

"But why were you waggling that spoon up and down in your mouth?" she asked, still concerned.

"See Popeye over there, the old guy mending nets? Well, he can whistle and suck on a pipe at the same time," I began enthusiastically. But before I was halfway through explaining the unique challenge, she muttered something under her breath and went back to her reading.

Forewarned that St-Raphaël's town centre was devoid of charm, we walked back to Twingo, which I'd remembered to park in the shade of plane trees. And then, believing that we qualified as discriminating tourists wanting to bathe in the history of Roman ruins, we set off to Fréjus—and an unexpected visit to a medical clinic.

22

Fréjus:

The Coloured Cross Conundrum and the Pink Elephant Man

It happened just as we were pulling up at a pay-and-display parking spot in Fréjus. Perhaps Mozzie had radioed ahead to Central Command reporting our recent movements and approximate coordinates. Once it spotted Twingo, the wasp locked on its target (ironically, a White Anglo-Saxon Protestant), banked sharply in through the driver's side window, and with pinpoint accuracy hit the tip of my nose. Not that its mission was a total success, as the wasp was unable to unleash its sting power at that instant of initial impact. Being that my nose was aerodynamically modified when I walked headlong into a lamppost some years ago, the wasp deflected off the tip and was trapped for two seconds against the frame of my sunglasses before it fired off its weapon at a secondary target: the side of my nose. An instinctive swat of my hand sent the wasp spiralling down, crash landing on the floor mat, the heel of my size ten sandal making sure it did not survive. The pain was instantaneous and excruciating. My eyes filled with tears and, within seconds, fine streams were running down both of my cheeks.

As she was aware of what had just happened, my first-responder wife sprang into action by screaming and springing out of the car. She has a phobia of wasps and bees. Opening the hatchback, she reached for our medical kit and retrieved the small first aid booklet. Not knowing if I was allergic to wasp stings, we became concerned that, if I *was* allergic, I could be dead within the hour. My wife looked at her watch. Precious time was ticking away. But she read on: *"Get to a doctor as soon as possible, and take along the insect that stung you. If the insect is nowhere to be found, inform the doctor of its name."* Given that the wasp was unable to tell me its name, I retrieved its corpse from the floor mat, locked the car doors, and asked the first English-speaking person for directions to a medical clinic.

Fortunately, just fifty metres away, cantilevered out from a dull, grey building, was a large, flashing green neon sign in the shape of a cross. This, we were advised by a bilingual teenager, signified a medical centre. As we dashed towards it, my face swelling by the second and only fifty-seven minutes to live, I asked myself why the cross was green. Why wasn't it red? I would have more confidence in my chances of surviving if I were running to a medical centre with a red cross, I thought. I had seen the Red Cross in action on TV, those dedicated professionals saving lives internationally for decades. But I couldn't recall having seen a green cross on the side of ambulances racing to and from accidents. Was the work done at a Green Cross clinic more environmentally friendly? Adding to the conundrum, I remembered that the out-of-country medical insurance I'd purchased in Vancouver was with Blue Cross. What's that all about? Why a blue cross? I asked myself as I neared certain death.

With only fifty-four minutes left on my earthly clock, we burst through the doors of the Green Cross medical centre carrying my deceased winged foe in hand. At first glance, I thought the receptionist-nurse, who had a wart on the end of her nose, was wearing a witch's Halloween mask. But, no, I suspected that she must be an unhappy person who didn't believe in applying anti-aging cream every night.

"Do you speak English?" I blurted, skipping the usual, *"Parlez-vous anglais, s'il vous plaît?"*

"Oui," she replied.

"So why didn't you answer yes? You idiot! Can't you see I'm dying?" came to mind.

Ooh-la-la Land

Nurse Frighteningale pointed to a sign—written in six languages, including Japanese—that informed new patients that they should provide not one, but four pieces of identification when returning their completed "Patient Information" form. The form, which asked for personal details such as address, telephone number, and occupation, also asked if I was allergic to anything. Below that, it asked for the name and address of my next of kin. If I am allergic to wasp stings it may only be for the next forty-one minutes, I thought as I passed the completed form, together with my passport, driver's license, VISA card, and Vancouver library card, to the witch.

"*Asseyez-vous, s'il vous plaît,*" ordered Nurse Frighteningale without making eye contact and succeeding in her deliberate effort to annoy me by not speaking a word of English.

"Do you mean, sit down?" I wanted to scream.

The first thing I noticed about the waiting room was its décor. The floor tiles were red, as were the walls, that is, up to about two metres above the floor. This reminded me of a tour we'd taken of a replica of an old Spanish galleon that was anchored in Victoria Harbour several years ago. The guide had explained that the floor and walls of the ship's infirmary, which was accommodated on a lower deck, had been painted red so that blood would not be as noticcable to those with gushing, open wounds. With the wounded out of sight and their moans and screams out of earshot, the rest of the crew was unlikely to become demoralized as they went about firing cannons, swashbuckling, and swinging from rigging while clenching daggers between their teeth.

With only forty minutes to live, I suspected that my ballooning face had reached the same blood-red shade, and it felt as though it was about to explode. How sad, I thought, that in the unlikely event that my head should explode, it would likely go unnoticed.

The second thing I observed about the room were the waiting patients. The three people, who were sitting apart and staring ahead at the red walls, each had a small dog at their feet. Perhaps we were mistaken about the green cross. Perhaps it signified a veterinary clinic. For a moment, I imagined leaving the doctor's office wearing a large cardboard collar to prevent me from scratching my face. And the three other patients were probably wondering where our pet was. That is, until I opened the palm of my hand and, with tears still streaming down my face, looked down at the lifeless winged creature lying on its back.

A forty-something man wearing green overalls and with his hair tied back in a ponytail—just like Muscle Mountain's—came out of one room, went into another, and then reappeared with a stepladder. He opened it and positioned it directly below a polystyrene ceiling tile. But before climbing the ladder, he pulled out a packet of cigarettes from one of his many pockets, placed a cigarette between his lips, and lit it. The smoke break, I assumed, was all in accordance with union rules. This was not an environmentally friendly clinic, I realized, as I grappled with the thought that if the wasp sting didn't finish me off, then the second-hand smoke would. The man in green overalls nodded to the other three patients, took another drag on his cigarette, and climbed the steps. All the dogs wagged their tails, one barked. Placing the fingertips of both hands on the tile, he pushed it up and set it off to one side. Reaching into the dark space beyond, he manipulated something that clicked into place. Immediately, we heard a distant humming sound and then felt a gentle flow of cool air begin to circulate his cigarette smoke. Back down the ladder, he folded it up, put it away, and re-entered the room he'd come from.

One by one, the three patients, together with their dogs, went into the doctor's office, and each came out carrying a prescription in one hand and a dog biscuit in the other. Each visitation took fifteen minutes, so, alas, by the time Nurse Frighteningale shouted, "Stef-fan!" and pointed to the doctor's door, my hour had expired, and yet, on the positive side, I had not. Meanwhile, my wife had been sitting with her head back against the wall, eyes closed, muttering something under her breath. I hoped it was a prayer for my quick recovery, but as the sole beneficiary of my estate, she might have been calculating the total of my life insurance policies and her soon-to-be, bottom-line inheritance.

Miraculously, I made it into the doctor's office, but then almost collapsed at the sight before me. It was not that of my ever-expanding, blood-red face reflected in the full-length mirror on the wall opposite me, but that of the pony-tailed, green-overall-clad, smoking janitor sitting behind a large oak desk.

"*Entre, s'il vous plaît,*" he started. "And what seems to be the matter?" he said in flawless English after noticing "ANGLAIS!!" written by Nurse Frighteningale in red ink at the top of my completed patient information form.

"My enormous, ever-expanding, blood-red face is the matter," I was tempted to shout contemptuously, expecting him to stand up at any moment and start sweeping the floor or changing a burned-out light bulb. "I've been stung by a wasp right here," I began, pointing to the epicentre of the inflamed area and then showing him the dead culprit in the palm of my other hand.

Pinned along the wall next to the full-length mirror were several colourful and graphic cross-sectional views of the human body. One illustrated the skeletal structure; another the muscles, tendons, and ligaments; next to it, the digestive system; and the last and always the most fascinating, the female reproductive system. Disquietingly, there were no framed certificates on the wall. Where was the parchment paper with the black lettering, red serrated edge seals, and illegible signatures to reassure me that Dr Janitor knew what he was doing? I half expected him to take a bottle of Liquid-Plumr and dab a little on the affected area, but he didn't. Instead, he had me hold an ice pack to it and then he dabbed on some calamine lotion.

"*Eh bien.* The stinger is out. You can expect the swelling to go down in the next twelve hours," said Dr Janitor as he dabbed more calamine lotion over a third of my face. "*Au revoir, Monsieur.* Have a nice day," he concluded, mimicking a North American farewell.

"What if the swelling doesn't go down within the next twelve hours?" I pressed sceptically.

"Then rush to a hardware store and talk to an expert," I expected him to say as he rubbed his chin in deep thought. "Get yourself to a hospital if you begin to feel nauseated or feverish or have problems breathing or become partly paralyzed," he answered, listing a few of the possible serious symptoms with the same nonchalant tone he would use when ordering countersunk-headed screws, two-inch spiral nails, a sheet of coarse sandpaper, and a can of gloss paint.

"What should I do with this?" I asked, as I opened my hand and presented the dead wasp.

"Just place it in the ashtray," he replied, pointing to the one full of butts on his desk.

"But don't you have to dissect it and analyze the poison?" I asked, visualizing him in the back room starting up a chainsaw.

"That will not be necessary. Do not worry, *Monsieur*. You show no serious signs of an allergic reaction. Some redness and slight swelling is normal," he said as he checked his watch.

I thanked him, and as I turned to leave, Dr Janitor reached inside a pocket of his overalls, presumably for another cigarette, or perhaps for a screwdriver.

When my wife saw me, she gasped. I assumed it was at the sight of my red face partly covered with a large pink blotch of calamine lotion, rather than a gasp of disappointment that I was still alive—the mental picture of her smiling at her lawyer and executor, as they handed her the cheque of bequeathed funds, disappearing in a blink of an eye.

"Feef-tee euros!" demanded Nurse Frighteningale, her fake smile revealing a missing front tooth.

"*Fifty euros!*" I exclaimed. "That's more than seventy dollars for just five minutes' work," I blurted, hoping that my agitation wouldn't trigger a shock to my nervous system, resulting in partial paralysis. Rather than prolonging the bad start to the afternoon, I paid her the money and turned to leave without further ado, hoping that she wouldn't cast a spell on me.

Stepping into the blazing sunshine, I was convinced I looked like the Elephant Man with a huge, pink blotch—a Pink Elephant Man. We walked back to Twingo, only to discover a parking ticket between the windshield and a wiper blade. We had forgotten to pay-and-display. The witch *had* cast her spell.

23

Fréjus:

Caesars, Monuments, Ruins, and Express Trains

Understanding only the number of euros handwritten on the parking ticket was enough to elevate my blood pressure to above hypertension levels. Feeling hot under the collar and, in my case, looking red hot above the collar, we decided to leave Twingo in what had become our no-pay-and-dismay parking spot. Placing the ticket back under the wiper blade, we walked into Fréjus-Centre rationalizing that the penalty was fair payment for several additional hours of parking.

Our priority, as we entered the narrow streets of the old town, was to sit in the shade and have a stiff drink or two. And having found an attractive café-bar near place Formigé within view of the ancient architectural splendour of Le Groupe Épiscopal—apparently, the most impressive monuments in Provence—we sat in the cool shade of an umbrella and beckoned a waiter to our table. Scurrying over, wearing a white apron tied about his waist and a folded white towel draped over his left forearm, the waiter hesitated, shocked at the sight of me. Gathering his wits but looking a little uncomfortable, he proffered the drink list to my wife and, with the exception of an occasional sideways glance, pretended I wasn't there. Perhaps he thought that I'd been buried in sand all day on the beach by a bunch of overzealous kids with buckets and spades, leaving only my head exposed to the scorching sun. I was tempted to quote John Hurt's famous line from *The Elephant Man*: "I am *not* an animal. I'm a human being." Instead, while my wife perused the multilingual drink list, I read from our guidebook.

As coincidence would have it, as I read that Julius Caesar had colonized Fréjus around 49 BC, my wife announced that she fancied a Bloody Caesar and searched under the Union Jack section of the drink list. Being partial to the popular Canadian concoction of vodka and Clamato juice with a dash of Tabasco and Worcestershire sauce, a lime wedge and a celery stalk, all served with ice in a glass, its rim coated in celery salt, I said, "Make that two, and tell him to bring them bloody quick." I then returned to my research, using our guidebook to hide my face from a little boy at the next table who kept pointing at me and tugging on his mother's skirt.

In learning that Fréjus was once a Roman port-city of over 40,000 inhabitants, and that Roman galleys set out from its harbour in 31 BC to defeat Marc Antony and Cleopatra at the battle of Actium, I recalled watching Richard Burton and Elizabeth Taylor onscreen in the enthralling, three-hour epic *Cleopatra*—the old movie reels now safely stored away in a can on a shelf in a vault at a Hollywood film studio. But what spoiled my big-screen recollections was the name of the battle: Actium. If memory serves me right, Actium is also the name of an over-the-counter product to help induce bowel movement. "QUICK ACTING!!" promises the packaging, implying that plugged-up consumers would be wise to be seated on the toilet before swallowing the recommended dosage. But I digress, most of Cleopatra's naval forces were killed and her ships destroyed in the battle.

Our waiter arrived to take our order, and as my wife tried her best to describe, charade-style, the ingredients of a Bloody Caesar, he responded with a dazzling, well-choreographed performance of his own dramatic gesticulations. However, by the time Act I was over, they both looked exhausted and we agreed to have two Bloody Marys instead: one each for the beauty and the beast.

When I read that Le Groupe Épiscopal was described as "an enclosed episcopal ensemble," I imagined a group of bishops arranged in a circle playing stringed instruments, a violin case open on the ground to catch loose change from members of their congregations on the way to worship inside the 11th and 12th-century cathedral naves. Clarification came—after finishing our Bloody Marys—as we strolled by the ornately carved wooden doors at the main entrance and then stepped inside the wonderful collection of historic buildings. Known as Cathédrale St-Léonce et Cloître, the main building has a parapet-topped tower that reaches high above the neighbouring rooftops and once provided a strategic position for archers defending the town during invasions.

In addition to the cathedral's two grand naves stands an octagonal 5th-century baptistery. Eight 2,000-year-old Corinthian columns that initially supported the roof of a temple under which thousands of pagan rituals of sacrifice took place were reused to support the roof of the baptistery under which, for centuries following, thousands of total-immersion baptisms have taken place. As we sauntered around, we noticed that the large font in the centre was empty of water. Sadly, at the bottom of the font, a deceased pigeon lay flat on its back, its wings spread, its eyes wide open and looking heavenward. I assumed it had been trapped inside the building, and its search for a droplet of water had ended, ironically, at a place where life begins again for thousands of Christians.

Outside the baptistery, we climbed a set of stairs to a magnificent cloister featuring painted wooden ceilings from the 14th and 15th centuries. Then we sauntered around the small museum, Musée Archéologique, where, set into the floor, we came upon a mosaic of a leopard that dates back to the 3rd century. Why a leopard? Why not a lion? I've never heard of Romans throwing Christians to the leopards.

With the heat of the afternoon and the effects of the Bloody Marys having stifled our capacity to absorb another interesting point of antiquity, we made our way into a beautiful courtyard and rested for a while in the shade. Had we been feeling brighter, we might have followed up on our guidebook's suggestion of closely comparing the cathedral's barrel vaults with the groin vaults that support the roofs of its two grand naves. But we'd had enough of the marvels of Gothic stonemasonry and the amazing accomplishments of the Romans; we just wanted to sit in the quiet courtyard, listen to the chirping birds, and watch fellow tourists coming and going, clicking cameras, and licking ice cream cones. In the centre of the courtyard stood a large stone well, which drew many tourists. Some of them had kneeled in the cathedral's pews, where they might have mumbled short prayers for the speedy recovery of a sick loved one, and then they hedged their supplications by closing their eyes, making the same wish, and throwing a coin down into the well.

Refreshed from our rest, we studied our map of the town and decided to visit the *arènes*, known commonly as the *amphithéâtre,* which is just a short chariot ride from the old town. I was not only intrigued that the amphitheatre was built almost 2,000 years ago to hold an audience of over 8,000 appreciative Romans but also that it's still in use today for two of the most popular but dangerous event-attractions: bullfights and rock concerts. Standing on the back row of stone seats, looking down at the stage, I wondered if those Bronze Age citizens of Fréjus would be rolling over in their graves if they knew that their appreciation of the performing arts has developed no further than bullfighting and rock music. During their time, the songs—played on lyres, flutes, and harps—were light and only the metal was heavy.

Not far from the amphitheatre, we came across a monument that commemorates the drowning of 421 people when a dam burst above the town in 1959. Sipping on ice-cold Perrier water at a busy café-bar, we read that water had played a significant role in Fréjus's history, and continues to do so. Today, of course, other than cool-looking tourists sipping on cool Perrier water, the safe swimming beach at Fréjus-Plage is the main attraction for thousands of summer-season tourists who bring with them their millions of euros.

And owing to the sea receding over 2,000 years, Fréjus-Plage now lies a kilometre south of Fréjus-Centre. To create the original Roman harbour, dozens of acres of lagoon were dredged, and wharves and a walled canal were built to link the harbour to the sea. To protect the harbour from a surprise naval attack at night, a huge iron chain, which through the day was submerged at the bottom of the canal, was winched above the sea's surface. A Roman guard would stand over six male slaves, whipping their perspiring bodies as they pushed on the levers of the huge hexagonal wooden capstan that raised and lowered the chain—the exhausted slaves wishing they'd been born Roman. The first slave to drop would be carried off on a flat-bed cart to the Roman temple for that evening's ceremonial sacrifice. Why kill a beautiful virgin maiden when an ugly old manslave is nearby and already close to death's door?

In those Roman days, water flowed out of a natural reservoir near Mons, and an enormous aqueduct carried it forty-five kilometres to the north of town, and eventually a smaller aqueduct fed the thermal baths. We walked to Porte d'Orée at the southeast end of rue des Moulins, and then stood in amazement at a remaining arcade of the thermal baths. Having been raised in a two-up-two-down, row house without an indoor bathroom or toilet, I'm always fascinated about the marvels of Roman baths. But I'm left in a quandary as to why plumbing hasn't advanced that much since Caesar first crossed the English Channel in 55 BC. For that first invasion, he brought with him 10,000 foot soldiers and 500 cavalry. A year later he returned with a further 5,000 foot soldiers and 2,000 cavalry in 800 boats. He even remembered to bring an elephant to scare the living daylights out of the Britons. What Caesar and all subsequent Roman emperors forgot to bring with them was an adequate number of plumbers.

As a poor family, our thermal bath was a galvanized steel tub that hung outside on a rusty nail in the wall at the back of our house. Once every three months, whether we needed a bath or not, my father and I would carry the tub through the back door into the kitchen and fill it with water from four large pans heating on the stove. One by one, ladies first, we would bathe in warm, soapy water. Being the only son and at the bottom of the pecking order, I was the last to immerse, by which time the water was slightly less murky than the River Mersey.

With the primary cleansing process complete, my father and I, using the single handle at both ends, would lift the half-full tub and waddle out through the back door. There, in the backyard, beside a small drain grid, we would carefully lift one end of the tub until it was empty. Nowhere near as sophisticated as the Roman aqueducts, our method of transporting water often proved ineffective. One poorly timed, out-of-sync footstep would create a tidal wave and drench my father at the front, and then me at the back. And *that* was the secondary cleansing process.

As we were getting hungry, we referred to our guidebook and found Restaurant l'Aréna, part of Hôtel l'Aréna, located on rue du Général de Gaulle. It was an attractive hotel with bright ochre walls and a swimming pool and a garden terrace with exotic greenery and colourful flowers. As soon as we entered the hotel, I headed directly to the washroom, where I washed away the remaining calamine lotion. Except for a small red blemish, the Pink Elephant Man was no more.

Although the restaurant is popular for its garden terrace, we chose to eat in the dining room, which is cozy, tastefully furnished, and decorated with deep yellow walls and olive trim. French doors opened onto the terrace by the swimming pool. We were at once taken with the ambience of the room, and by the time we'd been seated by a window, and served a bottle of white wine and a basket of bread sticks, the dining room and terrace were packed. It was a delicious meal: Scallop Salad with Truffle Vinaigrette for starters; followed by Oven-Cooked Sea Bass Fillet, Truffle Sauce, and Potato Gnocchi; and, for dessert, Hot Chocolate Sponge Cake with Coconut Cream. The service was excellent and the classical music helped enhance the romantic mood.

In the flickering candlelight, I looked across the table at my wife and whispered that she looked just as good as the day we were married. She smiled. "You have—" she began, but the rest of her sentence was drowned out by the nine-o'clock Nice-to-Marseille express. The clattering rose to a crescendo, the hotel shook, and the glasses and the crockery began to rattle. The rest of her sentence was far too difficult to lip-read, but I hoped it finished with "made me so happy" and not, "a piece of spinach stuck between your teeth." I mouthed, "I love you." And as the clatter of the last railway carriage trailed off down the track, she smiled and mouthed, "I love you, too."

24

Around Cap d'Antibes:

Two Lounging Walruses, One Slippery Eel, And One Telepathic Waiter

During the next several days, we didn't stray far from Hôtel Beau-Site in our quest to achieve a state of total relaxation. And while we were striving to reach this elusive state, we cultivated our suntans. Each day started with a café au lait and croissants on the crazy-paved patio, then we read, sunbathed, napped, swam until noon, and had lunch around the corner at Café Maxime's. After lunch, we'd walk through the neighbourhood or down to La Garoupe Plage, take another refreshing dip in the pool followed by a hot shower, change into dinner clothes, and then drive a short distance along the coast road into Juan-les-Pins or Antibes for supper. It was a very pleasant routine, a great improvement over our normal nine-to-five grind back home contributing to Canada's Gross National Product.

Talking of gross national products, a newly arrived couple spent most of their day lounging and snoozing at the edge of the pool. I'd heard from Cane and Able that the pair had driven down from Brussels. The man was bald and meticulously clean-shaven except for a white handlebar moustache. His body was over-sized and pear-shaped, his skin as white as snow, and though he was wearing a pair of skimpy white Speedo swim shorts, they were alarmingly unnoticeable. His wife, just as large and just as pale, did not have a moustache—at least, not one that was visible from our side of the pool. She was not bald either, but for some strange reason she preferred not to remove her skull-tight, white bathing cap. She wore a white one-piece swimsuit that not only contained most of her excessive rolls—from bust to bum—but also smoothed them out a little.

The sight of the bulging Belgians brought to mind a most fascinating TV documentary about a pair of albino walruses that came together and mated for life. Not that there was much action to the documentary because the focus was on the infinitely small chance of the two white mammals existing at all, not to mention them finding each other and then mating for life. And just like the inaction of the documentary, the Bulging Belgians would snooze side by side at the edge of the pool and occasionally manoeuvre themselves slowly off their bellies into the water for a brief swim, returning to the same spot for another snooze in the sun—the male of the species frequently raising his head to sniff the aromas wafting poolside from the kitchen.

Muscle Mountain's complexion was looking a lot healthier, the sun's rays having brought some colour to his massive body. And although his developing tan lessened the contrast between his skin and the tattooed roadmap of California, it accentuated the scar on his face by turning it purple-pink. Playmate, who had a darker tan than any of us, continued turning heads and popping eyeballs with her every elegant, high-heeled stride. My wife and I agreed that the tiniest of her thong bikinis had been crocheted from a one-metre length of string. Their daughter spent most of her time in the pool, and insisted I play with her each time I went in. Leaving my prescription sunglasses behind on my sun lounge gave her a distinct advantage as we dove to the bottom to retrieve euro coins thrown into the deep end by Cane, the game's charitable sponsor. With her 20/20 vision, she would see me falter and shoot for the coin like a slippery eel. And each time we rose to the surface, she would scream with delight at her win and then place her prize in a growing pile of coins at the pool's edge. Of course, her successful salvage operation was being watched and applauded enthusiastically by her parents who were standing close by, not only as encouraging spectators but also as lifeguards.

Back on my sun lounge, while applying a fresh coat of sunscreen, I heard the chubby-cheeked cherub counting her euros and babbling to her parents—probably recalling her seal-like dives and how she'd snatched each coin from under my dysfunctional eyes. Next, from behind a *People* magazine, I heard Cane inform Able that Britney Spears was performing in Manchester. Able's ears pricked up at this tidbit. "Is she that young barmaid down at the Red Lion?" he asked.

"No. Don't be bloody daft!" Cane recoiled, continuing to read her magazine rather than make eye contact. "No. I'm talking about the pretty young thing you like to watch on telly," she corrected, then slurped her thumb with her tongue and turned the page.

But Able was back behind his three-day-old newspaper, the few times he lowered it coincided with Playmate striding towards the shallow end of the pool to perform one of her cooling-down routines.

To tourists driving by, Café Maxime's was easy to miss. From the road it looked more like a newsagent or a gift shop. Racks of French Riviera postcards and newspapers from around Europe took up most of the small, raised, concrete patio in front. Inside was dark, noisy, and smoky, and as our eyes adjusted to the lack of daylight it became obvious that Café Maxime's was where local workmen came to drink a few beers, smoke cigarettes, tell dirty jokes, and comment on every kick of the World Cup soccer ball that zigzagged across the TV screen. Some were eating lunch; others sat back with toothpicks systematically advancing along their uppers and lowers, dislodging trapped food particles. All were facing the monster TV screen, their backs to us as we hesitated at the front door. With the exception of the extra-large woman who was placing glasses of frothy beer on a tray behind the bar to our left, my wife was the only woman in the room. After making a quick assessment of the establishment, we turned to leave, but the woman behind the bar caught our attention. *"Bonjour, Madame et Monsieur, s'il vous plaît,"* she said, stretching her left arm above the bar and pointing towards a garden terrace on the other side of the room. *"Je m'appelle Maxime,"* she announced. *"S'il vous plaît,"* she repeated, her arm remaining outstretched.

"Parlez-vous anglais, s'il vous plaît?" I asked.

Suddenly, there was a deafening silence. No one spoke; no one laughed. But, en masse, the workmen turned their heads. Not only had two foreigners entered their domain, but one of them was a woman. Even the soccer players on the TV screen stopped, protesting to the referee for some unknown reason.

"Yehz, I speak Eeng-leesh. Pleaz seet on *la terrasse.* Lunch weel come *immédiatement,"* Maxime answered, without removing the cigarette hanging from her lips, her left arm still outstretched.

"Merci beaucoup, Maxime," my wife responded, setting off across the room filled with paint-stained overalls, steel-toed boots, and loaded leather tool belts.

"Merci beaucoup," I repeated, then followed in my wife's footsteps heading to the terrace.

A wolf whistle from the back of the room pierced the silence, followed by a few whispered utterances and louder snickers, and then it was quiet again. No one was watching TV; they were all gazing upon my wife as she neared the sliding door. Even the soccer players on TV stood waiting with their hands on their hips, and tens of thousands of soccer fans in the stands sat quietly. My wife stepped out onto the terrace, but I failed to notice the floor-mounted aluminium track that guided the sliding glass patio door, and I tripped headlong onto the terrace to the thunderous cheers and applause of the workmen. Embarrassed, I turned around to acknowledge their appreciation of slapstick humour, but the referee had blown his whistle, the game had restarted, the fans were cheering, and we were no longer of interest.

On the terrace, we were shaded from the sun by an overhead wooden latticework covered with vines whose leaves and flowers provided a ceiling of fragrant vegetation. Palms and flowers flourished in large pots and in the soil at the base of the tall hedge that created three walls of the lush, natural-looking enclosure. Many more workmen, sitting at the dozen or so tables, were being served by one hyperactive, multi-tasking, ambidextrous waiter who was buzzing on caffeine, or perhaps something stronger. No sooner had we sat down and reached for our phrasebook than the waiter rushed by and deposited a basket of bread and a bottle of water onto our table. Without breaking his stride, he scooped up several dirty plates and a salt shaker from the next table. Then, while dumping the plates from one hand into a large plastic tub, he simultaneously slid the salt shaker, using his other hand, across another table into the open palm of a customer who nodded and shouted a request at his back as he took off for the kitchen, picking up more dirty dishes as he went.

Opening our phrasebook to "Lesson 12: At the Restaurant," we turned to the subheading "I would like…" and found, *"Je voudrais une carafe de vin rosé, s'il vous plaît."* As if by magic, even before I had practised our request *en français*, the waiter slid a carafe of rosé wine in front of us, and then disappeared to the far end of the patio. We returned to our phrasebook. I practised, *"Je voudrais la carte, s'il vous plaît,"* and hoped there would be an English section in the menu when it arrived. We scanned our phrasebook for "mixed salad," but our jaws dropped when two mixed salads were put in front of us as our waiter flashed by. Amazed by this coincidence, we put away our phrasebook, certain that whatever dish came to mind, it would be brought to us by the waiter who couldn't wait to be asked.

Sitting back after our salads, we both agreed that a piece of grilled fish, garnished with vegetables and drizzled with a rich lemon-herb sauce would be our first choice for main course. So we closed our eyes, imagined the dish, and counted to five. We opened them wide on the count of five, only to see two thick, juicy steaks with French fries.

Looking around, frowning in disbelief, and wondering which table had mistakenly received our grilled fish, I noticed the daily special handwritten on the chalkboard on the wall: "Le Menu du Jour: Salade—Bifteck aux Pommes Frites—Crème Caramel—Vin Rosé." Laughing at the discovery that it was a fixed menu, we cut into our steaks and began to devour them. Then, noticing that our carafe of wine was almost empty, I was about to request a refill, but before I had time to ask, another one was slid onto our table and the empty one carried off by the waiter who couldn't wait to be asked.

25

Cap d'Antibes:

A Birthday, a Death, an Operation, and a Wrong Word

On the morning of my wife's birthday, I had breakfast delivered to our room. Listening intently to my secret request the night before, André the Man agreed that it would be a delightful surprise—so romantic, so French—to start the special day with breakfast in bed. Of course, I hoped that *breakfast* would not be the start to the special day.

"*Et champagne et jus d'orange?*" asked André the Man, starting to get carried away with my celebratory plans.

"Yes, okay. Champagne and orange juice," I agreed hesitantly, seeing our dream house with an ocean view in West Vancouver slip out of focus. Even Pawn the Bellboy smiled at me and nodded his approval from his black floor tile by the doorway.

"Happy birthday, darling," I said after kissing my wife on her cheek.

"Thank you," she responded, smiling and turning her face to receive another soft kiss on the lips.

Fifteen minutes earlier, I had opened wide the floor-to-ceiling French windows to our balcony, drawn back the inner lace curtains, and positioned the small table and two chairs in front. The sun had barely risen, but its rays were already hot. As usual, the chirping birds, rustling palm fronds, and the rippling swimming pool provided a peaceful background serenade. No other sounds could be heard—no voices, no thuds, no clatter, no clank.

Ooh-la-la Land

I had placed a small gift-wrapped box on the table. In it was her birthday present: dainty, frilly lingerie—oh so brief, oh so see-through, oh so French, oh so ooh la la! While my wife had been rummaging through racks and shelves in a boutique in Cannes, I'd dashed across the road, hastily purchased her gift, and then smuggled it back to the hotel in our shoulder bag. I hoped that I'd selected the correct size. A shapely, young bilingual woman had assisted me with my selection based solely on my description of my wife whose overall body type was not much different from her own. Had I not been in so much of a rush, I may have been tempted to agree to the sales assistant's suggestion that she model it for me. I consoled myself with the thought that, should my wife be really pleased with the lingerie set, I could always return to the store and spend time picking another one out—with the assistant's help, of course. I have always believed that it is far better to give than to receive.

Having ripped off the fancy wrapping paper and taken the lid off the box, my wife opened the envelope that sat on top of the hot pink tissue paper. The small card had been slipped inside by the assistant, and I had signed it later with the usual, "With all my love." There was a colourful pattern on the outside and only French words printed on the inside, so I had no idea what the card actually said, though I hoped it was something like, "Happy Birthday to the woman who is and will always be the woman of my dreams." For all I knew, however, it may have read, "Guaranteed rip-proof. Wash in cold water. Do not iron."

Forty-five minutes after my wife modelled her lingerie, we sat back at the table wearing our soft Hôtel Beau-Site bathrobes and discussed our plans for the day. I liked the idea of shooting off to Monaco and celebrating the day pretending we were super-rich jet-setters who had just popped over from Rome to be photographed by the paparazzi before rolling dice and placing chips at the gaming tables in the most famous of casinos. But my wife wanted to go to Grasse, to walk through fields of lavender and jasmine and to take a ninety-minute course on all you need to know about perfume. Considering that it was, after all, her birthday, and no member of the paparazzi would even blink an eye at seeing us pull up in front of the casino in our sub-compact Renault Twingo, I agreed that we'd go to Grasse, the town of six thousand fragrances.

Looking a little startled by the sound of the knock at our door, my wife got up to see who was there. Jacques the Ass was standing behind a serving cart that was draped in a white cloth upon which was a basket of chocolate croissants, a silver pot of coffee and another of milk, silver dishes of marmalade and butter, two fine-china coffee cups, a red rose in a vase, a carafe of freshly squeezed orange juice, two fluted champagne glasses, and a bottle of champagne. "'appy birthday, *Madame*," he trumpeted as he pushed the cart through the doorway.

"Thank you so much, Jacques," my wife said, looking first at him and then at me.

"Happy Birthday, darling," I repeated, blowing her a kiss.

"I 'ope you 'ave a wonderful day, *Madame*," said Jacques, smiling as he removed the breakfast items from the cart and set them upon the sunlit table. "Where are you go-eeng today?" he enquired as the champagne cork whistled by my head, missing it by inches, and sailed out through the French windows at a speed and trajectory that, I was convinced, would have had it splash down at the far end of the pool.

"We're going to Grasse," my wife replied, as she reached for a glass of champagne and orange juice.

"Grasse is so wonderful. You weel lurve eet there. Eet ees where my mother lived until last week," he added, his smile disappearing.

"Oh, where did she move to?" I asked, as I reached for my glass of champagne and winked at my wife.

"She went to 'eaven. Yehz, she deed pass away juz last week."

So there we were, the three of us standing at the table, my wife and I drinking a toast to many more healthy happy years while Jacques was on the verge of tears.

"We're so sorry to hear that," my wife empathized.

Realizing that the poor guy had been mourning the death of his mother for the last week while he worked behind the reception desk, and not knowing what else to say to a stranger, I asked him what he'd recommend we see in Grasse. "You moost viz-eet *une parfumerie*, the Musée de la Parfumerie, and the Cathédrale Notre-Dame een la Vieille Ville," he began, his smile returning as he poured the steaming coffee and milk and we bit into our croissants. "You moost see the flow-eurs and un-der-stand the im-por-tance of *un bon nez*, or—'ow you say?—a good nose," he continued, touching the tip of his nose with the tip of his right index finger.

Oh, that's just great, I thought. Instead of pretending to be James Bond with a beautiful woman hanging off my arm in Monte-Carlo's Casino, we were going to drive for an hour to discover the importance of a good nose. Now, if anyone understood the importance of a good nose, it was me. I will explain.

Many years ago, because I'd had problems breathing through my nose, my doctor referred me to a surgeon who suggested I undergo a surgical operation: a septoplasty. The problem, the surgeon explained, was that because of some earlier trauma—like walking headlong into a lamppost when I was a child—the wall of cartilage that divides the two nostrils was so badly bowed that it obstructed one of my nasal passages. Not only was it difficult to breathe through my nose, but it also lessened my sense of smell. While examining my nose, the plastic surgeon—realizing that his annual golf club fees were due—also recommended that, while he had his tools handy, he could perform a rhinoplasty which, at significant cost, would improve my breathing and, though difficult to believe, would improve my looks too.

For a couple of weeks immediately following the operation, I had to take extreme care that nothing came into contact with my nose, not even my glasses. Because I was so dependent on my bifocals to perform my engineering design work, the surgeon suggested I make a supporting contraption. He explained how as he drew a sketch for me. "Get a sun visor. Pierce two holes through the peak, about here. Thread two large paper clips through the holes, secure the clips with duct tape, and then attach two more paper clips from the secured clips, like this. Once you've threaded the stems through these last two clips, they will hold your glasses in position without the weight of them pressing down on your nose."

It looked a little odd, but the contraption worked well and enabled me to return to work earlier than I had expected. Naturally, everyone in the office was curious to examine the extent of the black-and-blue swelling that once was my nose. Most of my colleagues, being engineering types, were equally intrigued by the contraption supporting my glasses. To clients visiting our office I resembled a croupier who had been punched in the face the night before by a sore loser.

When I first returned to work, I sat opposite my boss at his desk and explained to him behind closed doors that the surgeon had corrected my deviated septum. My boss expressed concern for my black-and-blue face yet great admiration for my ingenuity for the simple but effective way of suspending my glasses. "You should patent that," he suggested, with genuine interest. I smiled and shrugged my shoulders but refrained from admitting that it was the surgeon's idea.

Before leaving his office, my boss called the human resources manager to advise her that I had returned to work. Although my boss was a brilliant man, he had questionable oratory skills. From time to time, especially when nervous, he would choose the wrong word or mix up a well-known expression—his mouth got ahead of his brain. I had witnessed this tendency towards malapropism several times in meetings and during presentations to clients.

"Good morning, Mary. Just to let you know that Steve has already returned to work after his surgery. (Pause) No, nothing serious—just a deviated *scrotum*. (Pause) Yes, that's right, a deviated *scrotum*. You should come take a look at it. (Pause) No, I'm sure he won't mind. (Pause) He's wearing a contraption that keeps his glasses from touching it. It's badly swollen and all black and blue right now, but when the swelling goes down he's hoping to be able to breathe through it. (Pause) Yes, *really*. It's a miracle of modern plastic surgery. Are you sure you don't want to pop down and take a look? (Pause) Of course, I've seen it. (Pause) No, I don't think he'll let you touch it."

26

Grasse:

10,000 Flowers, 6,000 Scents, Five Noses, and Three Certificates

"*Bonjour, Madame. Joyeux anniversaire!* 'appy Birthday!" said André the Man, as we walked past the front desk.

"Thank you very much," replied my wife, beaming back at him.

"'ow was your *petit déjeuner?*"

"Delicious, thank you," we responded in unison.

"And the champagne; it was good?"

"Excellent, *merci*," I smiled, recalling the cork flying by my ear.

"'ave a wonderful day," shouted Jacques, smiling and waving from *Réception*, showing no trace of mourning.

"*Joyeux anniversaire, Madame!*" chimed Pawn the Bellboy, as he entered the lobby carrying the suitcases of two pale new arrivals who trailed behind wearily on the checkerboard floor.

One of our guidebooks described Grasse as a pleasant day's trip from the coast. What it really meant is that tourists can drive there and back, and spend several hours touring Grasse's pleasant sights in one day. The trip there and back is not that pleasant. And the promise of walking through fields of jasmine and roses diminished as we crawled the seventeen kilometres on the N85 from Cannes to Grasse, which sits on a plateau 300 metres above sea level. The N85 is also known as route Napoléon because it was the road that he and his gathering army took from the beach at Golfe-Juan to Grenoble after being exiled for a year on the Isle of Elba. Further research revealed that Napoleon and his army of over 1,200 soldiers hiked the 324 kilometres in only six days and arrived in Grenoble to a hero's welcome. With his popularity and support growing, he eventually went on to Paris and reclaimed his title as Emperor.

One tourist leaflet listed a dozen or so quotes that are, supposedly, attributed to the tactical general who turned politician and then mighty emperor. I found the following ones particularly of interest:

- A Constitution should be short and obscure.
- An order that can be misunderstood will be misunderstood.
- Glory is fleeting, but obscurity is forever.
- In politics, never retreat, never retract, and never admit a mistake.
- In politics, an absurdity is not necessarily a handicap.
- Never interrupt your enemy when he is making a mistake.
- The best way to keep one's word is not to give it.
- The French complain of everything, and always.

Traffic congestion worsened as we neared Grasse, and in the stop-and-go traffic I wondered if Napoleon, France's mightiest military mastermind, politician, and hero of the history books, rolls over in his grave at the mention of his name when associated with a road that is now used to take busloads of tourists from Cannes' lifebuoy-rated beaches to Grasse's perfume factories.

Turning onto boulevard du Jeu de Ballon, we crawled through the town centre, hemmed in on all sides by frustrated drivers. Plans to turn down side streets were thwarted by "no entry" signs, and we found ourselves involuntarily leaving town.

Hopes of seeing row upon row of purple-on-green lavender had been dashed the night before in reading that we'd have to drive forty minutes due west of Grasse to see the most popular of sweet-smelling plants that appear on postcards and covers of southern Provence guidebooks. However, just five minutes out of Grasse, we turned onto a country lane that wound its way several kilometres around fields of flowers. We parked Twingo, sat in the shade on a bench by an old stone church, and looked out over a field of pink roses. To our left, a long row of plane trees separated the pink-on-green striped carpet from the bright yellow carpet of sunflowers in the adjacent field. All was quiet except for the sounds of the birds and the bees.

It takes 10,000 flowers to produce one kilogram (just over two pounds) of petals, and nearly one ton of petals (that's ten million flowers) to distil three pints of essence. And it's these astronomical figures that justify the sky-high cost of perfumes, which are priced by the proportion of essence in the final blend. *Parfum* contains 20 per cent pure essence, and *eau de toilette* and *eau de Cologne* contain between 2 and 6 per cent. After reading this to me from our guidebook, my wife suggested that I keep these facts in mind before complaining about the exorbitant prices of minuscule bottles the next time I go looking for a gift for her.

One thing that I've always thought rather odd is, why call it *eau de toilette?* Why would the perfume industry, knowing that it takes millions of delicate, fragrant petals to distill small amounts of essence, and knowing that those essences go into their products, and knowing that those products are sprayed on soft female body parts to heighten their attraction to the opposite sex, call the final blend "water of toilet." And while we're on the subject, why is it called *eau de Cologne?* Why name a blend after the water of an industrial German city? Well, further reading revealed that the *toilette* was a cabinet in which Europeans kept their clean, refreshing water to wash away their body odour. And *eau de Cologne* was created by Giovanni Paolo Feminis of Cologne in 1695, and his descendant, Jean-Marie Farina, established "Eau de Cologne" as a brand name in 1816. Interesting, yes, but surely it's about time for a change of names—if for no other reason than to persuade men that their expensive purchase at Christmas and birthdays is a worthwhile investment. *Essence de Erotica,* for example, would be simple to understand and would also hint at pleasurable rewards. Such a name change would have men rushing to the stores with credit cards in hand—wild horses couldn't hold them back.

Grasse was also founded by the Romans, and in the Middle Ages it became a centre for trading tanned skins and oil, and then perfumed gloves in the 1500s. As people seldom bathed in the 18th century, perfume became a fashionable necessity and high-society members never left home without the fragrance of water of toilet wafting behind them. Over time, the perfumed glove makers split from the tanners and set up their own industry, which led to the start-up of perfumeries. Today, even though there are over forty perfumeries in the area, only Molinard, Fragonard, and Galimard are open to the public.

A "nose" is the name given a master perfumer who selects the most famous of fragrances. At last count, there were only five "noses" sniffing around the world, and each trained from between seven and fifteen years before ever extracting an essence. After two years, sniffing students have memorized around 2,000 smells, and a master perfumer can identify, with just one whiff through unobstructed nostrils, about 6,000 scents. And between 200 and 500 of these fragrances are used to make just one perfume. With so few of them around, "noses" are sought-after professionals who are compensated extremely well and are required under contract to protect their precious snouts. Drinking alcohol, smoking cigarettes or pipes, and eating spicy foods are forbidden. And, although this requirement is not posted on the perfumeries' noticeboards, employees are requested to refrain from eating beans of any kind.

Returning to the centre of Grasse, we had a choice of vacant pay-and-display parking spaces just a short walk from the Vieille Ville. The small, old town is made up of tall, narrow houses packed onto the hillside along with many steep, narrow, cobbled streets and stairways. Following our noses, we found our way to rue Mirabeau and ambled around the labyrinth of picturesque back streets. From the shadow of a pizzeria umbrella, I captured a photo of a teenage couple sitting on the rim of a fountain. They were locked in a statuesque embrace, their lips glued together. I swear they didn't move during our entire lunch. If it were not for their clothes, they could have been mistaken for part of the fountain—two oversized sculptured stone cupids. Pigeons could have landed on their heads and pooped, and they wouldn't have noticed.

"Look, honey, they're in love," my wife said, sighing. "Do you remember when we used to kiss like that?" she asked, her voice trailing away dreamily at the sight of the pair conjoined at the lips. "Do you remember when we were teenagers, how we would neck for hours with our first loves, oblivious to everyone around? Do you remember…?"

Oh no, here we go again, I thought. Soon she'll reminisce about how we met, asking me about my first impressions of her and requesting that I recite the list of reasons why I fell in love with her. Then she'll move on to our wedding day, recalling each moment from waking up to switching off the bedroom lights eighteen hours later. Somehow, I needed to derail her train of thought, change the subject, and bring her back to reality.

"Would you look at that?" I began, peering at my camera.

"That's so romantic," she continued, ignoring my exclamation.

"I didn't have it on auto-focus, the F-stop is set wrong, and I forgot to screw on the filter," I cried, not knowing what I was talking about.

"I wonder if they'll marry."

"Is that a crack in my lens?" I continued.

"Why do we stop kissing like that when we get older?"

"You know, I think I should get new batteries or else the flash won't work," I said, knowing full well they were fully charged.

"Isn't she pretty?"

"Not as pretty as you, darling," I responded, switching tracks and relying on flattery. Her gaze turned from the cupids.

"Really?" she asked, her tone implying she wanted to hear more.

"*Really*. You're like a vintage wine getting better with age. You're like a classic perfume, its fragrance never deteriorating."

"You're so sweet, darling. But you're wrong about the classic perfume because even the world's best deteriorate. All perfumes have a shelf life. They may not stamp expiration dates on the bottles, but they all deteriorate in time."

"Okay, forget about the perfume bit. You really are getting better with age. It's true, you are."

"Actually, come to think of it, I'm all out of perfume," she said.

"Well, let's go get you some in one of those minuscule bottles. It's your birthday, remember?" I prompted, full of enthusiasm and relieved that I'd escaped having to recall years of romantic moments, but prepared for the exorbitant price tag ahead. We got up from the table and left the motionless, life-size cupids inhaling each other.

Although Jacques had recommended we visit the museum and the cathedral, we only stopped to look at them from the outside, preferring instead to stroll along arm in arm observing the multitudes of tourists and our charming medieval surroundings. Having read up on both tourist attractions, my only regret at not visiting the museum was not seeing the second-floor exhibit: the 3,000-year-old scented hand and foot of a mummy. Why only the hand and foot, I wondered? Where was the rest of the body? And was the mummy a mummy or was the mummy a daddy?

As for the cathedral, our guidebook described it as being rather uninteresting. That is, with the exception of having three fine religious paintings on display: *Christ Washing the Feet of the Apostles* by Jean-Honoré Fragonard, and *The Crown of Thorns* and *Christ Crucified between Two Thieves* by Peter-Paul Rubens. However, our decision to pass on them too was an insignificant sacrifice.

Fragonard is a name a visitor will not miss, even on a short outing to Grasse. There is the Musée Jean-Honoré Fragonard, which displays the works of Grasse's famous artist, and the Fragonard Parfumerie. Our guidebook enticed us to visit the museum by challenging us to view his paintings of everyday scenes to see how many sexual organs and acts (that are cleverly concealed within) we could identify. But we passed on that too.

La parfumerie Fragonard is written up as being the most convenient to walk to, which is one reason it is considered by some the best of the three that are open to the public. Another is that it contains the Musée du Parfum, which is located on an upper floor and exhibits the world's largest collection of perfume bottles, dating from Roman times to Chanel times. But it was the description of parfumerie Molinard—its turreted Provençal-style villa, immaculate lawns, and blooming flower beds—that swayed us to drive a little way back down the road and visit the ritzier property.

The guided tour of Molinard was extremely interesting. To start, our multilingual hostess was a tall, shapely young woman who wore a badge announcing her name: Jacqueline. Below her name was her job title, which included a typo that made her, aptly, a "Hotess." Jacqueline showed us around the factory of pot-bellied vessels and explained each stage of perfume production—the olfactory process—from extraction to distillation and beyond to the works of the "nose." She told us that Habanita de Molinard was their best-selling *eau de toilette*. Then, with the men hanging on her every word, she recited their promotional blurb: "Every woman loves it because it is magic. She wears it because it reveals the disconcerting personality and intense seduction slumbering within every woman."

Speaking for the men, she could have told us that the perfume was made from dead rats; we wouldn't have cared. What was important to us was that once a woman has sprayed herself with the magical blend, it would "reveal the intense seduction slumbering within." But perhaps in my hasty judgment I was unwise to overlook the fact that it also "reveals the disconcerting personality": Could this include throwing temper tantrums or even carving knives?

Jacqueline informed us that a new batch was about to be released: "It is of the moment; it's very agreeable and has a few hints of humour." And although it sounded like a new clean joke, it was the men who raised their hands when she asked: "Would anyone like to order a bottle at a special pre-production price?" But then, we would have raised our hands had she asked for volunteers to test their new guillotine.

After the tour, I was coerced (by the birthday girl) into signing up for the ninety-minute "sniffer" course: the Molinard *tarinologie*, a theoretical and practical initiation into the perfumer's art. And, as I expected, I was the only male trainee-perfumer in attendance. Meanwhile, the other men who had been on the tour with their partners were down the road in a bar telling dirty jokes, drinking twelve-year-old Scotch whiskey, playing poker, spitting on the sawdust floor, and eyeing the young barmaids when they walked by.

The olfactory session gave us the opportunity to create our own perfume from eighty essences displayed on pivoting trays labelled Jasmine, Patchouli, Blackberry Bud, Galbanum, Mimosa, Vanilla, Rose, and so on. At the completion of the course, each of us took away a bottle of our own *eau de parfum* creation whose formula was stored in a computer so that we could reorder miniscule bottles at exorbitant but worthwhile prices. I named my blend Hottest Host.

I was happy to receive a Molinard Trainee Perfumer diploma to frame and add to the impressive collection of certificates on the back wall of my office. I could visualize it hanging between my Certificate of Completion: Swimming 25 Metres Breaststroke, which was presented to me at Bramhall public swimming pool when I was a schoolboy, and my Certificate of Completion: Beginner Ballroom Dancing, which I received a few years later. From a distance, these two framed papers with their red seals and fancy signatures had impressed many clients and co-workers who hadn't bothered to look closely at what they could only assume to be proof of my engineering qualifications. Surely, a third certificate would add to my credibility.

27

Juan-les-Pins:

A Disconcerting Personality, a Volunteer, and a Few Hints of Humour

The delectable fragrances of Habanita de Molinard and Hottest Host wafted around in our wake as we passed by *Réception*. "'ow was your day? 'ow was Grasse?" asked Jacques.

"Fabulous! Grasse was beautiful and very interesting," I replied.

"You 'ave much smell," he continued, proving that his septum was not deviated.

"Isn't it wonderful?" I said, hoping he thought so too. Realizing that he may have detected "the intense seduction slumbering within her," I escorted my wife straight to our room.

After showering away all traces of Hottest Host, I lay on the bed surfing the TV channels. In addition to the daily coverage of the World Cup soccer tournament, there was the Tour de France. Until watching several stages, I'd never been interested in seeing cyclists race along country roads and through city streets. Hence, I hadn't taken the time to understand the many aspects of the race: the types of stages, the vast distances, and the strategies of the individual cyclists and their teams. And I'd never fully appreciated the tremendous fitness and determination required—with or without banned drugs.

Of particular interest was the preview of each stage. From a helicopter high above the route, the cameraman brought a bird's-eye view of the route to be covered that day, in effect creating a series of spectacular tourism commercials of much of France. Over the course of the event, a worldwide audience gets to see a wide variety of majestic rivers bordered by poplar trees; quilt-pattern fields of yellow rapeseed, red poppies, and purple-and-green lavender; snow-capped mountains; rocky and sandy coastal stretches; small towns and villages with old steeple-churches of stone walls and blue grey slate roofs; and the final sprint on the grand boulevard of Paris: Avenue des Champs-Élysées.

We drove to Juan-les-Pins for a celebratory meal—a romantic birthday dinner at Les Arcades, on boulevard President Wilson. Coming upon a vacant pay-and-display parking space close to the town centre was a good start, and then seeing my wife squirt another fine spray of Habanita de Molinard to her neck provided promise for a wonderful evening. I just hoped that the "intense seduction slumbering within" wouldn't be revealed to anyone else in the restaurant and that her "disconcerting personality" would be a no-show. Warily, I checked the cloudless sky for a full moon.

A crowd had gathered in a circle on a pedestrian-only street near the restaurant. Curious, we elbowed our way to the inner circle. In the centre, four men were juggling balls and clubs. At the conclusion of each mini-routine the four of them shouted, "*Voilà!*" as they struck a dramatic, statuesque pose. The audience cheered and applauded and shouted "*Encore!*" Suddenly, everyone hushed as the troop leader addressed the crowd. When he finished, all remained uncannily quiet.

Breaking the silence, my wife shouted, "*Encore!*" I looked at her in disbelief, and then checked the sky again for a full moon. The troop leader smiled and walked over. Feigning comprehension, she nodded and then shouted, "*Oui! Oui!*" The next thing I knew, I was sitting on a wooden box in the middle of the circle of cheering spectators while two jugglers hurled clubs within inches of my head. The cheers grew louder the closer the clubs came to my nose. Yikes! Had I kept the telephone number of the surgeon who straightened my deviated septum?

Ooh-la-la Land

As the clubs flew by on either side of my head, another troop member darted between two of the twirling missiles and stuck a loaded cigarette holder between my lips—much to the delight of the cheering crowd. Not daring to protest the fact that I don't smoke, I then watched as the clubs were switched for flaming torches. As their trajectories grew steadily closer to the end of the cigarette, I feared that I'd soon find myself flat on my back in intensive care suffering from first-degree burns. My fear increased as I inhaled the smell of singed hair through unobstructed nostrils. At hearing a very loud roar, I opened my eyes. The cigarette was gone from the holder and the flaming, twirling torches had stopped.

"Let's hear it for the Canadian," is what I think the troop leader shouted to incite the audience to cheer and clap even louder for their skillfully executed grand finale—and to help boost the collection of loose change underway the instant the cigarette fell to the ground. Trusting that my hair was no longer on fire and that I hadn't soiled my pants, I got up from the wooden box and bowed to the crowd, or at least to those who hadn't scampered away eluding the entertainers and their up-turned berets in outstretched hands.

By the time I was reunited with my wife, she was surrounded by young Frenchmen who were not simply practising their English as I'd thought, but whose glazed eyes revealed that they'd fallen under the spell of her fragrance.

"Happy birthday, darling," I said as the rim of my champagne glass touched hers across the candlelit table.

"Thanks for such a wonderful day," she smiled. "Were you scared when those torches came so close?" she asked, her eyes sparkling.

"Scared? No, not at all," I lied, as I ran trembling fingers through my remaining singed curls.

Sitting at our street-side table we enjoyed five delicious courses, including a sumptuous, never-to-be-forgotten chocolate mousse with fresh raspberries. Several people strolling by smiled at me. A couple gave me a thumbs up; one shouted, "*Ca-na-di-an! Bravo!*"

"It was nothing," I managed to convey to my non-English-speaking fans by pouting and shrugging my shoulders. Bringing my attention back to the birthday girl, I winked at her and proposed a toast: "Here's wishing you many more happy birthdays, darling."

She then proposed a toast: "To my hero, for surviving flaming torches unscathed." After clinking glasses, I realized that, similar to the sales pitch for Molinard's new fragrance, I was "of the moment, very agreeable, and with a few hints of humour."

28

En Route to Saint-Tropez:

Brigitte Bardot, Peter Sellers, and Madame Eagle

At breakfast, while trying to decide where to spend the day, we overheard the Bulging Belgians tell Cane and Able that this was their eighth consecutive year holidaying at Hôtel Beau-Site. The main reason was that the French Riviera receives an average of 2,750 hours of sunshine a year. For comparison, I quickly checked the Internet and discovered that Vancouver receives about 1,750 hours; Brussels about 1,550; and Manchester, about 1,350. In 1962, Manchester received a miserable, record low of only 920 hours, which is probably why hundreds of pale-faced Mancunians left for Australia.

And it came as no surprise to hear that all the Bulging Belgians wanted to do while on holiday was to lie by the pool. Cap d'Antibes is worth revisiting, but to return eight times to lie by a pool requires a lack of imagination and no sense of adventure; in short, a walrus brain. Perhaps, unbeknownst to them, their yearly trek south was an annual migration. Had they had the inclination to walk down to the beach and go for a swim, they may have found themselves instinctively sunbathing on the rocks with the local seals.

"Good morning," said Cane as we got up from our table.

"Good morning. It's another beautiful day," my wife responded.

"Where are you young folk off to today?" Able asked.

"Saint-Tropez," I replied.

Thinking that the pleasantries would end there was naïve of us.

"Brigitte Bardot made St-Tropez famous, you know." Cane began. Her expression brightened as she switched from listening to the immobile Bulging Belgians to talking about her favourite subject. Able's newspaper went up in front of his face as she continued, "Yes. It was in the mid-1950s when she and Roger Vadim arrived in St-Tropez to film *And God Created Woman*." Cane looked around to make sure there were no children or undercover porno police about, then she continued: "She bared all, you know? She was naked in a scene that shocked the world. Of course, she was only a teenager in those days, but quite voluptuous, mind you. You can blame her for starting the topless and nude sunbathing thing." Just then Able lowered his newspaper, his eyes following Playmate as she strode across the patio in her white chiffon sarong cover-up that failed to cover up anything. "No, they don't make women like that anymore, do they?" Cane elbowed her husband, the usual prompt for him to agree.

"Oh, I don't know," he replied, his blood pressure rising at the sight of the vision in chiffon at the buffet table.

En route to St-Tropez, we thought it only right to stop in Fréjus and pay our parking ticket. Assuming that we could pay it at city hall, I stopped to ask a policeman for directions to the Hôtel de Ville. Winding down her window, my wife smiled and asked if he spoke English.

"*Bonjour, Madame.* Yehz, I speak *anglais,*" the young officer said, then leaned forward and almost put his head inside the car. "'ow can I 'elp you?" he asked, touching the peak of his cap.

"We have this," my wife began, showing him the parking ticket.

"We want to know where we can pay it," I added, as would any decent, law-abiding citizen.

"You want to pay eet?" asked the *gendarme*, who made no attempt to disguise his investigatory gaze down my wife's low-cut top.

"Yes, please. We want to pay it," I grovelled.

"Well, we don't *really* want to pay it," my wife added, then turned and gave me an eyebrow-raised glare.

"Are you Eeng-leesh?" he asked, prolonging his vista.

"No. We're Canadian," she replied. "From Vancouver, actually."
Had we answered, "Yes, we're English," he may have arrested us and
transported us handcuffed to the nearest guillotine.

"Vancou-vair 'as beautiful moun-tains, yehz? I lurve moun-tains,"
he said, his eyes peering down at the scenery before him.

"I can see that," I mumbled under my breath.

"You are on 'oliday, yehz?" he asked. Quite the piece of detective
work, I thought. Even a child would have seen Twingo's special non-
resident licence plates that advertised to everyone and their yapping
dogs that we were tourists.

"Yes, you are correct, we're on holiday." My wife smiled and then
outlined the circumstances that had led to us getting the ticket—the
wasp sting, the clinic, my swollen blood-red face, the hideous Pink
Elephant Man, who, by the way, was about to suggest to the ogling
officer that he need only go down to a top-optional beach to see many
more peaks and valleys.

"I weel take eet weez me," he said, as he took the ticket from my
wife's hand. "You can con-see-der eet no more," he concluded, in an
authoritative tone that one would associate with a Supreme Court
judge, yet with an accent that sounded more like Peter Sellers'
Inspector Clouseau.

"*Oh, merci beaucoup,*" exclaimed my wife, as I let out the clutch
and sped away before he had time to change his mind or ask my wife to
step out of the car and frisk her for concealed weapons.

From Fréjus, we continued along the coastal scenic route D559,
passing through the smaller towns of Saint-Aygulf, Les Issambres, Cap
des Sardinaux, and Sainte-Maxime. Just before entering the outskirts of
St-Tropez, we pulled into a parking space on the fringe of Port
Grimaud and walked into its vehicle-free centre. Impossible to miss its
uniqueness, Port Grimaud, like a mini-Venice, is made up of houses
that are built on the banks of canals. Each house has its own mooring
and, it appeared, every family has its own boat. The tower of the
attractive church, St-François d'Assise, is the focal point of the town

and drew us past the many orange-and-beige tile-roof row houses to the port's main quay. Butting up to the quay is a row of cafés and restaurants that enticed us to seek shade from the blistering sun and partake of our mid-morning refreshments. Sheltering from the heat, we sat under the colourful awning of Le Relais des Coches sipping cafés au lait and wondered why we hadn't ordered a glass of iced tea instead. An Internet search of Port Grimaud revealed that the port and the 2,500 canal-side houses including moorings were created by François Spoerry (1912–1998), an architect. In 1966, when he conceived of his "dream" plan, the 222-acre site was marshland. Today, Port Grimaud is one of France's major tourist attractions.

On our walk back to the car, we stopped at a *fruiterie*. I knew how delicious and juicy peaches are at that time of year, and I espied a crate of them on display outside the store. Perfect in shape and colour, each peach sat in a cup of white tissue paper. Reaching over, I picked one up and gently squeezed it to check if it was ripe. Just as I reached for a second peach, I heard a squawking noise and turned to see the owner swooping down on me like a wild-eyed eagle with wings outstretched. She fixed me with her beady eyes and stuck her talons into me (actually she slapped the back of my hand). Taking the peach from my hand and nursing it as if it were an injured chick, she carefully returned it to the crate. Then she beckoned us into the store, where we were deposited at the end of the line of customers. When it came our turn to be served, Madame escorted us back to the crate of peaches and, wearing surgical rubber gloves, lifted out the same peach and rotated it at eye level for our inspection. Having nodded our approval of several, she weighed them, bagged them, took payment for them, and then handed us the bag of fruit, and did so without smiling—or pecking out my eyes.

Leaving Port Grimaud, my wife read from our guidebook. St-Tropez is exposed to cold blowing winds (mistrals) in winter. Consequently, its population of only 5,700 seldom sees a tourist at that time of year, which is welcome relief from the 65,000 visitors the locals see clogging the town daily during July and August. The summer-season masses create horrendous parking problems that keep tow-truck operators busy twenty-four seven. A large clock located on the outskirts of town indicates to frustrated inbound drivers the estimated time they will have to remain in the stop-and-go traffic before arriving at the town's centre. Traffic jams have been known to back up around the bay and past Port Grimaud all the way to Ste-Maxime. Be forewarned, a two-hour crawl into town is not uncommon.

In 1944, St-Tropez was reduced to rubble as the Americans advanced on the German garrison. Unlike other Riviera towns, it stood shattered for more than a decade. However, its rapid transformation began with the arrival of Brigitte Bardot. All of which goes to show that while it took thousands of men and countless armoured vehicles many months to reduce the town to rubble in one big bust-up, it took only one woman with a big bust to get it rebuilt almost overnight.

29

Saint-Tropez:

Trop, People-Watching, a Four-Star Fairy Tale, Torpès, and Torpedoes

St-Tropez has been described as a resort town of excesses that has thrived on its sexy image ever since Brigitte Bardot arrived and undressed for the cameras. Cynics declare that too much skin is revealed, too much hedonism is exhibited, too much wealth is displayed, and, as a result, too much traffic brings too many tourists to visit. Consequently, the town has been nicknamed St-Trop, as the French word *trop* means "too much."

And it would seem that the People-Watching People World Championships are held at St-Trop every summer, and of the hundreds of thousands who enter the tournament, only the very best advance to sit at the front tables of the fashionable cafés and restaurants on quai Jean-Jaures and quai Suffren alongside the Vieux Port. Those who qualify are generally under thirty and able to look cool while looking at others looking cool on a hot, midsummer day.

The coolest women are pretty and dressed in designer-label clothing that consists of little more than the label. An occasional, nonchalant flick of one's long hair or an exaggerated flick of a cigarette scores big with the judges. Wearing expensive sunglasses perched skyward or backward scores well too, as does having a yappy little dog on one's lap or on a chair alongside. The most difficult part of this pleasurable pastime seems to be trying to look bored. It sounds easy enough, but it takes years of practice to perfect, particularly in such exhilarating surroundings.

The coolest men are accompanied by the prettiest women while appearing to avoid making eye contact and meaningful conversation. Not bothering to shave for a day or two is very important because shadowy facial stubble proves their contempt of their relationship while advertising their non-conformist masculinity. These men realize that their bad-boy image always scores points with men-crazy women and, of most importance, with the people-watching judges. And while the less-threatening contenders sit through lunchtime sharing a single glass of Coca-Cola sipped through two drinking straws, the coolest men order a couple of sandwiches and a bottle of wine, thereby proving that they have access to large amounts of cash or credit. Wearing a Rolex watch (real or fake) helps in appearing to be of celebrity status or the owner of one of the many stern-to-quay moored yachts. Both are of paramount importance in gaining championship bonus points. Cunning competitors, who succeed in their phony charade, always have in the forefront of their minds: "The secret of success is sincerity. Once you can fake that, you've got it made." (A line made famous by George Burns and French novelist Jean Giraudoux.)

Having shaved that morning and unable to fake sincerity, I was disqualified from the tournament. However, we managed to find a vacant table set three rows behind the front row of people-watching finalists at Sénéquier, the quayside café most renowned for its glamour-seeking people, bright red awning, bright red triangular tables, and exorbitant prices. No longer championship contenders, we were free to smile, converse with each other, and keep a running commentary of the poseurs at the tables in front of us and of those ambling by between the front-row tables and the moored yachts.

The yachts came in many shapes and sizes, but the powerful, sleek, white gin palaces and gleaming teak classics were given the most attention, not just because of their enormousness and in-your-face opulence but more because of their pretty, female deckhands. Most of these women wore short, white skirts and tight-fitting, midriff-revealing tops, and they served drinks from silver trays to overweight, cigar-smoking, non-sailing businessmen. A small anchor or rudder wheel embroidered in navy blue on the side of the deckhands' skirts or front and centre on their tops conveys to their non-sailing clientele a degree of authenticity as crew members who may have sailed the seven seas. More likely, the women are well-paid waitresses who think that "port" is either the place where they go to work each morning or a bottle of Spanish dessert wine and that "starboard" is when a Hollywood celeb steps on deck.

After sharing a single Coca-Cola sipped through two drinking straws, we left our people-watching platform and walked to the lighthouse at the end of the harbour's breakwater, môle Jean-Réveille. Along the way, looking back at the colourful quayside cafés and the gleaming sleek hulls, I wondered where SEEKING SUNSHINE and her motley crew were cruising at that moment.

It was a minor disappointment to discover that there were only two small sandy beaches on the town's north shore and that we'd have to drive some distance to see the seven-kilometre stretch of glorious sand that includes plage de Tahiti and plage de Pampelonne. Instead, we headed for the Old Town, just back of the Vieux Port, and were delighted by the postcard-worthy scenes throughout the cobblestone streets. The walls of some houses were painted in soft pastels, their doors, window frames, and shutters in bold contrasting colours. Some walls were painted ochre, dusty pink, and bright yellow, and many supported oleander, jasmine, and bougainvillea in their quest to climb to the orange-and-beige tile roofs. Sitting on the ground at the front of many houses and up on their windowsills were pots and boxes of geraniums. Nothing about the mishmash colour scheme clashed; everything lit by direct sunshine contrasted beautifully against the deep blue sky. And *that* is why artists have continued to come to St-Tropez with their canvases and paint palettes since Paul Signac, the famous post-Impressionist, first arrived in 1892.

Ooh-la-la Land

Making every effort to keep in the shade while strolling through the Old Town, we came across Château de Suffren, a 10th-century square tower located behind quai Frédéric Mistral. The Hôtel de Ville was next, and just around the corner from it was the 18th-century parish church, l'Église Notre-Dame-de-l'Assomption. Standing tall above the rooftops at one corner of the church was its pink-and-yellow bell tower with Provençal wrought-iron belfry atop, which has become the town's symbolic edifice and emblem. After taking several artsy photographs, we stepped inside the church to luxuriate in its cool shade and seek out the statue of Torpès, the town's patron saint.

Torpès, we read, was a Roman and steward in Emperor Nero's household. He was converted to Christianity by Apostle Paul, and in AD 68 he solemnly professed his Christian faith during a feast given in Pisa by the emperor in honour of the goddess Diana. This so angered Nero that he ordered Torpès to be tortured and beheaded. For some strange symbolic reason, his body, a hungry dog, and a nervous cockerel were placed into a small boat and pushed out to sea. The boat eventually landed at a small fishing village on the shores of southern France—now the bustling summer resort town of St-Tropez. For centuries, the parish church has held a colourful parade to commemorate the bizarre event when Torpès lost his head in Pisa and the rest of his body was discovered on what is now, coincidentally, a topless beach.

Looking at the model of Torpès's headless body lying in his small boat with the dog and cockerel standing guard over him, I pondered the tremendous courage he demonstrated in confessing his belief in Christ, especially in the knowledge that it would not be appreciated by his notoriously quick-tempered, barbaric boss Nero. And I wondered how many people today, trying to climb the corporate ladder, have the courage to put their jobs on the line and stand up for what they believe is right and ethical.

Knowing that the town was named for Torpès, I pondered why it became St-Tropez. And considering that he is a revered saint, I wondered why someone would place an empty beer can and cigarette packet in among the paper hearts and flowers on top of the glass case that contains the model of him in his boat. And finally, I wondered why the townsfolk carry a wooden bust of him—complete with moustached head—through flag-lined streets during the La Bravade parade, which is held each May in his honour. If the body in the boat was headless, what had become of his head? And if Torpès had never before been to St-Tropez, how could the craftsman who carved the wooden bust have known what the saint's head looked like and if the Roman had sported a moustache. Then I wondered if I wondered too much.

More narrow streets, colourful houses, and quieter squares bordered by plane trees made up most of the Quartier de la Ponche, another section of town that inspires the painter and photographer with sights of exotic birds singing inside cages that hang from shuttered windows, and of local old men playing pétanque in shaded parkettes and sipping pastis under vine-covered trellises. Plenty of attractive specialty shops, cafés, boutiques, and restaurants invite tourists to enter and dispose of their disposable income.

We escaped the blistering sun by taking a leisurely lunch at the terrace restaurant of the Hôtel La Ponche, a charming old building that has been renovated and redecorated with great taste and looks out over the small sandy beach of the Port de Pêche, an old fishing port just east of the Tour Vieille—the Old Tower.

While savouring each delicious morsel of our entrée—a platter of *fruits de mer* comprising mussels, scallops, lobster, and giant prawns— and sipping chilled Côtes de Provence rosé, we scanned the hotel's promotional leaflet. In it, Hôtel La Ponche proudly describes itself as *"the smallest and most secret of four-star hotels in St-Tropez—a fairy tale hidden behind humble fishermen's cottages."* As I sucked on the meaty end of a succulent lobster claw and tried not to annoy the distinguished four-star diner's with my slurping and finger-licking, I wondered about this typically romantic, carefully crafted spin. One would assume that *"smallest"* refers to the fact that the hotel has only eighteen rooms, and not that each room barely accommodates a bed.

That *"most secret"* would appeal to those wishing to rendezvous clandestinely. However, if the hotel's management was *really* intent on ensuring that their hideaway remained most secret, then surely they would discontinue their website. As for the *"fairy tale,"* the fantasy came to an abrupt end when our waiter handed the four-star bill to me on a silver platter. Later, below a photograph in a real estate agent's window, we were equally shocked to see the outrageous "asking" price of a humble fisherman's cottage.

The hotel's promotional leaflet also maintained that part of Brigitte Bardot's movie *And God Created Woman* was filmed on the same beach that we looked out upon from our table. Another promotional snippet recommended guests: *"Don't miss the pleasure of going down for a swim with a glass of champagne in your hand."* That would account for the terrace restaurant having its own lifeguard, and for the barman having to order a case of champagne glasses every week.

Although we would love to have collapsed onto a hammock in the shade and slept off lunch, instead we stepped out of Hôtel La Ponche into the relentless sunshine and ambled along rue des Remparts to rue de la Citadelle. The citadel was a ten-minute, uphill walk from the centre of town and was well worth the visit, if only to experience the commanding views looking west over the old town and its port, and north across the Golfe de St-Tropez at Ste-Maxime. The 16th-century stronghold, with its impressive multi-sided perimeter stone wall, was encircled by a dry moat on a grassy hill. We'd been told that the grounds were patrolled by peacocks, but we didn't see any. I suspected they were lying on shaded hammocks sleeping off lunch.

We had no burning desire to visit the Musée naval de la Citadelle, but we entered it anyway as we had the burning desire to escape the burning sun. Located in the citadel's dungeons, the museum exhibits items that recount St-Tropez's maritime history with an interesting collection of naval relics, including some from World War II. Of all the weaponry, the torpedoes interested me most because I'd read that conventional torpedoes are still manufactured at a factory just outside of St-Tropez. I was curious if there was a connection between the words, "torpedo" and "Torpès," our headless martyr whose stiff body was propelled horizontally across the sea from Pisa. But as I delved for more information, I realized I was dealing with too much mythology, too much conjecture, and too much guesswork. And after too much wine and too much sun, it all became too much. In short, it was all *trop!*

30

Saint-Tropez:

Friendly Japanese, a Smart Car, and a Burst Bubble

Walking back down rue de la Citadelle, we were swept up in a wave of immaculately dressed, elderly Japanese tourists who had just flooded out onto the hot sidewalk from two air-conditioned buses and were following their guide—a fellow countryman—who held high a sign displaying Japanese characters that may well have read, "If you can't see this sign, I've either stepped off the curb or you're lost." Each time the guide stopped on the narrow sidewalks to describe a point of interest, we had no option but to stand and stare at whatever he was pointing at and to wait for a salvo of camera clicks and a chorus of "*Ahsō!*" before moving on to the next point of interest. At the first stop, two of the gang had their lenses pointed at me—their first-ever close-up (I presume) of a live Caucasian male standing head and shoulders above anyone in their group. After hearing the click of their shutters, I turned and faced my Asian fan club. Cognizant of their embarrassment, I smiled and winked at them, setting off a series of bows, giggles, and hand-over-mouth whispers that spread throughout their group. By the time we arrived at place des Lices, my wife and I were standing in the back row of the assembled group, posing for the guide who'd been asked to take a photograph of everyone and for everyone on their tour.

Place des Lices, a large square situated behind quai Suffren, was crowded with people seeking the shade of the gently swaying plane trees and the colourful awnings and umbrellas of the many attractive cafés and restaurants. After waving goodbye to the Japanese tourists, we strolled over to the famous Le Café, St-Tropez's most historic eatery—formerly known as Café des Arts. This is where Brigitte Bardot and her friends would hang out for refreshment when they were not required on set. Having just played a starring role myself in several demanding group photos, I could well understand how draining it must be to be *on* all the time for the cameras, one's fans, and the ever-prying lenses of the paparazzi.

It's common knowledge that, when compared with North America, most side streets in Europe are barely wide enough to accommodate two-way traffic. Some would argue that North Americans are generally larger than Europeans and, therefore, need larger cars. Regardless, en route to the Musée de l'Annonciade, we got our first close-up look at a parked Smart car. Sitting in the car was a young man and woman. The driver, the man, was peering at a map and looking confused, and the woman was peering out of the window and looking beautiful. Stopping to photograph the metal and glass bubble on wheels, I nodded and smiled at the woman who turned and stared directly and seductively into my lens as if on a photo shoot for a fashion magazine.

"Hi," I said, not daring to zoom in on her face and take a shot of her high cheek bones, sultry green eyes, and full pursed lips for fear of being punched in the mouth by the driver or, more likely, elbowed in the ribs by my wife.

"Hello. Are you by any ch-ah-nce from Ameri-cah?" asked the English beauty queen.

"No. We're Canadian," I responded, then turned to my wife to check on the proximity of her bony elbow.

"From Vancouver, actually," added my wife.

"Oh, I see," replied the beauty queen in a tone combining equal amounts of condescension and disappointment.

"Are you lost?" I asked the driver.

"Not ex-ah-ctly, old chap; I know we're in Saint-Tropez, but I'm not sure ex-ah-ctly where," he said, his eyes still set on the map resting on his lap. "Would you be so terribly kind, old chap, to show me ex-ah-ctly where we are?" He lifted the map onto the dashboard.

Reaching across in front of the beauty queen, being careful not to brush up against her twin cupolas, I touched the map. "Just here. This is where we are, just here," I said, noticing that my hand was trembling at the temptation of putting a stranglehold on the driver should he call me "old chap" once more.

"That's ex-ah-ctly where I thought we were. Jolly good, that's awfully kind of you, old chap," he said, continuing to sound like David Niven in one of his classic black-and-white movies.

"How do you like the Smart car?" I asked, smiling and managing to retract my arm from the car's interior without striking him.

"Absolutely marvellous, my good, old chap. It's manufactured here in Fr-ah-nce, you know, by Daimler. It's got all the bells and whistles."

"But does it have a horn?" I queried. The beauty queen giggled, and then feigned biting her bottom lip like all sexy models (and innocent girls with hairless legs) do.

"Of *course* it does," he replied, pointing at the horn button, missing my pun by a mile. "There's not much room for one's luggage, old chap, but it's nippy about town and very easy to park. It has a tiny, 600cc, three-cylinder engine in the back, you know. It rides rah-ther smoothly and holds the road frightfully well, you know, even doing a hundred on the motorways. There are air bags in the front and, as you can see, there's plenty of headroom. You know, it's terribly efficient on petrol, old chap, but far too affordable for Daimler to put a Mercedes' three-spoke-wheel emblem on the front," he rambled, like an enthusiastic car salesman salivating at the prospect of closing a deal.

"Wasn't she beautiful?" asked my wife, on cue, no sooner had we left the Miss United Kingdom and David Niven impersonators and their rented Smart car.

"Who, darling?" I queried, feigning innocence.

"The pretty young Englishwoman in the bubble car," she said.

"Oh, *her*. She isn't prettier than you, darling," I duly replied in accordance with my happy-wife-happy-life script.

Changing the subject, I said, "By the way, honey, that was a Smart car, not a bubble car." And that clarification provided me the perfect segue to tell her the story of Mrs Bubble.

Mrs Bubble was a short, middle-aged woman who lived in our Coronation Street–type neighbourhood when I was a teenager growing up just outside Manchester. Of course, Mrs Bubble was not her real name but rather a nickname given to her by the neighbourhood kids because she had bought a "bubble" car. Popular in the 1950s and '60s and probably no longer in production, a "bubble" car was much smaller than a Smart car. It was a three-wheeler—two at the front, one at the back—with a small motorbike engine and only one curved door that made up the entire windscreen and front panel of the car. The steering wheel was attached to the door and pivoted when the door was opened. Inside there was barely room for two small people to sit side by side on the tiny bench seat. The almost-spherical body, which was 50 per cent windows, certainly resembled a bubble.

Now Mrs Bubble had a severe limp, a deformity since birth that left her with one leg shorter than the other, or was it one leg longer than the other? When she began to take driving lessons in her "bubble" car, she discovered that although she could reach the gas pedal and brake with her right foot, her deformity made it difficult to reach the clutch pedal with her left foot. Her nervous driving instructor, a retired jockey who had qualified for the job because of his short, skinny stature, solved the problem by attaching a wooden block to the clutch pedal. Had he been an engineer, he would have attached the wooden block to her left shoe, thereby eliminating her severe limp also. Our backstreet gang witnessed the first couple of test drives during which Mrs Bubble zigzagged across the road, hopped the curb, and drove along the sidewalk while the instructor looked more terrified than when he was thrown from his saddle and dragged over most of the Grand National steeplechase course with his right foot caught in the stirrup.

The third lesson began inside her garage, one of several prefabricated, timber-framed structures with thin, corrugated, asbestos-sheet walls and roof that had been erected on a scrap of land on the banks of the Micker Brook, which eventually flowed into the River Mersey. After both Mrs Bubble and the instructor had squeezed onto the "bubble" seat and secured the front door, she started the engine, checked the rear-view mirror, depressed the clutch, shifted the gear stick into position, released the handbrake, revved the engine, and then let out the clutch. Not realizing that she'd put the car in first gear instead of reverse, it shot forward, crashed through the back wall of the garage, plummeted off the thick concrete base then rolled like a ball for two revolutions down the steep embankment. Had it made one more revolution, it would have splashed down into the brook and been swept out to the Irish Sea, possibly never to be seen again.

Escaping from the vehicle like astronauts emerging from the hatch of a space capsule, the driving instructor and Mrs Bubble, both of whom suffered only minor bruises to their bodies and egos, limped back up the embankment and off down the street in opposite directions. That life-threatening event put an end to Mrs Bubble's driving career, and wrote off her damaged bubble car. In more ways than one, her bubble had burst.

We retraced our steps along quai Suffren and quai Jean-Jaures, past the bobbing white gin palaces, the cafés, and their people-watching people, up through the Old Town, and back to Twingo.

Before setting off, we considered visiting the famous stretch of beach located just four kilometres southeast of town, between Cap du Pinet and Cap Camarat, but we were hot and tired and the crystal-clear, cool swimming pool at our hotel seemed more inviting. Besides, we had been forewarned that sections of that beach are for those who choose to bare it all—à la Brigitte Bardot—and although many of the nudists may have been worth observing, apparently several senior citizens of both genders operate food concessions and patrol the beaches along that stretch carrying trays of hotdogs and wearing nothing more than toothless grins and Coco Chanel tans.

31

Monaco—Monte-Carlo:

Palaces, Princes, Parades, and Privies

Hôtel Beau-Site's patio was busy that evening. All the familiar faces were there as well as a handful of new arrivals. Both André and Jacques were scurrying around with trays of drinks, plates of sandwiches, and dishes of tasty, crispy things. As usual, the evening air was still and warm, and the buzz of conversation drowned out the soothing sound of the rippling pool but not the shrill, non-stop singing cicadas. Everyone was happy, but that was expected—everyone was on holiday and most had a drink in their hands. Even Jacques was smiling and being particularly hospitable.

Playmate and Muscle Mountain were sitting at a table in the centre of the patio—Playmate in another tiny, ultra-feminine number that left little to the imagination. Muscle Mountain wore Bermuda shorts and a white T-shirt, the latter cut from a king-sized bed sheet. They were the hub of attention, like a pot-bellied stove (of sorts) glowing hot in the middle of a log cabin on a cold winter's night with people huddled around staring at it, appreciating the crackling warmth. Their daughter was sitting at a table with Cane and Able, and the three of them were playing cards—a strange game whose ever-changing rules only the chubby-cheeked gambler understood. Cane and Able rarely took their eyes off her and never stopped smiling, even though they didn't understand a word she was saying and even though they were being fleeced. Frequently, we'd hear the little girl scream as she discarded the last of her cards and then scooped up several euros. Looking a little bemused, Able would say something like, "You sure are good at this game, you little beauty." And Cane would reach for her purse again and say, "Well, I better get some more money out,"—not wanting their fun to come to an end, not wanting to return to the solitude of her *People* magazine. Who knows how much the child gambler conned from Cane and Able that evening, but it was plain to see that they thought it was worth every penny.

Lounging on sun chairs, strategically positioned closest to the kitchen, the Bulging Belgians were propped up in a semi-reclined position quietly devouring a plate of sandwiches and a dish of sardines. Occasionally, one or the other of them would pick up a sardine, reach across to their mate, dangle the little fish over their loved one's mouth, and then let it fall into the open chasm—much like a trainer rewarding its star performer, a sea lion or a walrus, perhaps, at Marineland. This seemed to be their way of showing affection to each other; they were being romantic. They didn't need a candlelit table, soft music, and a rose. No, just open a can of sardines and watch the sparks fly.

Within eavesdropping range was a group of six new arrivals—three middle-aged English couples—drinking martinis. The men were telling "adult" stories and becoming louder and more inebriated. To the non-English-speaking guests, they appeared to be having a very enjoyable evening. Undoubtedly, the men were in competition with one another, each trying to outdo the others with a funnier story while the women listened and then laughed hysterically at each punchline. Cringing with embarrassment as their stories grew sillier and more vulgar, we moved away and enjoyed the rest of the evening at a table with soft-spoken French-speaking guests.

The next morning, we drove east on the Grande Corniche, heading into the blazing sun en route to Monaco. The tiny, glamorous principality is a fantasyland of chic boutiques and extravagantly opulent 19th-century pleasure palaces, home of a photogenic royal family, host of one of the world's most famous Formula 1 Grand Prix races, and a tax haven for high-rollers and jet-setters—a place that never seems to go out of style.

After parting with handfuls of euros at several toll booths, we careened off the scenic A8 raceway at the Monaco turnoff, braked sharply, and then cautiously followed a series of hairpin bends down the steep, ear-popping mountainside to the narrow one-way streets of the jam-packed principality. We entered an underground parking lot just a stone's throw from the steep ramp that leads to place du Palais. After taking a ticket and parking Twingo, I studied the rates printed on the pay booth and gasped at the double-digit numbers. The daily rate had an asterisk beside it, and I believe the associated sentence—in small, italicized print at the bottom—was informing drivers that loans could be arranged inside the booth; just ask the scar-faced attendant wearing the charcoal-grey pinstripe suit, black shirt, and white silk tie.

We hiked the long ramp to the top of The Rock—a 141-metre (459 feet) tall monolith—on which the Palais Princier is located. From the centre of the cobblestone place du Palais, the palace looked very impressive. Four floors high, it had light beige walls with white trim, many huge arched windows, a grand stone doorway, and four square battlemented towers that rose above its flat roofline. In front of the palace, and dotted all over the square, were dozens of old cannons and piles of cannon balls—the latter possibly used by the princes and their guests in after-dinner games of pétanque. Either side of the grand doorway stood a sentry box, and in front of each was an armed soldier—his uniform entirely white, pith helmets and gun holsters too—standing to attention and trying not to blink as tourists took photos galore.

The Palais Princier is the private residence of the ruling Prince, however, the State Apartments are open for public visits part of the year. According to the official website, the original fortress and ramparts were built by the Genoese in 1215 and throughout the centuries was transformed into one of the most luxurious residences in the style of Louis XIV. Prince Honore II was responsible for reassembling the rich collections of art, which had been auctioned off during the French Revolution when the palace was turned into a hospital for the Italian Army. However, Prince Rainier III (1923–2005) is credited for restoring the palace to its former glory and the magnificent state in which it can be seen today.

At the admissions counter, we exchanged a small fortune for a tape player and earphones that led us on a self-guided audio tour of fifteen rooms of the State Apartments, including the Throne Room. Listening to the voice inform us about the history of the palace, its furnishings, and its residents, we moved like robots looking up at ceiling frescoes, at walls lined with paintings and tapestries, at floors inlaid with marble, and at a spectacular Carrera marble staircase.

From the State Apartments, we shuffled into another wing of the building and into the Musée Napoléon, where we listened to fascinating descriptions of the items on display and accounts of historical events. The rooms were filled with antique furniture, ancient letters, nautical charts, and battle records that once belonged to Napoleon. One framed note recorded that Napoleon's only son was born after twenty-six hours of labour and that, after being delivered by forceps, the boy refused to cry until he was fed a drop of brandy. Sure! A likely story, I thought, but one that has helped sell container loads of Napoleon Brandy ever since.

Back on the square, we looked out over Port de Fontvieille, which was chock-a-block with super-yachts and large sailboats. Bordering its quays were dozens of attractive, packed-in-tight apartment buildings, many with exotic roof gardens. And sandwiched in the middle was the spectacular sports stadium, stade Louis II, which had been shoehorned into place on land reclaimed from the sea. With a population of 37,831 in an area of only 2.02 sq. km., Monaco is the most densely populated sovereign nation in the world. Claustrophobics tend to keep away.

At ten minutes to noon, we headed over to join the crowd gathering in front of the palace to watch the famed Changing of the Guard. Alarmed at hearing shrill whistles, we turned around to see what all the commotion was about. Two policemen were blowing their whistles, their cheeks puffed out like Louis Armstrong hitting high "C" on his trumpet, and frantically waving their hands in our direction. We froze, assuming they were waving at someone behind us, a suspected terrorist perhaps. We were about to hit the deck to allow a clear shot, when double doors opened to one side of the palace's main entrance and a black sedan drove out and headed right towards us. Continuing to blow his whistle, one policeman ran ahead of the car with one hand on his holstered pistol, the other waving at me to move. I pointed at my chest, and mouthed, "Do you mean me?" With a powerful tug, almost dislocating my arm, my wife dragged me off to one side and the sedan drove by. And there, sitting in the back seat, was Prince Albert II.

Compared with the Changing the Guard at Buckingham Palace, where Foot Guards, resplendent in their full-dress uniforms (red jackets and tall black fur busbies), parade their colours during the royal ceremony in which a New Guard exchanges duty with the Old Guard, this one was a bit of a letdown. There were not many guards in the parade and a trumpeter of the accompanying Guards' band was marching out of step; another missed a few high notes. Nevertheless, we were happy not to have missed it and relieved that we'd not been arrested by a gun-toting Louis Armstrong impersonator.

Before setting off along the scenic footpath that winds its way around the cliffs from place du Palais to Monaco's cathedral, I stopped to use a public washroom. Sitting at a table between the entrances to HOMMES and DAMES was a middle-aged woman. As I approached, she pointed to a sign on the wall and then stuck out her hand, palm up and cupped. According to the sign, I owed her one euro. Now, I realize that she needed to pay the rent on her Monte-Carlo apartment and I understand that toilet paper, liquid soap, and paper towels have to be purchased, but surely anyone who climbs to the top of The Rock and parts with a small fortune to enter a priceless palace in one of the richest places in the world should be able to use a public toilet without having to hand over more cash.

Ooh-la-la Land

Not wanting to argue the point, I dropped a euro into her open palm—studiously ignoring the engagement ring with a diamond the size of a walnut on her other hand—and turned right through the open doorway into the men's room. Self-conscious that there was no door, I positioned myself strategically at the urinals. As I was pointing Percy at the porcelain, a busload of Italian women converged on Diamond Lil, and given that DAMES could only accommodate two at a time, she directed two of the women into HOMMES, to the cubicles behind me. The first woman smiled as she passed by, and said, *"Buongiorno."*

"Hi, how ya doing?" I responded, nodding in her direction, while shaking Percy before retracting him into the privacy of my underwear.

32

Monaco—Monte-Carlo:

Fascinating Sights

Monaco's St Nicholas cathedral has been described as an uninspired 19th-century version of Romanesque architecture, which is known by its massive quality, thick walls, round arches, sturdy piers, groin vaults, and large towers. Reading that, one may think that it's not worth visiting. But it was. We thought that its exterior was extremely attractive, and its interior is graced with a magnificent altarpiece and the floor-level tomb of Princess Grace. The latter is the main reason the cathedral attracts so many visitors. Millions around the world remember the day when Grace Kelly, the beautiful American film actress, married Prince Rainier. But millions more remember the day, September 14, 1982, when Princess Grace plunged to her death after crashing her Rover through a barrier on a hairpin bend. Her younger daughter, Princess Stéphanie, who was only seventeen at the time, was also in the vehicle but miraculously survived.

Curious to see the tomb of Princess Grace, we joined the long line of people waiting to enter the cathedral and soon realized that everyone ahead of us was being turned away. A huge man in a beige suit and sunglasses stood at the front doors shaking his head and wagging his right index finger at anyone who began to climb the steps to the entrance. Judging by the shape of his nose—it had been broken, the septum severely deviated—he was a former boxing champion. And those who persisted to the top of the steps were physically blocked by

Bouncer, who pointed to a multi-lingual sign upon which was written: CLOSED—SILENCE AND PRAYER DAY.

As we started up the steps against a steady stream of rejected tourists, I mused that the cathedral was not closed because of building renovations, an electrical power outage, falling ceiling frescoes, or a private function, but because it was a day for silence and prayer. And I found *that* rather fascinating.

As expected, when we got to the top of the steps and presented ourselves in front of Bouncer, he shook his head and pointed at the sign. Rejected and dejected, I turned to follow the others back down the steps, but my wife smiled at him and said, "We're going in to pray and we'll do so silently." I winced and braced for a knockout punch, but instead he almost floored me with, "Certainly, *Madame*. Here, let me get the door for you." And in she went with me following on tiptoes. And I found its colossal interior, with grand organ, white marble altar, incredible apse mosaics, and the tombs, including Princess Grace's, rather fascinating.

Next door to the cathedral, just across rue de l'Église, stands the Palais de Justice, another magnificent building. Built of light beige stone, its front elevation embodies a magnificent rotunda section with decorative arched windows, a portico, balustrades, a battlemented central tower, and twin semi-circular stairways that lead up to a set of large, wooden double doors. The building *has* to rate as a masterpiece of stonemasonry. Those tourists who were in the area with the sole purpose of visiting Princess Grace's tomb at the cathedral, even those who were not normally attracted to the art in architecture, *had* to have found it rather fascinating.

From the cathedral, we strolled through the pretty St-Martin Gardens to the Musée océanographique. Another popular tourist attraction and impressive building, it stands perched on the edge of The Rock and houses specimens collected on expeditions around the world—Jacques Cousteau, the renowned marine pioneer, having led several of them. An immense aquarium of many illuminated tanks containing hundreds of species of fish and other sea life is the museum's main attraction and was well worth the visit. Together with divers, snorkelers, anglers, tourists, and children of all ages, we found the museum and most of its exhibits—especially the shark lagoon—rather fascinating.

Feeling hungry and weary, we stumbled upon L'Aurore Restaurant on rue Princesse Marie-de-Lorraine. It's large enough to handle a busload or two of tourists, but several archways subtly divide the room into smaller, intimate dining spaces. Even though it was mid-summer, an artificial fire flickered in a huge brick fireplace. All the tables were covered in pink linen tablecloths, and most of the chairs were occupied by suntanned customers wearing shorts, sandals, and summer tops and looking healthy and relaxed.

Sitting by himself, just tables away from ours, was a guy I thought might keel over face first into his meal, and I couldn't help myself from peeking over at him—like a motorist driving by mangled wreckage, not wanting to see the carnage but looking anyway. His face was pale, drawn, and wrinkled and he wore a grey suit. At his feet was a briefcase, and I guessed he might be a salesman. Propped up against the vase on his table was a folded newspaper, which he stared at intensely, while pressed against his right ear was a cell phone. His brow furrowed and his face contorted in reaction to what he was reading or perhaps to what he was listening to on his phone. At the same time, he was scooping pyramids of food into his mouth and, after every third forkful, taking a drag on a cigarette that lay burning in an ashtray to his left.

When he'd finished eating, he spent a few minutes sucking on his teeth, running his tongue around them, and then used his pinkie fingernail as a toothpick. With his phone still held to his ear and another cigarette smouldering between his fingers, he drained the last of his red wine, flicked ash into the empty glass, blew his nose on a napkin, threw some money on the table, picked up his briefcase, and walked out onto the street scratching his backside as he went. Not a pretty sight, but a rather fascinating one.

33

Monaco—Monte-Carlo:

A Map, a BLT Prince, a Senile Senator, and a 007 Wannabe

Monaco tourist maps remind me somewhat of the maps you receive as you enter Disneyland, only there's nothing Mickey Mouse about Monaco—there's just less elbow room. Remarkably, Monaco covers only 196 hectares, or 485 acres, of which nearly forty hectares were recovered from the sea. To help you visualize 485 acres, London's Hyde Park has 344 acres, New York's Central Park has 840 acres, and Vancouver's Stanley Park has 1,000 acres, which is twice the area of Monaco. And as small as the principality is, Monaco is divided into five areas: Monaco-Ville, Fontvieille, La Condamine, Monte-Carlo, and Moneghetti, the last of these encompassing Les Révoires and the Exotic Gardens on its western border with France.

And one has only to look at a Monaco tourist map to understand why Prince Rainier III was known as "The Building Prince." Among his principal developments were congresses, convention centres, and sports facilities, including the stade Louis II, the stadium we'd seen earlier which is home to AS Monaco soccer club and seats 15,223 fans. It's not a particularly large stadium by international standards, but it is different from most as it's built above a car park. Another of the prince's developments, the Espace Fontvieille, lies just south of the stadium. This "big top," made of a special tent canvas, is sixty-two metres (200 feet) in diameter and when it is not accommodating the world's greatest circus acts, it is used for all types of shows, conventions, exhibitions, and banquets; its "theatre-in-the-round" seats over 4,000 people comfortably.

Four more convention centres lie within striking distance of the casino. The Monte-Carlo Congress Centre and its auditorium, which is named for Prince Rainier, are perched over the sea beyond Port Hercule. The building is a wonderful example of contemporary architecture, and hosts symphonies, rock concerts, and variety shows. A little farther east, at the water's edge, is yet another state-of-the-art conference centre—the Grimaldi Forum Monaco, which can accommodate events for up to 3,000 delegates. And a little farther, past plage Larvotto, is Sporting Monte-Carlo, a futuristic-style building that contains luxurious entertainment facilities, including restaurants, a casino, a night club, and a Cuban smoking parlour—not that many Cubans visit Monaco.

In addition to the spectacularly modern buildings, there are several elegant ones from the Belle Époque: the Monte-Carlo Casino, the Opéra de Monte-Carlo, Hôtel de Paris, Hôtel Hermitage, and Café de Paris. Then there are the world-famous hotels that are rich in history for rich clientele—the Monte-Carlo Grand Hôtel, Hôtel Mirabeau, Hôtel Métropole Palace, and the Monte-Carlo Beach Hôtel. These are the places where you're likely to bump into retired tennis stars, Formula 1 drivers, aging actors and rock stars like Bjorn Borg, Daniel Coulthard, Roger Moore, and Ringo Starr who are said to live in Monaco. But I doubt you'd bump into one of them in a Monte-Carlo 7-11 convenience store; there are none!

La Condamine is the quarter that skirts the main port and is the hub of Monaco's restaurants and nightlife. After descending The Rock and walking through La Condamine to boulevard Albert 1er, we caught our first glimpse of a family of four-and-a-half riding along on a Vespa scooter: father at the controls, mother on the back with a bag of groceries, two small children standing between the handlebars and their father, and a yappy little dog sitting in a basket over the front wheel. That's how many of the locals get around! It's particularly difficult to get around by car since a huge train station was built in the town centre—supposedly to ease congestion by making it easier for visitors to get in and out of the principality by public transport.

To improve traffic flow and provide more useable space, many tunnels have been carved out of the mountainsides and much land has been reclaimed from the sea. And that is why I like to think of Prince Rainier as the "Building, Land-reclaiming, Tunnel-boring Prince" or, in short, "The BLT Prince." His son, Prince Albert, is now the head of government and has more plans of his own on the drawing board.

Despite its claustrophobic environment, Monaco has a surprising number of landscaped areas, public gardens, and parks. Jardin du Casino, Jardins du Larvotto, Jardin Japonais, Jardin St-Martin, Parc Princesse-Antoinette, and Parc Paysager de Fontvieille et Roseraie Princesse-Grace are among the main ones. But we read that the Jardin Exotique, located to the northwest of The Rock, is the most popular and is often referred to by Monégasques (as citizens of Monaco are known) as an "escape hatch."

The farther we hiked along avenue d'Ostende, which ramps up the eastern side of Port Hercule and leads to place du Casino, the better the view became, particularly looking back west over the port to The Rock. The place du Casino, bordered by magnificent Belle-Époque buildings, has to be one of the most visited tourist sites in Europe. The Monte-Carlo Casino is spectacular and elegant. Unlike the jet-setters who turn up at the foot of its grand stairway in Ferraris or Rolls-Royces, we turned up in a sweaty mess with bulging shoulder bag, camera, and a 3D tourist map. Realizing that the casino would have a strict dress code, we'd come prepared.

In need of washrooms to change into our dress-code attire, we walked across to Café de Paris. The maître d' raised an eyebrow at the sight of my shoulder bag, but after an up-and-down glance at my wife, he said, "*Bonjour, Madame et Monsieur, s'il vous plaît. Thiz way, eef* you pleaz," and led us to a front-row table on the patio. As we sat down in the welcome shade of an umbrella, the refined-looking gentleman sitting at the next table turned to the maître d' and said, "François, tell the waiter, another gin an' tonic; don't forget the ice." He had an American accent, from the Midwest, I guessed—a man of power and wealth, a senator or a captain of industry who felt it unnecessary to add "please" to his requests, a man who never had to plead for anything, a man who was used to giving orders.

"*Oui. Certainement, Monsieur. Immédiatement, Monsieur,*" the maître d' responded, then rushed away, smiling in anticipation of being slipped a large tip when Senator Midwest left. Without even looking at the drink list—and it's as well we didn't—we too decided to order gin and tonics. The waiter returned with the senator's drink, a side glass of ice, and a small dish of roasted peanuts. Senator Midwest handed him a folded banknote and the waiter smiled, "*Merci beaucoup, Monsieur. Merci.*" But the senator just nodded and took a sip of his gin and tonic.

The waiter turned and began to walk away. "Excuse me," I said, trying to catch his attention. He stopped and looked back. "Would you bring us two gin and tonics, please?" I asked. The waiter nodded, turned, and walked back towards the bar, but stopped en route to take orders from wealthier-looking customers.

"Are you here on vacation?" I ventured, looking across at our distinguished American neighbour. That was enough to start him off on his own question-and-answer period.

"Am I here on vacation? You can betcha bottom dollar I'm here on vacation. Do I deserve the break? Ya damned right I deserve the break. Have I been here before? Sure, I've been here before. What do I like about it? I like the weather, the priddy ladies, and the gamblin'. What don't I like about it? It's too damned crowded and the streets are too damned narrow. Would I wanna live here? Never! Ask me what I'd change. I'd ban those noisy motorcyclists and yappy dogs. Do I...?" And on and on he went, and all the time staring off in the direction of the casino's impressive green-domed roof, not once making eye contact with us.

Our waiter returned with our G&Ts, ice, and peanuts, and after placing them on the table, he stood and looked at me expectantly. "Thank you," I said, and then realized that his statuesque pose was his prompt for me to hand over some of our gambling money as reward for his two minutes of service. As we were not as forthcoming as Senator Midwest, the waiter placed a small, silver tray down by the side of my glass, and on it was a ticket, which I assumed was the bill. Not wanting to go into shock prematurely, I decided not to peek at it until we were ready to leave.

Concerned that we may trigger more prattling Q&A monologue if we asked the boorish senator another question, we read up on the casino: the fascination of the *salons privés*, the gilt-edged Rococo ceilings, the stained-glass windows and domes, the bronze lamps held aloft by nude nymphs, the entrance stairway that boasts a sculpted palm, and the magnificent and ornate opera house, Salle Garnier, with its eighteen-ton, gilt-bronze chandelier and extravagant frescoes. But one thing that we found intriguing was a sign, hung at the entrance to the casino, forbidding ministers of religion and Monégasques from entering the gaming rooms. And that even when the Prince or others in his family want to attend an opera in the adjacent Salle Garnier, they can do so only by entering the room through a side door and not by way of the casino.

Before picking up our bill from the silver tray, we spent a moment guessing the amount. Nothing could have prepared us for the shock. As I placed a large euro note on the silver tray, I half expected to see a Wells Fargo armed guard accompany our waiter. "*Merci beaucoup,*" I said, "Keep the change." He looked at the banknote and just nodded. Then he turned around, looked at Senator Midwest, smiled, and asked if he'd like another drink.

"Would I like another drink? You're damned right I'd like another drink. Would I like more ice? Of course, I'd like more ice. Do I think that…?" And, in a flash, we were on our way to the café's washroom to change into our casino attire.

Emerging with her hair combed and her make-up applied, a strand of pearls around her neck, a fresh squirt of Habanita de Molinard spritzed on to her neck and wrists, and her feet slipped into dainty, high-heels to enhance her summer dress, my wife looked ready to be led off on the arm of James Bond. But as Agent 007 was nowhere to be seen, her next best option was to link the arm of the spectacled guy standing outside HOMMES—the one dressed in a creased navy blue blazer, long pants, and a pair of beige loafers, and holding a blue shoulder bag. At best, I looked like 006; however, had the gorgeous woman on my arm known that I was accidentally wearing one beige sock and one black one, my rating would surely have slipped to 005.

We felt special as we walked up the grand stairway under the scrutiny of several bystanders—tourists who were cursing because they hadn't known about the strict dress code. As we reached the top of the stairs, I nodded casually at the uniformed doorman, a nod of familiarity that said, "Hi. It's us again, back to lose another bundle. By the way, you're doing a great job of keeping out the riff-raff, not to mention those cunning religious ministers and Monégasques."

"*Excusez-moi, Madame et Monsieur.* What ees een your bag, *s'il vous plaît?*" the brute asked curtly, demonstrating a lack of intuition.

"Just a couple of pairs of sandals, a cosmetics bag, a camera, and a tourist map," I answered feebly, deliberately not reporting the overripe banana and the half-eaten chocolate croissant.

"Pleaz, I weel look inside."

"Sure you can," I answered as I opened up the bag.

"'ave you passports?" he asked.

"Yes, we have passports," I replied, wondering if the screening process would include a drug-sniffing dog and a full-body search, and if 007 had ever endured such humiliation.

"All ees een order. *Merci.* Pleaz check your bag and 'ave your passports ready," he said, as he pointed in the direction of the admissions counter.

"Passports," a woman said from behind the counter. "That will be twenty euros, please," she said, after checking that our faces matched the photos in our passports and that we were not religious ministers or Monégasques.

"*Twenty euros!*" I exclaimed. "That's thirty dollars," I moaned, not at all like James Bond. "You mean we have to pay thirty dollars just to get inside? Thirty dollars for the privilege of possibly losing our life savings," I ranted.

"Is there a problem here?" A huge man in a suit had appeared from out of nowhere and was now standing next to me, looking down. His mouth smiled, but his eyes were as cold as steel. He repeated his question: "Is there a problem here?" His voice was soft but raspy.

"None whatsoever, but thank you very much for asking," my wife responded, as I reluctantly produced a twenty-euro note and handed it to the woman behind the counter.

"*Bonne chance,*" said the woman, as we turned and walked out of the shadow of Odd Job, the steely eyed enforcer.

Not knowing where to go, I suggested we follow three women who were laughing and looking like they knew their way around. The five of us turned right into a short corridor and then turned immediately left, in single file, through an open doorway. The mirrored room was a hive of activity. We'd entered DAMES. I was not off to a good start.

Exasperated, my wife dragged me back through the atrium and into the Salon de l'Europe. Her expression communicated in no uncertain terms that my secret agent rating had slipped again, probably to 004— and she still hadn't noticed my mismatched socks.

34

Monte-Carlo Casino:

Who is This Mysterious Woman?

As I looked around the airy Salon de l'Europe and marvelled at its 19th-century frescoes, its many sculptures and wonderful paintings, its early 20th-century carpet, and its eight huge chandeliers made of pure bohemian crystal, my wife was scanning the various gaming tables. "I see we can also play Trente et Quarante in this room."

"Is that right?" I responded, not really listening, still focused on one of the magnificent chandeliers. "Er, sorry darling, what was that again, tronty something or other?"

"Trente et Quarante. It's played with six packs of cards at an odd-shaped table. That's one over there. The cards have a nominal value. The face cards are worth ten. There are four single bets: *rouge, noir, couleur,* and *inverse* that are paid equally. The croupier deals two rows of cards: a first row of black cards, a second row of red cards. The total of each should be between thirty and forty. That's why it's called Trente et Quarante—French for "thirty" and "forty." The player with the total nearest to thirty wins."

I was dumbstruck. "How do you know all that?" I asked, staring at her wide-eyed and wondering if this revelation was yet one more side-effect of Habanita de Molinard.

"You know, from that guy. The one who worked as a croupier," she answered casually as she continued to scan the room.

"What guy who worked as a croupier?" I enquired, frowning.

"You know who I mean, that guy that I dated from Quebec. He worked as a croupier at a casino in Montreal," she replied sheepishly. "He taught me many of the games. You know how I love playing games," she said, looking down at the roulette table.

"Which guy from Quebec?" I asked, taken aback.

"You know."

"No, I don't. What was his name?" I asked, wracking my brain trying to recall our life-before-you-came-along conversations when we first fell in love. "How long did you date for?" I continued before she'd had time to tell me his name.

"Oh, I forget now. It was such a long time ago. I told you about him, didn't I?"

"No, you did not!" I shot back. "Wait a minute, you've forgotten his name and yet you still remember the rules of tronty quonty. You've got to be joking!" I ranted.

"Dominique LeBlanc. That's it, I'm sure I told you about him."

"No, you did *not*. And now you can remember his *surname* too," I stated incredulously, as I realized that 007, or even 004, would never have reacted this way.

"Don't be silly. We only dated for a couple of months. Besides, we really didn't see that much of each other. We were just friends, really," she added skillfully.

"Hmmm. So what other games did Domin-eeek teach you?" I asked, not really wanting to hear the answer.

"Well, there's Roulette, Craps, Blackjack and Punto Banco. Not that I used to gamble; I was just interested in knowing how to play," she clarified, probably hoping that I would delve no farther.

"Hmmm," I repeated, sulking.

"I read that Banque à Deux Tableaux and Chemin de Fer are also played somewhere in the casino. I've never heard of Banque à Deux Tableaux, but I think that Chemin de Fer is also known as Shimmy and is based on the same principles as Baccarat," she said.

"You know how to play Baccarat?" I blurted, my eyes bulging.

"Yes, I've watched it but never actually played it," she replied as calm as a politician. She switched her attention to the little white ball as it circled the roulette wheel in front of us. "You do know how to play roulette, right?" she asked, trying to get us back on track.

"I think I do," I answered, realizing that if I were to probe deeper into her past my rating may drop to 003.

"Okay. The wheel has thirty-seven compartments numbered from zero to thirty-six. As you can see, these same numbers are found on the green table layout where we place our bets. Half the numbers are red; half are black. Zero is not red or black, it's a neutral colour. If you place a bet on a single number, which is called a *plein,* and your number comes up, you will win at the highest rate of odds: 35 to 1. If you place your chip so that it straddles two numbers, which is called a *cheval,* the odds reduce to 17 to 1. A *carré* is a bet placed on four numbers and pays out at 8 to 1, and so on. If you place a bet on red or black, or on *impair* or *pair,* or on *manque* or *passe,* then your odds are even."

What is all this? I struggled to get my head around this insight into her games' knowledge and her pre-Steve history. Who is this mysterious woman who knows that there's a subtle difference between Chemin de Fer and Baccarat? What other unknowns lie slumbering beneath that beautiful exterior? What other surprises may be revealed when I least expect it? One thing was for sure: I was beginning to regret having bought her that minuscule bottle of perfume. Curse those side-effects!

"Come on, honey, let's go and explore some more. Let's go play the slots and the VPMs and win lots of money," she said as she took my hand and then kissed me on the cheek.

I looked at her questioningly, "The slots and the VPMs?"

"Yeah, the slot machines and the video poker machines," she clarified, as I was led off in a fragrant trail of Habanita de Molinard.

After cashing a large euro banknote for two rolls of slot machine tokens, we each took one and headed for the VPMs in the Salle Blanche. This was another magnificent arched room with a high ceiling and outstanding décor, including beautiful burgundy drapes, more grand chandeliers, and multi-globe wall lights. It took me less than five minutes to lose my roll of tokens to a single slot machine. And no sooner had I left my seat than a middle-aged woman took my place, inserted a token, pulled down the lever and—wouldn't you know it?—won what sounded like a small fortune. Such was my luck. My wife—wouldn't you know it?—was having better luck. I'd heard the dink, dink, dinking of each machine as she moved from one payout to another.

Exercising great self-control, my wife suggested that we cash out her winnings and move to the Salles Touzet, which is actually two private gaming rooms in one large hall—a partition wall covered in paintings creates the two. It was designed by architect Jules Touzet and opened in 1890, the year electricity first lit the gaming rooms and the year in which it became exceedingly difficult to hide one's cards up one's sleeve. The rooms were decorated with precious woods and many large, beautiful paintings of rural settings hung on the walls.

A brochure that we picked up at the entrance stated: "*Although the room was renovated in 1988, the spirit remained unchanged and, today, players can indulge in Black Jack and Craps.*" On the subject of spirits, I noticed that indulging in alcoholic beverages in the games rooms was prohibited—gambling being the only permitted addiction. Studying the brochure, my wife said, "Look, there's a typo. It should be spelled as one word: Blackjack. It's a common mistake," she said nonchalantly. "Black Jack spelled as two words could be a can of wax, a ring-necked duck, or a small town in Montana."

I was dumbstruck, again. "What about Craps?" I asked, thinking I might stump her.

"Craps was a spin-off of the word 'crabs,' which was the lowest throw in an earlier English version of the game. Craps is played with two dice in which a first throw of 7 or 11 wins; a first throw of 2, 3, or 12 loses the bet; and a first throw of any other number must be repeated to win before a 7 is thrown, which loses both the bet and the dice." She checked that I was following along. "Craps is both the name of the game and a losing throw of the dice. In North America, when two dice are thrown and both come up showing one spot, the losing throw is not only called 'craps,' but also 'snake eyes.' And when a player loses, he or she is said to have 'crapped out,' which is not to be confused with what a camper does in the woods," she explained with a wry smile. I smiled back while looking at her through snake eyes.

Of all the gaming rooms, the Salle Médecin was my favourite; it was the epitome of all that I'd imagined a casino to be—a set in a James Bond movie—with plush décor, including panels of mahogany engraved with gold inlay and large colourful tapestries. Sauntering from table to table, I was amazed to see the vast amounts of money being wagered in tall piles of chips.

"How about we buy some roulette chips?" my wife suggested. "We could just play safe by doubling up on red or black. That way, we can't lose," she added nonchalantly.

"Run that by me again," I said, trying to grasp the concept.

"Well, we start by placing just one chip on red. If black comes up we lose our bet, but then we double our bet by placing two chips on red. If black turns up a third time, we double up again by placing four chips on red. If we lose again, we place down eight chips, and so on. There's a 49 per cent chance of the ball landing on red, so it's bound to come up sooner or later and when it does we win at even odds. And provided we keep on doubling up on consecutive spins of the wheel, we can't lose," she explained.

It made perfect sense. So we bought thirty-one chips—all of our remaining gambling allowance. My wife smiled at me as she placed a single chip on red. The croupier spun the wheel and sent the little white ball spinning around its outer rim. We waited for it to stop bouncing around on the wheel, and when it did, it came to rest in a red compartment. We'd won. The croupier cleared the losing bets and paid us our winnings, a single chip. We smiled at each other. My wife picked up one of the chips and left the other on red. The croupier spun the wheel. The ball stopped on black. We'd lost. My wife smiled and placed two chips on red; our "double-up" plan was underway. It came up black. We smiled, and then she placed four chips on red. It came up black. I stopped smiling. She bit her bottom lip and placed eight chips on red. It came up black. We started frowning. We only had seventeen chips left. She placed sixteen of them on red. I crossed my fingers and—wouldn't you know it?—the ball stopped on black.

"So, what do we do now?" I asked, looking at the single chip.

"We could buy more chips, at least thirty-one more, and double up again on red, or we could quit," she answered, smiling and raising her eyebrows. "Which do you want to do?" But we were too late; the croupier had announced, "No more bets" and had spun the wheel. And—wouldn't you know it?—the little white ball came to rest in a red compartment. Such was my luck.

"Where should we put this last chip?" I asked, taking it from her hand. "Where would Domin-eeek put it?" I added.

"He'd probably tell you to shove it where the sun don't shine!" she said, and burst out laughing.

Who is this mysterious woman who looks even prettier when she laughs? I asked myself. Who is this woman who says she loves me, quirks, odd socks, and all? Well, she's my Casino Royale special agent, my confidante, my lover, my best friend, and she's my wife. And—wouldn't you know it?—such was my luck. So eat your heart out, James Bond!

35

Cap d'Antibes:

Mad Merce and One-Time Strangers

Before leaving Vancouver, while searching the Internet for the French equivalent of bed & breakfast accommodation, we'd discovered the Gîtes de France website. And after searching it at length, we made a five-night reservation at a hobby farm in Puget-sur-Argens, at a place called Le Mas du Centaure. Curious, I searched for the translation. We were going to be staying at The Farmhouse of the Monster that has the Head, Arms, and Torso of a Man, and the Body and Legs of a Horse, which we had soon nicknamed The Farmhouse of the Half-Man, Half-Horse Monster.

And it was while we were driving back to Cap d'Antibes in the slow lane of the A8 autoroute during rush hour (with cars flying by as if we were stuck in third gear) that we realized we had only two more nights remaining at Hôtel Beau-Site. And as much as we were enjoying easy access to the beaches and Antibes' old town, our spacious room, the pool, and our poolside acquaintances, we were looking forward to a change of base camp.

Still on the A8, I was pulling out of the slow lane to overtake a truck that was straining to climb a long gradual incline when the dull grey dot in my rear-view mirror suddenly became the gleaming grill and flashing headlights of a full-sized Mercedes. Just as I was passing the truck, to my horror, I saw four more trucks ahead of it—all crawling along bumper to bumper. Panicked by the menacing threat behind, and with too little space between the trucks to pull back into the slow lane, I slammed my foot flat down on the gas pedal. Gripping the steering wheel with white knuckles, I negotiated a very poorly lit, twisting tunnel. For the minute or so it took to pass the trucks and pull back into the slow lane, the idiot in my rear-view mirror stayed on my tail flashing his headlights.

Livid, I glared at him as he drew level. He was red in the face, eyes bulging, shouting, and shaking his fist. Pumped up with adrenalin, I made a gesture typical of other road-rage idiots and by doctors about to probe for the prostrate. This was like waving a red cloak at a raging bull. The driver of the Mercedes swerved into the slow lane ahead of us and slammed on his brakes, which forced me to swerve into the fast lane to avoid rear-ending him. Then he accelerated alongside us, shaking his fist at my wife who screamed something at him that needed no translation. Then he accelerated and cut in front of us, slamming on his brakes again and forcing us to swerve back into the slow lane. Heeding my wife's screams, I pulled over onto the hard shoulder and came to a stop. Shaking and dry mouthed, I turned to my wife and gasped, "Honey, are you okay? That guy was an absolute idiot. It's all right now; it's over," I reassured her.

Sitting wide-eyed and staring straight ahead, she slowly shook her head. "No, it's not," she whispered. "Look!"

With renewed horror, I saw that Mad Merce had also pulled over onto the hard shoulder ahead of us. His door opened, he got out, and he started to stride towards us. Tall and broad, he glared at me, the veins in his neck bulging. Everything seemed to be moving in slow motion as my life passed before my eyes. This is it, I thought: Shootout at the OK Corral. I may never see Vancouver again. Will Domin-eeek get back in touch with my wife? Will they marry and move to Las Vegas or Monte-Carlo? I'd made a Will, but who will get my golf clubs? Surely not Domin-eeek. Mad Merce was only strides away. Was it time to call his bluff, time to stand tall like a man, time to look him square in the eyes and threaten him through clenched teeth? No, it was not. Instead, I put the car in reverse, let out the clutch, and hit the gas. With the engine screaming, we shot backwards on the hard shoulder with Mad Merce running after us.

Still travelling in reverse, I'd managed to put about a hundred metres between us. Just short of re-entering the tunnel, I slammed on the brakes, selected first gear, shot off the hard shoulder, and sped into the flow of traffic, leaving our relentless and intimidating pursuer cursing and shaking his fist. It was a long walk back to his car. "Hey, Bozo! Would you like a ride back to your car?" my wife shouted out of her window as we drove by and accelerated into the fast lane—her perfume's side-effects still raging within her.

Back at Hôtel Beau-Site, we ventured out on to the patio. Two chairs at a table for six were occupied by black poodles, both of them sitting upright and looking aloof. The accompanying family of four, who were also sitting upright and looking aloof, all had a mop of curly black hair, which gave them an alarming resemblance to their pets. I overheard Cane complain to Able that the management should discourage hotel guests from bringing their dogs to the patio during mealtimes. "I'm sure the Queen and Duke of Edinburgh don't allow their corgis to sit at the dinner table," she said as she turned to face her husband. Able nodded, patted her hand, and said, "You got that right, dear." Wow! They were actually communicating lovingly with one another.

Cane and Able looked towards the palm tree, beamed the broadest of smiles, and began to applaud. The chubby-cheeked cherub had just finished a dance routine and was bowing to her appreciative audience. I was surprised that after she took a second bow she didn't pass around a hat for loose change—to add to her card-game winnings and the euros salvaged from the bottom of the pool.

We passed the three English couples, who were sitting at a table sipping martinis. One man was in the midst of telling a joke that involved an actress and a bishop, but the plot had nothing to do with the theatre or the church. A moment later, a chorus of laughter rose up and one of the women shrieked, "Oh, that's bloody dis-GUS-ting!" And they burst into laughter again.

Ooh-la-la Land

The Bulging Belgians were lounging contentedly in sun chairs between two serving tables that were loaded with empty dishes and sardine cans. André and Jacques were the busiest I'd seen them, and they'd conscripted Pawn the Bellboy to double as a bus boy. The three of them were smiling; the wine was flowing and so too were the tips. There was no doubt that we'd miss these poolside acquaintances, these one-time strangers, when we moved on to Le Mas du Centaure.

But that's part of what makes vacations interesting: you never know who may be sitting next to you at the pool or the breakfast table. They could be sailors, scallywags, Scandinavians, schoolmasters, Scots, scientists, scoundrels, sculptors, secretaries, seismologists, senators, señoritas, shahs, sheiks, sheriffs, Sikhs, simpletons, socialites, sophisticates, steeplejacks, surgeons, or even swashbucklers. Yet, strangely, after only a few words of introduction, they would no longer be strangers.

36

Antibes:

A Car, a Stone, a Phone, and a Hi-Tech Toilet

The next morning we strolled down to Le Garoupe Plage. It was another beautiful day: a blazing sun, a soft breeze, and a Mediterranean deep blue sky. Blossoms burst forth from every shrub, vine, hedge, garden, and flowerpot. Birds chirped as if there was no tomorrow. Families headed in droves down to the clean, golden sand; many had already set up their beach paraphernalia. Adults in their next-to-nothings lay glistening on sun lounges, mats, and towels. Children built sandcastles, kicked balls, and splashed at the water's edge. The sweet scent of pine blended magically with the salty smell of the sea. Beachside restaurants were already preparing for lunch. Newly laundered table linens, shining cutlery, and sparkling glassware were being set into place by smartly dressed young waiters. The delicious smell of garlic cooking in olive oil wafted from kitchen exhaust vents that faced the pay-as-you-lay sundecks, intermittently overpowering the pine scent and salty air. It was mid-summer and everyone on Le Garoupe Plage was happy; it was heaven on earth.

Speaking of heaven, the sight of a brand new Rolls-Royce Phantom sparkling in the sunshine in the parking area set back from the beach, surrounded by drooling dreamers, brought to mind the words of the most revered preacher: "It is easier for a camel to go through the eye of a needle than for a rich man to enter heaven." I guessed that the owner was having brunch somewhere close by, sipping champagne and orange juice, and eating caviar and a smoked salmon omelette. His camel was probably running up and down the beach in a futile attempt to slim down, clueless as to the size of the eye of a needle.

Standing guard over the marvel of gleaming, precision-pleasing engineering was a chauffeur wearing a uniform and a smarmy smirk. Obviously, the four-wheeled eye-catcher was his pride and joy. Other than getting his boss to wherever he wants to go, whenever he wants to go, and getting him there safely, his job would be to ensure that no damage, no theft, and no rust occurs to the 500,000-dollar vehicle. The French Riviera exudes such materialistic wealth. But then, who needs a Rolls-Royce Phantom when a Renault Twingo will do? Not that that alone would improve our chances of driving through the eye of a needle or parking permanently on the other side of those pearly white gates; it would not.

We strolled a considerable distance observing and photographing the natural beauty, the old architecture, and the hustle and bustle and colour of life. For the most part it was very relaxing and enjoyable—a lazy, impromptu day on holiday in the sun. However, a couple of incidents stand out.

The first occurred at a tourist information office at place Charles de Gaulle in the centre of Antibes. Initially we'd popped in to browse the racks of tourist-attraction brochures and postcards. But while we were there, it occurred to me to investigate the Stone of Terpon. I'd read that the stone had been found centuries ago when Antibes' original harbour wall was being demolished and reused as filler material during the 17th-century construction of Fort Carré. The stone had been linked to Antibes' beginnings—a time when it was nothing more than a place where ships would dock so that sailors could dock with prostitutes. An expressionless middle-aged woman was standing behind the counter. She stared at me as I asked, *"Bonjour, Madame. Parlez-vous anglais, s'il vous plaît?"*

"Bonjour, Monsieur, bonjour. Off course I am speaking Eeng-leesh, *off course* I am," she replied with a pout and a shrug of her

shoulders at each pause, her eyes as dull as a mid-November day in Vancouver. So why do you keep telling me that you're off course? I wondered. "'ow can I 'elp you, *Monsieur?* 'ow can I 'elp you?" she asked, determined to repeat a phrase in every sentence.

"What do you know about the Stone of Terpon?" I started. Just then, the telephone on the counter began to ring. The assistant placed her hand on the receiver but didn't pick it up. I looked down at the phone; it continued to ring. I looked back at her. She just stared back at me expectantly. "Where is it kept? How big is it? What is written upon it and in which language? Of what historical importance is it, if any? When did they find it?" I asked. The phone kept ringing. "I understand that it dates back centuries. Is that so?" I prompted. Her hand remained on the receiver. I looked down at it. She had long fingernails; they were painted crimson. An engagement ring and a wedding ring, partly hidden within the creases of wrinkled skin and captive below a swollen knuckle, were proof that she had a husband and arthritis. She looked bored. There was no sparkle in her eyes, no charisma to her personality. The phone kept ringing. "Is it true that the port of Antibes was once an early sailor's retreat, little more than a seaside bordello?" I asked, recalling the passage in our guidebook. "Is the message that is carved into the stone written in Greek?" The phone kept ringing and the woman just kept staring at me. I stopped speaking and waited for a few seconds. She raised her eyebrows and opened her mouth a little. She was about to speak. I could tell she was thinking and forming a reply. I raised my eyebrows too and then nodded my head in encouragement. "Go ahead," I said, expecting her to recite the entire history of the Stone of Terpon. Instead she picked up the receiver and spoke into it: "*Bonjour, Informations Tourisme. Oui. Bonjour, Informations Tourisme.*"

I was flabbergasted. Then, rather than ask the person on the other end of the line to hold for a moment until she'd finished attending to me, she held a five-minute conversation in French with someone who, if I understood correctly, wanted to know how to get to the railway station. When she eventually put down the receiver, I looked at her incredulously and waited for her to respond to my questions, but she just stared back at me. A few seconds passed before she said, "*Bonjour, Monsieur, bonjour.* 'ow can I 'elp you, *Monsieur?* 'ow can I 'elp you?"

I gave up. "I just want to buy these two postcards."

"*Off course, Monsieur, off course,*" she said, then took my money.

The second incident happened after our picnic lunch on a bench that faced the sea and overlooked the golden sand of plage du Ponteil. Having consumed several cafés au lait in the morning and a bottle of water with lunch, I got a sudden and intense call of Nature. Looking around, I spotted a public toilet less than fifty metres away. It was one of those modern toilets that's often found at the side of the road: a hi-tech, fully automated, coin-operated facility enclosed within an oval-shaped metal cabinet. I rushed over to it and began to read the instructions. From the graphics I realized that I needed to insert fifty cents into the slot. I dug deep into my pockets and pulled out my loose change, but, as is often the case in these desperate times, I found that I didn't have the correct amount. Bursting, I turned to leave, thinking that I'd jump down onto the sand and rush fully clothed into the sea. It was then I noticed that the cabinet door was slightly ajar. Relieved that I would soon be relieved, I pushed it open, got inside, slammed the door shut, turned the lock, unzipped my zipper, took two strides over to the stainless steel bowl, and released my bladder valve.

Standing in place, I heard the whirring sound of an electric motor, and then, to my utter surprise, the stainless steel bowl that I was aiming at suddenly began to retract behind the cabinet's interior wall panel. As best I could, I shuffled forwards, adjusting my trajectory to hit the moving target, but the bowl disappeared before my bladder was empty. Alas, my jet splattered onto the floor. No sooner had the bowl disappeared from sight than a cloud of superheated steam came billowing out from behind the wall panel and engulfed me, scalding my exposed parts. Another motor whirred, and up popped four sprinkler heads from the floor panel. A split-second later, they started to revolve, shooting forth high-pressure jets of water and disinfectant. All I could do was stand in the midst of it all, like a "flasher" in a car wash, exposed and getting soaked and disinfected, just waiting for the thirty-second wash cycle to end.

Wet, bedraggled, and smelling like a hospital, I unlocked the door and stepped out into the sunshine. My wife, who was still sitting on the bench, looked my way. "What on earth happened in there?" she asked, then started laughing.

"I thought I'd just get cleaned up a little after taking a whiz," I replied, wringing out my T-shirt. "I tell you, it was like a steam room in there." She laughed louder. "I guess I entered just before the cleansing cycle. It's probably a trick developed by the locals who know they can use the facilities for free *as long as they don't lock the door.*"

Streams of tears rolled down my wife's cheeks as I described the activity inside the hi-tech trap, and especially so when I added, "I'm not joking. *Really*, I'm dead serious. Not only has Percy been pickled, he's been badly scalded too."

Part Three

37

Puget-sur-Argens:

Bon Voyage and Bienvenue

André and Jacques beamed when we presented ourselves at the front desk and laid our room keys down on the counter. Pawn the Bellboy, who had just returned to his black square by the front door after loading Twingo with our bags, was also smiling.

"*Voilà! Madame et Monsieur,* I 'ave for you the bill. I 'ope you are 'appy with the spe-ci-al price. *Oui, Monsieur?*" asked Jacques. "Eet ees for stay-eeng weez us for many nights," he added, still beaming from ear to ear.

"*Merci beaucoup,*" I responded, feeling a little ashamed at earlier having suspected we were in for a tourist ripoff.

"I 'ope you were very 'appy 'ere. I 'ope you weel tell everyone een Vancou-vair about Hôtel Beau-Site," smiled André the Man.

"Yes we weel tell everyone een Vancou-vair," I replied, realizing that I was mimicking him.

"Thank you for a wonderful stay," my wife added as I put away my credit card.

"Eet ees our ple-zure, *Madame. Au revoir et bon voyage,*" they replied in unison.

Much of the area just outside of Puget-sur-Argens was an unattractive industrial estate of box-shaped buildings. At one intersection was a drive-through stonemasonry outlet where it was possible to conveniently drop by and drop off an order for a custom-made gravestone, pre-engraved in readiness for the time when you permanently drop out. Driving amid these ugly factories and warehouses, we were beginning to wonder if our Gîtes de France selection had been a wise one. The Internet photographs had revealed Le Mas du Centaure as a picturesque stone building in the midst of lawns and paddocks and located near a forest: the Forêt Dominion de Terre Gastes. And sure enough, after crossing a bridge that spanned the A8, we left behind the ugliness and the traffic and found ourselves in the countryside. The contrast was incredible, like being in a theatre at the end of an act when the backdrop and lighting are changed in seconds, without the curtain even dropping.

We had the address of Le Mas du Centaure but we were uncertain how to get there. So we pulled into the sleepy town centre of Puget-sur-Argens and parked in front of the post office to ask for directions. As luck would have it, the young couple we approached could speak English. But I discovered this only after mispronouncing *Mas* and *Centaure,* when the young couple explained that they thought I'd asked, "Is there a lump of smell nearby?" Ironically, it wouldn't be long before we'd be tiptoeing around nearby smelly lumps in the paddocks of "The Farmhouse of the Half-Man, Half-Horse Monster."

I showed the couple the name and address that was printed on our copy of the Gîtes de France website. "No, we know not of thiz place," the young man replied. "But we weel tel-e-fon," he suggested. "I weel call Le Mas du Centaure and tell them you are 'ere." It took him less than two minutes to explain the situation to the proprietor. I couldn't help but notice that while he held his phone with his left hand, he moved his right hand continuously as he spoke. I thought it especially odd because the listener couldn't see his animated performance. So, then, why gesticulate? Suppose his right arm was broken and set in plaster, would he be unable to speak? At least, he'd be tongue-tied. When he put down the receiver, he smiled and said, "Wait 'ere for two mo-ments. Madame Flora, she weel come 'ere for you." And not once did he move his hands.

Within seconds of saying goodbye to the young couple, a Renault Laguna raced into the main square and, in a cloud of dust, came to a screeching halt in front of the post office. The driver, an attractive woman of about forty with long, flaming red hair, leaned out of the window and waved at us. *"Madame et Monsieur, s'il vous plaît,"* she shouted without getting out of her sporty machine, which she kept revving as if on the starting grid of a race track. *"S'il vous plaît."* She waved again, beckoning us to follow. We ran to Twingo, started the engine, and raced off—à la Monaco Grand Prix—in pursuit of the rapidly accelerating Laguna and the flowing red hair of its spirited driver, Flora.

Entry onto her property was via a narrow dirt lane, the start of it concealed by a hedgerow of flowering bushes. A small sign, LE MAS DU CENTAURE, was set back a few metres from the paved country road and was almost impossible to read in the cloud of dust, which was the only clue to where Flora had turned off. A dusty, bumpy lane wound its way several hundred metres through an area of scrub, across a lush field, between railed paddocks, and eventually ended at a magnificent stone farmhouse.

By the time we'd parked the car, which looked as if it had just crossed the finish line of the Paris–Dakar Rally, Flaming Flora was standing with her husband in the shade of a wrought-iron gazebo on a large stone patio. The two were smiling and waving. A jug of iced lemonade, crystal glasses, a pot of steaming tea, china cups and saucers, a plate of homemade cookies, and a vase of roses had been lovingly set on the wrought-iron table. Three black dogs—a Scottish terrier, a bloodhound, and a mongrel—sat obediently beside the attractive proprietors. It was indeed an impressively warm welcome to "The Farmhouse of the Half-Man, Half-Horse Monster."

38

Puget-sur-Argens:

Pregnant Pauses, Black Dogs, and Single-Handed Achievements

"*Bienvenue,*" greeted our host, smiling broadly and extending his hand, "*je m'appelle Philippe. Asseyez-vous, s'il vous plaît,*" he said, motioning for us to sit, as he and Flora joined us at the table. We were pleased with what we'd seen so far: the rural setting, the farmhouse, the paddocks, and our welcoming hosts. However, it was only a matter of minutes before we discovered that the proprietors could speak no more English than we could speak French. And so our fifteen-minute interaction, though very pleasant, proved somewhat awkward. In anticipation of such an eventuality, Flaming Flora had placed a French-English phrasebook beside her teacup, but referring to it and experimenting in broken English did little to improve communications. Likewise, after several unsuccessful attempts at understanding what they were saying, I retrieved our English-French phrasebook and opened it at "Lesson 17: Table Talk." But, alas, after making several requests for them to repeat what they were saying, and to "*parlez lentement,*" all attempts at conversation dried up and we resorted to hand gestures, questioning looks, nods, and smiles.

During a rather long pregnant pause, when I found myself smiling like a simpleton and gazing blankly at a mule in the paddock,

Flaming Flora went to retrieve an extra-thick photo album from the farmhouse. The photos, arranged chronologically, recorded the progress of construction of their farmhouse, ancillary buildings, patios, and swimming pool. The focus of each action-packed shot, whether it was of topsoil being removed by a bulldozer, concrete being poured over steel reinforcing bars, a nail being hammered into a wooden frame, or a final coat of gloss paint being applied to a door, was a sole construction worker, a fair-haired, slightly built man wearing blue jeans. It was none other than our host, Philippe. We were able to interpret from her gestures that Flaming Flora's unassuming husband had built Le Mas du Centaure single-handedly. And I thought, for anyone so driven and so strong, there was, perhaps, a half-man, half-horse monster concealed within Philippe's small frame. More surprisingly, Flaming Flora conveyed to us, by opening her mouth wide, touching a molar with a finger, and making a buzzing sound, that her mild-mannered husband was a dentist by profession, not a general contractor. Monday to Friday he filled tiny cavities using delicate instruments at his surgery in Fréjus and on weekends he filled huge cavities using bulldozers while landscaping their hobby farm in Puget-sur-Argens—an amazing visual contrast in physical activities.

Another distraction that eased the awkwardness of the pregnant pauses was the three dogs. The long-haired Scottish terrier had been sitting beside my chair looking up at me, waiting patiently for a morsel of butter-rich cookie to be thrown its way—reminiscent of Noodle the Poodle back in Cannes. Although at first glance the terrier looked cute, it never stopped growling while showing a little of its glistening pink tongue and two gleaming white fangs that protruded from its mess of straggly black hair. With tail wagging, ears pricked up, and eyes hidden behind hair, it played the role of the smiling, friendly dog. But I knew better. Moreover, it smelled terrible; its matted hair was evidence that Terrible Terrier had rolled around in patties in the paddocks. I was *not* going to be petting *this* dog.

Ten long seconds into another pregnant pause, I turned around to admire the front of the farmhouse—Cavity Phil's enormous single-handed achievement—but then quickly averted my eyes from the bloodhound that was sitting back against the farmhouse wall, with a hind leg cocked up in the air, licking itself. Obviously excited by the commotion created by our arrival, it too was exhibiting something that glistened pink.

The third dog, unlike the exhibitionist, Horny Hound, and the growling Terrible Terrier, was not a thoroughbred but a mongrel—an expectant bitch. And, unlike her two male canine cohabitants, she lay demurely in the shade of a plane tree—saving her energy for the imminent birth of her litter. Black all over, with the exception of her snow-white paws, she was an attractive dog with a well-shaped head and an adorable sad-eyed expression. And although she was only a mongrel, Pregnant Paws was a dog worthy of petting.

Loaded down with our heavy suitcases, I staggered behind Flaming Flora who showed us to our room. Rather than help me carry our suitcases, Cavity Phil strode off in the direction of a stone storage building where he kept his earth-moving equipment, cement mixer, machine tools, and work benches. He had, no doubt, assumed that I could manage to carry a couple of suitcases by myself. Besides, he probably had a "Today's Job List" to be getting on with. Earlier, over tea and butter-rich cookies, while I was looking forward to collapsing on the bed, taking a refreshing shower, or slumping into a hammock, he was probably looking forward to strapping on a tool belt, starting up a chainsaw, or driving around in a bulldozer. He'd be spending the afternoon single-handedly removing topsoil, excavating craters, relocating boulders, chopping down trees, and building stone walls. And I'd be single-handedly watching him sweat.

We knew, from interpreting Flora's web page, that access to our room "Cigales," was "*par escalier*"—by a staircase. But what came as a surprise as I staggered around the corner, sweating like a pig, wobbling like a jelly, and wondering why I hadn't made use of the mule in the paddock, was that the staircase was a circular type—the type that you'd find in a lighthouse. Step by step, I lugged our heavy suitcases and wondered why someone (perhaps a dentist) hadn't single-handedly installed an elevator or an escalator. Thankfully, when I reached the top, my cardiovascular workout was rewarded.

"Cigales" was a fairly large, airy room of white walls. The *"grand lit"* had a bright yellow bedspread and pillows. The bedside lampshades, drape tassels, and other decorative accessories were also bright yellow. Painted around the walls at waist height was a narrow, bright yellow strip that incorporated a stencilled winged insect at one-metre spacing. On the back of the door was a large, decorative coat hook in the form of a yellow-winged insect. Cigales, we learned after a five-minute charade by Flaming Flora, is the French word for "cicadas": the shrill, winged insects that we'd heard, but never seen, especially around dusk, since setting foot on the French Riviera. Three wooden beams, also painted bright yellow, supported the white plaster ceiling. Two sets of plain, white drapes hung from two lengths of one-inch-square wrought-iron rods that had been heated in a forge and then twisted several times along its length. The heat-treatment process would have been repeated to form the decorative curlicues at each end. Apparently, there had been no need to have them made by the local 300-pound blacksmith because the slightly built Cavity Phil had made them himself, single-handedly.

The small room (and I do mean small) that accommodated the shower and toilet had white walls and bright yellow towels. As a welcoming treat for my wife, an assortment of sample-sized toiletries had been wrapped in white tissue paper and placed in a little bright yellow bag with two loops of white silk ribbon for handles and then placed on top of the pile of folded towels—likely by Flaming Flora. My wife was delighted. She loves surprise treats and she loved her first impressions of "Cigales." I too enjoy surprise treats. So I took a quick look around the bedroom to see if Cavity Phil had prepared a little bright yellow bag of assorted "masculine" goodies for me— hooks, tap washers, electrical fuses, some solder, and a length of duct tape, or a small bag of hazelnuts to break my teeth on. But there was nothing, not even a toothbrush, a roll of dental floss, or a toothpick.

Flaming Flora wasted no time in showing us how to operate the air-conditioning unit, and then pointed at a corner table on which stood an electric kettle, two bright yellow mugs, and a container of tea bags, sachets of coffee, sugar, and powdered cream. With a smile and a flick of her long, flowing red hair, she handed us a huge metal key. It looked like the type that might have hung on a huge ring on the huge belt of the huge dungeon master of a huge medieval castle during the Crusades, but it was probably made single-handedly a couple of years ago by the less-than-huge Cavity Phil. Then, in a flash, Flaming Flora departed, her long red hair shooting after her. As soon as the metallic clunk, clunk, clunk of her heels finished descending the circular steel staircase, we tested the firmness of the mattress, unpacked, and drank a cup of refreshing mint tea.

So, all was good with our new base camp. That is, until I stepped into the clear-plastic upright coffin that served as our shower cubicle and discovered that the shower head receptacle, the part normally anchored to the wall, was broken. Consequently, the shower head just dangled on the end of its hose and, with no other way of anchoring it into position at normal shower height, it had to be held with one hand. Having only the other hand free to hold the soap, lather up, and wash with, the showering procedure was considerably frustrating. Reluctantly, we agreed that we would not complain to our hosts and accept the fact that while staying at the "Farmhouse of the Half-Man, Half-Horse Monster," we would shower single-handedly.

39

Puget-sur-Argens Environs:

Mr Clampett, Mr Wayne, and a Cowgal

Frothing at the mouth and with fangs clearly visible, Terrible Terrier was running alongside Twingo barking and snapping at the driver-side front tire as we drove up the dusty, bumpy lane and onto the paved country road in search of a local restaurant for dinner. Leaving behind the hound from hell to snarl and pant in our dust, we elected to turn left at LE MAS DU CENTAURE sign, but it soon became apparent that we were heading away from urban sprawl. The farther we drove, the prettier and wilder the countryside appeared— undeveloped land except for the paved road beneath our fang-scarred tires. For certain this road would not lead us to a quaint restaurant serving fine French cuisine. For *that,* we'd have to turn around and head in the opposite direction, back past Le Mas du Centaure and the recuperated hound from hell.

Soon a large sign informed us that we were entering the national forest, Forêt Dominion de Terre Gastes. The paved road turned to gravel and wound its way through the bush, and after several kilometres, the gravel road changed to dirt. Deeper into the forest, with darkness falling rapidly and our sense of direction fading by the minute, we were startled by the sound of gunshots. I hit the brakes and skidded to a stop.

"Did you hear that?" I asked, aware of my quavering voice.

"Probably hunters," my wife responded, as she depressed the

shutter button after framing an artsy photo of the base of a large tree bordered by fungi.

"Did you see that?"

"Yes, do you think they're truffles?" she asked, as she zoomed in on the mushroom-shaped protuberances.

"No! I don't mean those dumb mushrooms. Look! Over there! I saw something move over *there*. Something's behind those bushes," I whispered, wide-eyed and pointing.

"It's probably the hunters," she said, as she leaned out of her window and took an almost-vertical shot of the leafy canopy above.

Just then, I swear I saw the shadowy images of three men stealthily picking their way through the bush. Thoughts came to mind of the shotgun-wielding, banjo-duelling hillbillies who stalked Burt Reynolds, Jon Voight, Ned Beatty, and Ron Cox in *Deliverance*. In particular, I was recalling the haunting scene that ended with a well-aimed arrow. Having no immediate access to a crossbow, I stepped on the gas and, in a cloud of dust, spun Twingo around and headed to the safety of urban sprawl and the promise of gastronomic delights.

We didn't get to dine at a quaint, countryside restaurant serving fine French cuisine after all. For *that,* I blamed urban development and the proliferation of fast-food establishments, especially in the area southeast of Puget-sur-Argens where we ended up. Relieved at having avoided a close encounter with shotgun-wielding Billy-Bob Clampett and his redneck friends, I parked Twingo in the parking lot of the Buffalo Grill on Route Nationale 7.

If you were to drive that section of RN7, regardless of your speed, it's highly unlikely that you would miss the Buffalo Grill's two-metre-high red banner advertising the weekly special—steak with something—that is anchored to the front of the building. Should you fail to see the red banner, I doubt you would miss the three-metre-high totem pole erected front and centre of the property line. However, should you have limited peripheral vision bordering on blindness and miss the totem pole, I guarantee you would not miss the twenty-five-metre white wooden verandah that spans the entire length of the front of the North American cowboy-style structure.

As we entered the swinging doors—Western saloon–style ones—we were greeted by a young man dressed as a cowboy in leather boots, blue jeans, huge shiny belt buckle, fringe shirt, shoestring tie, black Stetson, and all. He grinned and yelled "Howdy!"

"Howdy! How ya doin', partner?" my wife yelled in an accent typical of a Southern belle. Startled by her uncharacteristic response, I knew immediately the cause and wondered what other disconcerting personality traits may soon be revealed.

"Howdy!" was the limit of our cowboy's English vocabulary, and from that point on he rattled on in French faster than the rattling tail of a rattlesnake. After showing us to our table—which was covered in a red-and-white gingham tablecloth—our greeting cowboy, Jean Wayne, also became our waiter. As soon as we were seated, he placed plastic menus on the table and then disappeared into the kitchen where he lassoed a steer, wrestled it to the ground, and roped it in less than nine seconds—breaking the Calgary Stampede record. Minutes later, he two-stepped out of the kitchen carrying two bowls of mixed salad and a basket of bread, which he placed in front of us with a "*Voilà!*"

"Yahoo!" exclaimed my wife.

"Oh no," I muttered under my breath, as I prepared for the imminent embarrassment of her climbing onto the table, lifting her skirt, and dancing the Cancan.

"Doggone it, I'm gonna have *this* one," she said, looking up first at Jean Wayne and then pointing to the colour photo of Steak 'n' Mushrooms, #7 on the menu.

Not buying into the whole cowboy scene quite as much as the smiling cowgal sitting opposite me, I pointed at picture #1, Steak 'n' Fries, and asked Jean Wayne if the steak was cut from a buffalo or a cow and if I could have the moat of blood served "on the side." Not understanding a word coming from the corner of this sidewinder's mouth—a stranger from out yonder, west of the Canadian Rockies—

Jean Wayne frowned and said *oui,* left with our order, and went to inform the sheriff to assemble a posse, lickety-split.

Though far from being a quaint restaurant serving fine French cuisine, the food and service were surprisingly good, and we had a pleasant evening. And much to my relief, the Cancan dancer didn't make an appearance. And so, with slabs of meat in our guts, and thousands of sticky globules of fat rushing through our veins, we skedaddled out of town in our chuckwagon (no posse in pursuit), found our way to our homestead, and climbed into our bunk bed. Yahoo!

40

Les Arcs:

A Nightmare, a Bat Cave,
a Rolex Watch, and a Drowned Rat

It was a tremendous relief to wake up in our sun-filled room, as I'd been dreaming vivid dreams—no, nightmares actually. Lying there in the comfort of our *grand lit*, staring up at the yellow ceiling beams, and listening to the slow breaths of my sleeping wife, I tried to recall my dream, scene by scene, and piece it together.

It was weird. I was frightened. I was being chased by a gang. I was running, but a mad dog was snapping at my heels. It was wearing a tartan collar with shiny metal studs. There was an ugly guy wearing a toothless grin and carrying a shotgun and, behind him, a slim guy wearing a leather tool belt and carrying a small high-speed drill. Following him was a female racecar driver wearing a long, flowing, red scarf, and right behind her was a long-horned bull with a ring through its nose. In close pursuit was a cowboy wearing a silver star and a blood-red neckerchief, and galloping behind him were a dozen more riders carrying banner flags and nooses. But then, all of a sudden, I was saved by a beautiful woman who was wearing a frilly dress and two black-lace garters. It was scary and it was weird and I couldn't make any sense of it.

After showering single-handedly, my wife and I clambered down the circular steel staircase, made our way to the front of the stone farmhouse, and entered the kitchen-cum-dining room where Flaming

Flora was preparing breakfast. The room was large with a huge stone fireplace at one end. In the middle, a large rectangular wooden table, with enough chairs to seat twelve or more, was laden with pots of homemade jams, baskets of freshly baked croissants, and bowls of fruit and yoghurt. Wooden beams, spaced a metre apart and spanning the width of the room supporting the white stucco ceiling, added to the charm and quaintness of the interior.

Pregnant Paws lay demurely in front of the fireplace and barely raised one eyebrow to peek up at us as we greeted Flaming Flora. Horny Hound was more attentive. The dog pranced over and rubbed up against my leg, drooling at the prospect of humping it later. Terrible Terrier, still with matted hair partially covering its beady eyes, growled and smiled that familiar fanged grin.

Attempting to communicate with Flaming Flora while I was swallowing mouthfuls of warm croissant covered in homemade, tooth-decaying, strawberry jam proved somewhat stressful. Several times I resorted to bluffing a response rather than searching through my phrasebook in "Lesson 30: At the Breakfast Table While One's Leg Is Being Humped." Instead, I opted for an occasional affirmative nod, a shrug of the shoulders, and a smile while confidently saying, "*Oui. Oui,*" in response to her rapid-fire words. She may have been asking if we'd like to stay for another month or, perhaps, if either of us had done time in France's La Santé prison.

After washing down our croissants with a couple of cafés au lait, and administering a couple of not-so-subtle but effective kicks to Horny Hound's underbelly, we bid our host *adieu* and, with camera, maps, guidebooks, and sunscreen at hand, we drove up the dusty, bumpy lane, leaving behind the relentless, fangs-exposed Terrible Terrier in our dust.

Back on paved road, we set off to explore the neighbouring towns and the surrounding countryside. We came upon the small town of Le Muy, which, apparently, was one of the first places liberated in the Allied invasion of southern France in August 1944. Of no particular interest to us as tourists, we motored on to Les Arcs.

Les Arcs is a picturesque medieval village of narrow, cobbled streets and stone houses, all of which have been lovingly maintained and, from the outside at least, appear authentic and in excellent state of repair. To our surprise, Les Arcs had only a few shops for tourists to browse through and buy souvenirs. In contrast to Cannes and Antibes and even Monte-Carlo, there was not a single shelf stacked high with souvenir T-shirts emblazoned with place names and unimaginative slogans like "Oh My! I Survived Le Muy!" or "Les Arcs—Been There, Done That, Couldn't Buy a T-Shirt!"

Walking around the town, we came upon the medieval, stone-walled Le Logis du Guetteur. Our guidebook reported that this three-star hotel is famous for its *"restaurant gastronomique"* and that its beautifully appointed dining rooms are set in caves under the hotel's forecourt. Curious, I left my wife outside snapping artsy photos while I stepped inside the lobby. Standing behind the reception desk, tapping a pen on a reservation ledger, was a dark-haired, fit-looking man wearing a three-piece black suit—somewhat resembling Batman waiting impatiently for Robin to come out of the Bat Cave. I asked him (charade-style, that is) if we could walk through the premises and check out its caves and all.

As Batman was determined to speak to me only in French, I concluded we could only explore the Bat Cave if we were staying in the hotel as patrons. No sooner had I begun to shake my head sideways, declaring, almost ashamedly, that we were just tourists passing through, than his forehead furrowed in an expression of utter disdain. "Well, get the hell out of here," I interpreted his glare and overall assessment of me, The Joker.

"Hi, honey," my wife called, adjusting her sunshades to the top of her head as she came in from the street and the relentless sunshine. *"Bonjour, Monsieur,"* she said, smiling at Batman. "Do we have your permission to look around these beautiful premises?" she asked, her lips bright with a fresh application of ruby-red lip gloss. As my wife advanced towards us, I knew that Batman didn't stand a chance as I'd detected her unmistakable, secret weapon: a new application of her heat-seeking, bunker-blasting, man-attacking, libido-boosting, knee-knocking fragrance. Lookout, Batman! Catwoman has arrived.

Smiling from ear to ear, Batman proceeded to lead us on a tour of the charming, historic hotel and the famous fine-dining restaurant enclosed within its 10th-century grey stone walls. Ignoring The Joker and speaking only to Catwoman (in English, I might add), Batman showed us a few attractive and comfortable *chambres* before leading us out onto a patio where chic, Rolex-wearing patrons were sipping pre-luncheon martinis.

We strolled alongside the blue-tiled swimming pool of crystal-clear water that was next to the patio and that tempted anyone wearing a Rolex Deepsea watch to dive in to check if their wrap-around-wrist investment would withstand the pressure at the first two of the 10,908-metre depth that was reached when the prototype was strapped to the hull of the Deepsea Challenger submersible during the expedition to the deepest point of the world's oceans.

"It's amazing! The watch just kept ticking," is what Rolex representatives had hoped James Cameron would say after popping his head out of the hatch upon surfacing, and not what he was overheard to say: "Anyone got any idea what time it is?"

Lagging behind the attentive and cordial Batman and the eyelash-fluttering Catwoman, I slipped off a sandal and dipped my toes into the pool. It was the shock of the glacially cold water that caused me to lose my balance and fall in. Gasping for air when I resurfaced, I was tossed a life preserver and plucked from the pool by a concerned first-responder, who just so happened to be wearing a Rolex watch.

The two superheroes had re-entered the hotel and were standing cape-to-cape inside one of the beautifully appointed dining rooms as I arrived at their side looking like a drowned rat, but ever-so refreshed.

"*Voilà!* Eet ees so een-cred-ee-bla. *Oui?* You like? 'ave you ever seen any-thing so unique, so un-expec-ted, so sur-pri-zing?" Batman gushed, as if he'd just spotted the Bat-Signal projected against a dark sky somewhere in downtown Gotham City.

"It is indeed incredible," replied Catwoman as she looked around, then spotted me.

"No, I have *not* seen anything so unexpected and so surprising," she croaked as she stared The Joker up and down in disbelief, her frown disappearing in a burst of *purr-fect* laughter.

41

Towns in the Var Region:

The Magical Mystery Tour

After leaving Les Arcs, we had no planned itinerary. We didn't have to be anywhere by any particular time. We had no idea where we were heading and we didn't care. I recall a circular scenic route through quaint villages scattered amid lush fields, forests, vineyards, and olive groves, and alongside deep canyons, craggy cliffs, and meandering rivers. It was a Magical Mystery Tour.

From Les Arcs, we next came upon Trans-en-Provence, where we stopped to view a rather odd structure called a high-mass air well that was designed and built by the Belgian engineer Achille Knapen. I'm sure you remember him. His name even came up the other day at The Gap when I was buying an expensive pair of jeans with threadbare patches, frayed holes at the knees, and bleached-white blotches on the thighs and *derrière*. The air well, also known as a condenser, is a large bell-shaped stone structure that looks somewhat like a gigantic bee hive spanning a depression—a ground reservoir. Its intended function was to collect drinking water by promoting the condensation of water from ambient humid air. Now, I realize this may not sound enthralling, but I encourage you to read on.

Many air wells were built and used in the 19th century, and you'll be thrilled to learn that the simplest designs were passive, in that they require no external energy source and have no moving parts. Unfortunately this type of water generation system became obsolete, leaving behind hundreds of monumental stone structures and many more unemployed engineers and stonemasons throughout Europe.

Now here's the kicker. An air well must *not* be confused with a dew pond. Absolutely fascinating! The next time you're at a cocktail party when someone is pontificating about recent shifts in the geopolitical landscape, you interject that you've decided to donate your dehumidifier to charity and you're going to fill in your dew pond at the bottom of your garden, and replace both with a fifteen-metre-tall, limestone high-mass air well. Then raise both eyebrows, nod your head, suck your teeth, and walk away in search of someone more interesting.

Five minutes was sufficient to photograph the gigantic, obsolete dehumidifier. So, after driving slowly through the pleasant town centre of Trans, we headed north to Draguignan in search of something more interesting.

According to legend, Draguignan is derived from the Latin name *Draco* or *Draconem.* Central to the legend is a bishop named Saint Hermentaire who, somehow, killed a dragon and thereby saved many people. From this event comes the Latin motto of Draguignan: *Alios nutrio, meos devoro,* which translates, somehow, to "I feed others, I devour my children." If, after reading this additional piece of trivia, you think that you have, somehow, missed a piece of the puzzle, don't worry; you're not alone. Just stash it away ready to recall for another cocktail party exit story.

Draguignan has been proclaimed the Capital of Artillery. In 1976, the large town welcomed the École nationale d'artillerie, the National Artillery School, and then, in 2010, the École nationale d'infanterie, the National Infantry School. The arrival of the military was the main factor in the small town becoming a thriving city.

Most large towns and cities in Provence offer numerous points of interest and entertainment to attract fickle tourists with wallets bulging with credit cards and cash. But after passing a couple of high-walled military bases, this fickle tourist thought there was no way we'd be stopping to buy postcards and writing to friends, "Having a great time in Draguignan, wish you were here."

However, with our stomachs growling, we decided to stop and stroll through the town centre in the hope of finding a restaurant for lunch—say, at a four-rifle-rated establishment. Vacant parking spaces on the main street were impossible to find, so we turned onto a side street and, as luck would have it, a camouflaged Jeep pulled out from the curb in front of us, and I managed to squeeze Twingo in between an AMX Leclerc main battle tank and an armoured personnel carrier.

We were unable to find even a three-rifle-rated restaurant, so we settled for a two-mortar-rated pizzeria where we sat on a patio under a large tree and hoped that the birds squawking above would miss the thin-crust targets with their air-to-surface guided missiles. As extra punishment for our hasty decision, our waitress had decided that we were the enemy. She was not a happy soldier. Perhaps she'd just returned from a torturous interrogation or had recently received a dishonourable discharge for taking bayonet practice too seriously. Her displeasure at serving us was palpable from the moment I smiled and said, *"Bonjour, Madame. Pardonnez-moi, je ne parle pas français. Parlez-vous anglais, s'il vous plaît?"* She grunted something and stared at her notepad. I pointed at one of the pizzas on the menu, she wrote it down and then left without saying a word. Twenty minutes later she slid our fifteen-inch diameter lunch onto our table and then scurried away—possibly to a bomb shelter behind the kitchen. Fearful that the thin-crust disc was a disguised landmine, we cut into it warily. It tasted absolutely delicious—the best pizza ever. The war was over. It was time to forgive and forget. And peace returned to the land.

Our stroll around Draguignan's city centre, especially through the pedestrian-only streets of the old town, proved more interesting than we'd expected. The attractive, well-planned boulevards; the place des Herbes; the tree-lined allées d'Azemar; and the medieval "clock-less" tower built in 1663 (so the sign informed us) gave Draguignan a touristy appeal. But it was time to move on.

☼

From there we drove through the tiny village of Pierre de la Fée and then followed the road alongside the Naturby River, which winds its way through the beautiful Gorges de Châteaudouble. The superb scenic drive attracts tourists from far and wide, as do the craggy cliff faces for those who are beginner rock climbers. For advanced rock climbers, our guidebook recommended the limestone walls of the nearby Gorges du Verdon, which is also known as the Grand Canyon du Verdon and is considered one of Europe's most beautiful river canyons. Its walls stand several hundred metres high and offer many outstanding routes for those experienced enough to engage in multi-pitch climbing.

Memories of my rock climbing days are a little hazy—so much so that I can only recall one day. And I suppose a more accurate description of that day's activity would be rock *dangling*. I was eighteen and attending an Outward Bound school on a four-week physical endurance course in England's Lake District. It was dubbed: "A stepping stone from boyhood to manhood." I remember an ape of a climbing instructor running up a thirty-metre, near-vertical rock face hammering pitons into cracks and threading rope through them as he went; and arriving at the summit in minutes, barely winded.

"Come on then," he shouted as I stared up at him, wide-eyed. With safety rope attached to my climbing harness, I began my ascent with spindly legs trembling and knobbly knees knocking. Reminding myself not to look down, I managed to climb halfway at which point I lost my footing and slipped. I jolted to a stop and began to sway to and fro, like a pendulum, on the end of the rope. And *that's* when I began my one hour of incredibly tense multi-pitch rock dangling—somewhere between boyhood and manhood.

We stopped briefly in Châteaudouble. Other than it being another small, picturesque village, I'm at a loss to recall anything of particular interest. However, a quick Internet search informed us that its area code is 83038 and its postal code is 83300. Its population in 2006 was 476 but then declined to 470 in 2007, proving that six people agreed with me that there really wasn't anything of particular interest in Châteaudouble.

Farther along we came to Figanières, a medieval village sitting on a hill. Narrow streets, laneways really, wound among tall houses packed around St-Michael's parish church, and then entered pleasant squares with shade trees, benches, and fountains. Driving these narrow streets requires concentration, a keen sense of the width of the car, and quick reflexes to make minor steering adjustments. Making the slightest misjudgement will likely result in the door mirrors colliding with oncoming door mirrors, scraping against limestone walls, shattering against rock faces, or slapping unsuspecting tourists. Thankfully, with necessity being the mother of invention, *"Voilà!"*— cars have fold-back door mirrors.

By mid-afternoon, we had reached Callas, where we stopped to stroll through the village centre and then visit the Chapelle de Pennafort. Approaching the village from afar, we'd seen its white bell tower rising above the trees. The chapel was built in 1855; it stands next to an 11th-century Saracen tower and is topped with a dome. Inside, the vaulted dome is painted blue and, below that, frescoes of saints and angels frame its supporting walls. My wife looked subdued and reverential as she glanced up and down from guidebook to frescoes, her halo adjusting with every move.

"Don't you think that that one looks like Frank?" I asked while looking up at the frescoes and thinking that one saint had a striking resemblance to a friend of ours. "Nah, Frank wears glasses. It must be the hooked nose and grey beard," I added.

My wife turned and glared at me; her halo had disappeared. Now, after years of marriage, I've learned to sense her slightest mood change. I don't always know what causes the change, but my suspicion is that it's something I've said or done. So I knew that it was, once again, time to implement damage control.

Pointing up at a fresco of an angel dressed in a long white robe, I said, "Honey, look at her. She's beautiful. That white dress reminds me of your wedding dress." I turned back to see that she was looking up and smiling at the fresco—her halo was back in place.

Driving south, we passed through the beautiful Gorges de Pennafort with its scatterings of beige and orange rocks. Ready for an afternoon break, we stopped at Hostellerie Les Gorges de Pennafort: a lovely three-star hotel that faces the craggy rocks. Sitting on a shaded terrace that overlooked an attractive, peanut-shell-shaped swimming pool and sundeck, we enjoyed a pot of Earl Grey tea and shared a huge slice of Gâteau au Chocolat. Several guests were sunning themselves, some were swimming, and a tanned young woman with over-inflated twin cupolas pointing skyward floated on an under-inflated pink airbed. Rejuvenated from the jolt of caffeine and sugar, I sprang from my chair and started off towards the gate in the perimeter chain-link fence.

"I think I'll take a closer look at the pool," I said, as I half-turned to get the nod of approval from my wife. "Maybe I'll just dip my toes in," I added, while checking the location of the closest life preserver.

"Try not to fall in this time," she commented dryly.

I walked over to the gate. There was a knob at the top with a latch attached to it. I twisted the knob, but the gate didn't open. I lifted the knob. Nothing happened. I pushed the gate and twisted the knob. It refused to open. By this time, I had the attention of all the poolside bathers. They were smiling. I was not. I looked back at my wife. She was gesturing and mouthing words that I couldn't decipher. I noticed that the twin cupolas had docked at the pool's shallow end and the over-inflated young woman was coming to my rescue. She placed her hand on top of the knob and with a quick push downwards and a twist of the knob, released the latch, and, *"Voilà!"* the gate opened. I smiled and thanked the young woman; escorted her back to her berth; complimented her on her itsy-bitsy, ooh-la-la bikini; and then dipped my toes into the water without falling in.

Back at our table my wife remarked, "That was nice of that young woman in the bikini to show you how to open the gate. You have to push the knob down and twist, right? That's what you had difficulty with, right?"

"Yes, that's right."

"That's because it's childproof."

I looked at her. Her halo had disappeared. It was time for damage control again.

42

Le Mas du Centaure:

Our Fellow Guests

After a restful night's sleep, we used the electric kettle and enjoyed a pre-breakfast cup of Earl Grey tea while sitting in bed, propped up against pillows, and recounted the highlights of yesterday's Magical Mystery Tour.

We had noticed as we drove or strolled through the villages and towns—regardless of their size or antiquity—that on every main street, or in every square, there was at least one hairdressing salon. In some villages, these *salons de coiffure* were more commonplace than bakeries. Moreover, the hairdressing establishments seemed busy six days a week, their customers mostly women in their "golden" years. And who can blame them for wanting to treat themselves to a regular visit to (the French equivalent of) PERMANENT WAVERS or HAIR APPARENT to get a rinse and set, and to gossip with Francine who occasionally raises her painted-on eyebrows and exclaims, "*Sacré bleu!*" to the juicier ooh-la-la tidbits as she creates before-and-after magic with her arthritic fingers and thumbs?

Tourists and locals alike expect to see a church in the central square of a town or village—a cathedral in a city. Over the centuries, these remarkably designed and constructed buildings have become recognized less as structures built to glorify God, sanctuaries to pray and worship within, but more as their community's focal point, the spot from which directions are given and to which tourists are drawn. But it was clear that the *salons de coiffure* were thriving, possibly attracting more customers than the churches. The vain desire of those uncertain of the promise of eternal life seemed to be winning out to the certainty of a few days of enhanced beauty in the here and now.

Had we asked any local woman the way to the tourist information office, provided she could understand and speak English, she would surely have pointed down the road: "Follow this road about 100 metres, turn right at CURL UP AND DYE, go 100 metres more and turn left at PARTING WAYS. You'll pass BANGS FOR THE MEMORIES on the left and FROM HAIR TO ETERNITY on the right, but just continue until you get to the main square and you'll see the tourist information office next to HAIRWAY TO HEAVEN. I'm not positive, but I think it's directly opposite that big, old building, Christ Church Cathedral."

At some of the local markets, we also recalled having seen posters advertising the promise of truffles for sale during the upcoming season. These richly flavoured fungal delicacies, especially of the Var region, are traditionally sniffed out by pigs trained to discover, and then uncover, the golf-ball-sized goodies under the soil near the roots of oak trees. They are usually collected during winter when they are most fragrant, and their scarcity is the reason for their exorbitant cost. What our Internet search didn't convey was the method by which the pigs are trained, the length of their apprenticeship, the drop-out rate, and the number, if any, of experienced truffle-sniffing pigs that have been known to tremble, even collapse, at hearing their trainers say that they particularly enjoy truffles fried in bacon fat.

Having worked up an appetite thinking about bacon, we followed the tantalizing smell of coffee around to the front of the stone farmhouse and entered the large kitchen-cum-dining room.

"*Bonjour,*" shouted Flaming Flora, her red hair blurring across the five-metre stretch from fridge to stove, as she delivered a basin of crêpe batter. To our surprise, sitting at the table sipping coffee and eating slices of baguette covered in homemade jam were six other guests. Obviously, while we were away, these guests had checked in and Le Mas du Centaure had become a hive of activity.

As we adjusted our chairs and sat at the table, my wife smiled and greeted everyone with a hearty *bonjour* and then continued to smile and sigh happily, as one would when overcome with joy at discovering that the fellow guests were one's long-lost cousins, last seen carrying pickaxes and heading off to a hard-labour camp in the quarry lands of Siberia where there aren't any *salons de coiffure* signs and where not a single pig has received truffle training.

I was more restrained. I need at least two cafés au lait before I come close to cracking a smile. Besides, my mind was preoccupied. I was wondering about the whereabouts of the black canine trio. Whose leg was Horny Hound humping? Whose tires were being shredded by Terrible Terrier? And where was Pregnant Paws?

Halfway through my first café au lait and my second chocolate croissant, I began to feel human again, almost ready to smile. Sitting across from us were two young women, rather attractive identical twin sisters from London. My wife had already introduced herself to everyone, of course, and had established that Kitty and Katherine, who spoke with Cockney accents, were hitchhiking their way around Europe. As the caffeine began to stimulate my brain, I studied the twins. I compared their every feature, looking for an identifiable difference: a freckle, a scar, a piercing, a tattoo, a crooked nose, a moustache, a missing front tooth or a slight variation in eye colour, hair colour, hairstyle—anything that might help to tell them apart. They also dressed the same, and even their voices sounded alike. They were, indeed, identical.

Seriously, if you saw them together as you strolled the main street of a medieval village, you'd immediately call in at the closest *salon de coiffure* and ask directions to the nearest ophthalmologist, as you'd swear you'd just experienced a severe case of double vision.

"You can call me Kit for short, and you can call her Kat. Our friends call us the Kit-Kat twins. You know, like the chocolate biscuit," said one of them—don't ask me which one tomorrow. "I call her my 'skin and blister'. You know, that's Cockney for 'sister'."

"Cor, blimey! Will someone fetch me another café au lait, real quick?" I muttered.

Sitting to the left of my wife—my "trouble and strife"—were two girls from China. They kept quiet, sometimes whispering and tittering to each other behind hands raised in front of their mouths—a habit, I assumed, to hide teeth in need of straightening or whitening or both. And there was extensive tittering behind hands after my "trouble and strife" surprised them (and me more so) by smiling at them and saying, "*Nǐ hǎo.*"

"That's Mandarin for 'hello'," she informed me tactfully.

The Babes from Beijing had both their Mandarin-English and Mandarin-French phrasebooks open on the table in front of them. They turned the pages frequently, searching for Mandarin translations of one or two English words that stood out to them when listening intently to the small talk. Their greatest challenge, and that for the rest of us too, was trying to understand the Cockney rhyming expressions that crept into the Kit-Kat twins' lingo.

"So you 'ave to climb the 'apples and pears' to get up to your room?" asked Kit, or was it Kat, after asking my "trouble and strife" which room we were staying in.

Then, after spending awhile studying a sentence in her Mandarin-French phrasebook, one of the Babes from Beijing asked Flaming Flora a question in French. Now, having struggled my entire life to learn a few words of French and be able to string them together to form a sentence and then pronounce them correctly, I was particularly interested to hear Flaming Flora's response to the Babe's question, which sounded to me more like that of the French rapper, One True Killa, having an argument with an extremely annoyed duck.

"*Oui, un moment, s'il vous plaît,*" said Flora, as she collected dirty dishes from the table in a blur. And then, a few seconds later, she reappeared with a pair of chopsticks in hand.

"I give up. Will someone fetch me another coffee, real quick?" I muttered under my breath.

Sitting to the left of the Kit-Kat twins was a young couple from Sweden. Their Swedish-French phrasebook open on the table was the dead giveaway. The guy introduced himself as Svenn. He wore black horn-rimmed glasses with lenses thicker than bottle bottoms and had a head of platinum blonde hair and a complexion whiter than snow. I thought he looked like death warmed up and wondered if he was about to faint face first into the mound of whipped cream that he'd spooned over his crêpe. His baby blue, short-sleeved shirt revealed dark sweat stains around the underarms. For some reason, Svenn was nervous. Looking at my "trouble and strife," Svenn mentioned that he worked as a graphic designer for a gaming company in Stockholm.

"Yes, okay, I'm a nerd," he added as if confessing to a crime.

His wife, or partner, was fairly plump and had ruby red cheeks; evidently she had either applied too much rouge or, unlike Svenn, her heart was pumping blood to them at a great rate. Her shoulder-length hair, which she'd dyed in wide streaks of brilliant blue and yellow, reminded me of the Swedish flag.

"My name is Ika. I-K-A. Ika," she said, spelling it out so that we could better understand its pronunciation. Then, after a little gentle persuasive probing from my wife, Ika revealed that she worked as an interior decorator, also in Stockholm.

"Are you sure you spelled your name right? Shouldn't it be spelled I-K-*E*-A?" I mused.

Then, to my right. "These flowers on the table are beautiful," observed a Kit-Kat twin—don't ask me if it was Kit or Kat.

"They're orchids, aren't they?" added her "skin and blister."

"Yes, they're of the Orchidaceae family," Ika interjected. "Their Latin name is *Aerides odorata*. They're endemic to the Philippines."

Being a lover of flowers, I was so impressed that I cracked a smile. "Wow! It sounds like this woman really knows what she's talking about," I said, my smile widening, the caffeine waking my brain cells.

"Man!" Ika snapped back wearing a deadpan expression. "Man! I'm not a woman. I'm a man!"

My jaw dropped, my smile disappeared, and my "trouble and strife" choked on her chocolate croissant as we realized our IKEA-store-sized *faux pas*.

"Will someone *please* fetch me a double espresso, real quick?" I pleaded under my breath.

43

Grimaud, La Garde-Freinet, and Collobrières:

Here, There, and Everywhere

During the next few days while touring here, there, and everywhere, we came to appreciate the vast number and variety of places worth visiting in southern Provence. If you're inspired to visit the region, I recommend that you rent a car—a small one like a Renault Twingo. Try to avoid the lure of organized tours that visit eight countries in seven days. You know how the story goes.

"Hey! Fred. What's the name of this city we're driving through?" asked Helen, nudging her husband who, feeling the effects of jetlag, had dozed off with his head propped against the steamed-up window.

"Er, now let me see," said Fred as he glanced down at their seven-day itinerary. "According to this, Wednesday has us visiting London, followed by a stopover in Dover."

"But today's Thursday."

"Gee whiz! You're right. This must be Paris. And it says here that we're scheduled to stop soon for a bathroom break in Munich, and then again for dinner in Prague. By golly, look at this photo, Helen. We're stayin' at a fancy five-star hotel tonight in Moscow."

For sure, everyone takes photos or shoots video or both when they're on vacation. A man and woman travelling together normally share a camera. And it's usually the man framing the woman posing front and centre with a backdrop of a mountain range, a waterfall, a beach, or a historic structure like the Eiffel Tower, Big Ben, the Leaning Tower of Pisa, or the Pyramids. In our case, my wife appears front and centre in 95 per cent of our holiday snapshots. Far less photogenic, I appear in the remaining 5 per cent and, for some unexplained reason, I'm never quite front and centre, or my feet have been cut off, or I'm out of focus, or I'm frowning, or there's a lamppost sticking out of the top of my head. You've got the picture.

Not everyone takes notes of where they've been or of what they've seen or experienced. But I do. The journaling helps me better reflect on the mood, the smell, the sound, the feel, the temperature, the beauty of the place, and so on. When I read the notes later on a grey, rainy day, they trigger more memories than those while flipping through a folder of photos on my computer screen. For example:

—After breakfast, we heard Cavity Phil playing his trumpet in the barn next to the paddock—he needs lots of practice, he should keep to dentistry and hobby farming—the black canine trio was locked inside with him—howling along like a pack of wolves.

—Drove to **Grimaud***—another medieval village due west of the Gulf of St-Tropez—ordered two teas and a minuscule cake at the Tea Room—served by a miserable waitress who took umbrage when I asked for a receipt after she added the price up (to an outrageous sum) using a calculator rather than the till, which we saw her use when making sales to the locals.*

—5k farther west, we came to Bertolotto's holiday accommodation down Chemin du Prignon—B&B accommodation on a vineyard— fairly remote attractive area but surrounded by fire-blackened trees—spoke with owners, Paul and Christine—Paul very congenial while polishing his Porsche—business must be good—Christine tells us that they were terrified when fires recently swept through the adjacent hillside forest—3 firemen died up the road.

—*Returning to Grimaud we saw a young guy cycling "no handed" down a steep hill—a baguette in one hand, texting a message on his cell phone in the other hand—only in France!*

—*Still in Grimaud we hiked up to the 17th-century castle at the top of the hill—great views over the surrounding countryside—ate lunch (roasted chicken with rice and ratatouille niçoise, carafe of rosé, crème brûlée, café au lait) sitting on patio at brasserie "Le Clem's"—two local farmers at next table sipping pastis and blowing smoke into each other's face, killing themselves twice as fast by inhaling both first and second-hand smoke.*

—*Travelled north on the D558 to* **La Garde-Freinet**—*yet another pretty medieval village—noticed that almost all of the old houses had satellite dishes anchored to walls, rooftops or chimneys—enjoyed wine tasting and finger-food sampling in tourist information office— the start of a week of celebrating food throughout the region—seven days of eating food to celebrate eating food—only in France!*

—*Travelled south on the D558 back to Grimaud then headed west on the D14, a torturous winding narrow road over hills of charred trees to* **Collobrières**—*informed by local guy that oak trees often stripped of bark for production of cork—strolled through the town which was celebrating the harvesting of sweet chestnuts—the streets filled with stalls selling locally made products: baked sweet chestnuts, sauce, jams, bread, pork sausages, wine, cheeses, tarts, artwork, and pottery—also lots of puppet-making—saw a woman controlling the strings of a marionette of an old man—art imitating life!*

—*Sitting at a table under a large shade tree on the forecourt of La Petite Fontaine, ate a delicious five-course dinner: red wine, bread & liver pâté, salad, combo of duck, roast beef and ham with veggies followed by a cheese plate, caramel flan, coffee and a digestif—too happy to spoil the evening by converting the bill to Canadian dollars.*

Ooh-la-la Land

—Met Andy and Angela from England at the next table—went back to their four-bedroom home-away-from-home for more coffee—a large renovated medieval stone house with an ultramodern interior, nicely furnished and with all the latest stainless steel appliances.

—Back to our *Gîtes de France* by midnight—a full moon—the summer air still warm—no howling dogs—let sleeping dogs and trumpets lie—all is quiet—clunk, clunk, clunk up the staircase...

44

Mougins:

Horn Blowing, People Watching, Pipe Smoking, and Tango Dancing

We were the first to sit at the breakfast table, and I'd consumed a freshly squeezed orange juice, two cafés au lait, and half a baguette smothered in jam before our fellow guests began to arrive with smiles on their faces and phrasebooks in hand. And I was smiling. Yes, I was *smiling*, close to laughing actually, at the sight of Horny Hound being chased around the table by Terrible Terrier while Pregnant Paws lay in her usual comfortable position, raising an eyebrow each time her mad cohorts completed a circuit. What had Horny Hound done to upset Terrible Terrier? I needed only one guess.

The Kit-Kat twins, dressed in identical outfits, came into the room first and said *bonjour* in unison.

Then one of them—don't ask me which—said, "Cor, blimey! Isn't it a glorious morning?"

Then the other said, "Cor, blimey! It is a glorious morning."

They looked at my wife and said, "Isn't it a glorious morning?"

Then my wife said, "It is indeed a glorious morning."

Then I said, "I need another coffee, real quick."

Then my wife asked, "Did you two 'skin and blisters' have a good night's 'Bo Peep'?"

Then I said, "Make that a double espresso."

Svenn and I'm-a-Man Ika arrived next, with the Babes from

Ooh-la-la Land

Beijing giggling right behind. Flaming Flora was being her usual self: a carrot-topped blur stretching from kitchen to dining area, delivering food and clearing away dirty dishes faster than the speed of sound. Cavity Phil, as always, was absent from the table. The sound of the straining diesel engine of his Caterpillar d10 bulldozer coming from the paddock was evidence that it was the weekend—two days away from his "Open-Wide-Please" clinic in Fréjus—and he was out there somewhere grubbing the roots of a 100-year-old, thirty-metre-tall tree that he'd felled yesterday, single-handedly—just one of the many jobs remaining on his "Today's Job List." His next job: filling the hole left after dragging the mass of roots off behind the barn where he would chop it up into toothpicks tomorrow, single-handedly.

It took about forty minutes to arrive at Mougins. Svenn and I'm-a-Man Ika had recommended it. The Babes from Beijing, after referring to their English-Mandarin phrasebook, had giggled and nodded their agreement. However, getting there was not entirely uneventful. We experienced—no, *I* experienced—considerable frustration while trying to pay the toll at the *péage* station leaving the A8. I had misjudged my approach to the booth and stopped Twingo a little too much to the right, just beyond arm's reach of the toll machine. I couldn't reverse and manoeuvre nearer to it because the car behind was too close. I tried to get out, but the door banged against the machine's concrete base and there wasn't enough space for me to squeeze out. The delay is what triggered the first car horn to blow.

"Just ignore it," whispered my wife, who was nonchalantly flipping through pages of a magazine full of beautiful women wearing wedding dresses and looking happy with broad smiles, wrinkle-free skin, and dazzling white teeth.

With blood pressure rising, I wound the window down as far as it would go and then, with my head and shoulders cantilevered from the door frame and my wife hanging on to my belt, I was able to insert the ticket. As the amount displayed was distressingly significant, I elected to pay by credit card. It's always disconcerting to see one's

235

vacation lifeline being sucked into a machine, perhaps never to be seen again. Equally disconcerting is seeing it being spit out because it had been rejected by the bank. The red-and-white-striped barrier remained horizontal, which is when the driver behind started screaming at me in French—an instruction or an obscenity; it could have been both.

"Just ignore him," whispered my wife again after commenting that she prefers A-lines over ball gowns and sweetheart designs. With my blood pressure shooting way beyond hypertension level, and with horns reaching a crescendo in the ever-lengthening line of cars behind us, I retrieved my credit card and inserted a large banknote, and *"Voilà!"* the barrier rose, the cacophony of horns stopped, and we were on our way.

Low on cash and high on blood pressure, I mumbled a couple of expletives while mentally adding "autoroute *péage* stations" to the top of my short list of "Frustrations and Irritants while Touring." Ignoring my mutterings, as I accelerated to reach the speed limit, my wife turned, frowned quizzically, and asked, "Did you *really* love my wedding dress? Was there too much lace? I'm so happy it had sleeves and a high neckline. I don't think that an off-the-shoulder strapless number would have been the right choice for our church ceremony. I would love for us to renew our vows. Wouldn't you, darling?"

Talking of "Frustrations and Irritants while Touring," another that rates high on my list is that of being turned away from a parking lot by a short guy wearing a military-style peaked hat, a grey jacket with red armband, a leather satchel, a small, black moustache, and a threatening expression. Then having to backtrack half a kilometre to find a parking space on a side street, which is what happened when we arrived at the base of the hill that led up to the 14th-century fortified gateway to Mougins' Vieille Ville.

Our hike up the hill, on through the fortified gateway, and around the rampart was rewarded with splendid panoramic views of the surrounding countryside, especially those towards Vence and St-Paul.

Ooh-la-la Land

The ground floor of many of the ancient houses had been converted into high-end art galleries, charming cafés, and excellent restaurants. We were very impressed by the quality of artwork in the galleries' window displays and back rooms and by the attractive linens and table settings on the patios of the cafés and restaurants. We were also impressed by the well-preserved rampart, the cobblestone streets, the ancient buildings and fountains, and the attractive main square, in spite of a ten-metre-tall, twisted, twelve-inch steel I-beam painted red at its base and changing gradually to a bright yellow petal at its tip that had been erected in view of every dining, art-loving, souvenir-seeking tourist. Out of place and impossible to miss, this piece of modern art was likely the work of an unemployed structural engineer who had mistakenly consumed magic mushrooms instead of truffles.

By mid-morning we were sheltering from the heat and sipping on iced Coca-Colas while watching life go by from under the awning of Brasserie de La Méditerranée. The comings and goings of smiling brides and grooms in ribbon-bedecked horse-drawn vintage carriages, superbly preserved antique cars, and latest model Rolls-Royces and Mercedes captured my wife's attention. She was oblivious to the old English couple sitting off to my right. Neither of them could hear very well and they were shouting their observations at each other. He was smoking a pipe that had the largest bowl I have ever seen. I swear it had carvings of gargoyles all around it, and it must have taken a small trowel to fill and a blowtorch to light. The old Dragon had obviously left the optional smoke extraction system at home as visibility under the awning deteriorated with each puff.

His wife was also watching the brides and grooms parade in and out of the church across the square. She was not only partly deaf but severely cross-eyed, despite wearing a pair of 1970s Elton John frames and thick corrective lenses. As one bride emerged from a Rolls-Royce, my wife remarked, "Doesn't she look beautiful?"

But before I could respond, the Dragoness shouted, "DOESN'T SHE LOOK BEAUTIFUL?" her eyes squinting to eliminate double vision, her husband barely visible in the cloud of tobacco smoke.

"Does it remind you of *our* wedding?" my wife asked, her eyes focused on the bride, not the groom, nor the half-million-dollar Rolls-Royce Phantom.

"DO YOU REMEMBER OUR WEDDING DAY?" shouted the Dragoness. The Dragon snorted and I coughed, and then, like the cavalry charging over the hill to the rescue, our waiter placed our bill in front of me.

Escaping the tobacco smog, we strolled along the cobblestone streets, popping into several art galleries and souvenir shops. Attracted by the front of the Hôtel Des Muscadin, Restaurant & Spa, we stepped inside and were treated to a tour by the manager. He was proud to show us a modest suite on the upper level, the most expensive on the hotel's tariff list. He informed us that it was once used by Pablo Picasso before he bought a farmhouse down the road where he spent his final years until he passed away on April 8, 1973. There was a small, bright room, which the manager said Picasso used as his studio, and a darker room, which we assumed was his bedroom. It was a surprisingly modest place that was available at a high-season daily rate that only the likes of Oprah could afford.

Before leaving the Vieille Ville, we returned to the main square and entered the attractive Hôtel de Ville, where two rooms were devoted to an art exhibition of black-and-white photographs of tango dancers. Having seen tango dancers perform in clubs and on the streets of Buenos Aires, we were delighted to study the photos and reminisce. Each captured the intimacy and sensuality that characterizes the Latin dance. Tango music was playing in the background; its unique sound and rhythm helping viewers to appreciate the seduction that takes place on the dance floor.

The Dutch artist Ineke Stutvoet came up to us, introduced herself, and told us about her love of photography and the tango. For the collection hanging on the walls, she had travelled to Buenos Aires and followed tango dancers for seven months. As the three of us studied one of the full-length photos of a couple striking a typical tango pose, Ineke said, "As you know, it is typical for the man to be dressed in a black suit, a white open-necked shirt, black shoes, and a black fedora. Notice that the two of them are staring lustfully, but not into each other's eyes. See how seductive she looks. Notice his groin thrusting against hers as she submissively leans back in his arms. Look at her arched back, the slit in her short black dress exposing her long legs in black fishnet stockings. Notice her black high-heeled shoes, and how her right foot, calf, and thigh are intertwined with her seducer's thigh."

"Excuse me, may I have a glass of water and a long, cold shower too?" I would have asked, had the blood not drained from my head leaving me speechless.

45

Valbonne:

Mother of Markets, Public Washrooms, Snobby Women, and an Oboist

By noon, tourists began to select prime people-watching tables on the patios of the most popular restaurants bordering the main square of Mougins' Vieille Ville, and despite our guidebook's recommendation that the old town is the smart place to eat, we weren't hungry and decided to move on and have lunch in Valbonne.

Only a fifteen-minute drive north of Mougins, Valbonne was a delightful surprise. Its section of medieval buildings and cobblestone streets is spread over an area of ten-by-four blocks and, fortuitously, when we arrived, its central square was bustling with activity as the hub of a colourful and vibrant market.

This was the mother of all markets. Stall upon stall filled the square, and many overflowed down the streets leading to it. A variety of meats, fish, cheeses, vegetables, fruits, breads, pastries, wines, jams, nuts, candies, flowers, clothes, shoes, linens, kitchen wares, antique furnishings, tools, knick-knacks, souvenirs—you name it—were being sold. Mouth-watering smells wafted from rotisseries, pizza ovens, crêpe-making hot plates, and popcorn poppers, and from mobile carts selling candy floss, ice cream, and toffee apples.

After browsing many stalls, sampling food and wine, purchasing souvenirs, and taking photographs galore, we were famished. It was time to find a prime people-watching table on a shaded patio overlooking the market. But first I needed to search for a public washroom. Finding one has proven to be a bigger challenge than we expected in such popular tourist towns. The provision and upkeep of them in Provençal medieval villages must rank way down the local council's list of priorities when deciding on the allocation of funds for the various projects proposed by the town's residents, merchants, and councillors.

"I propose we allocate the remaining funds to improve our one and only public washroom facility. It has no hot water, the hand-dryers don't work, a few of the toilet seats are missing, most of the door locks are broken, vile graffiti covers the doors of the men's cubicles, and the sewer line often backs up causing the toilets to overflow," I imagined the petition from Councillor Hygiene.

And Councillor Restaurateur responding, "First, I just want to remind my fellow councillors that it was only last year that we allocated funds for the purchase of toilet paper and liquid soap for that washroom. Surely it makes better business sense if tourists are encouraged to seek out a washroom in a café, bar or restaurant, thereby making them feel obligated to purchase a snack, a drink, or a meal." He continued, "I propose we allocate the monies for the manufacture of signs that read: THESE WASHROOMS ARE FOR RESTAURANT CUSTOMERS ONLY."

After I left the ill-equipped HOMMES, my wife spotted two men paying their bill at a prime people-watching table on the packed patio of Café des Arcades. She grabbed my hand and, almost pulling my arm out of its socket, made a mad dash onto the patio. Noticing that other ravenous seekers of prime people-watching tables had also eyed the pending vacancy, she dragged me right up to the table and stood impolitely behind the two men who were finishing their espressos.

"*Excusez-moi,*" she interrupted. I lowered my head and studied my feet. The two men swivelled in their chairs and looked up at her. She smiled while lifting her sunshades to rest above her hairline. "*Avez vous—*" she started.

"No worries, darlin'. Sure, you can join us," replied the smiling Aussie on the left.

"Nah, my mate's just pullin' ya leg. We're just on our way. No worries, lady. The table's all yours," said the other Australian.

"We really don't want to rush you."

"Yes, we do. I'm starving hungry," I thought.

Amazing! In less than a minute the two blokes from Down Under were gone and we were seated at the prime people-watching table reviewing a menu while an attentive waiter went about replacing the table setting. It took only a few more minutes for him to take our order and deliver a basket of bread, a bottle of Perrier water, and a carafe of chilled rosé wine. And by the time our Caesar salad and Hawaiian pizza arrived, we'd eaten all the bread, sipped all the wine, and were singing along to the tunes being played on an oboe by a tall tramp of a guy standing to my left in the square.

"What a beautiful sound. The oboe has such a unique tone, don't you think?" I said, nodding in the direction of the musician.

"Yep, he's probably the best-est oboist soloist," she giggled as she took another sip of wine.

"He looks quite dishevelled, don't you think?"

"Yep, he's quite the lowliest oboist soloist," she slurred, then let out a belly laugh that everyone on the patio heard, and started me giggling like a schoolboy. Such was the result of drinking wine and sniffing Habanita de Molinard on an empty stomach. We were in a great mood and nothing could ruin it. Or so I thought.

At the table to our left were two English women who were speaking loudly enough for us to hear their every word. They lived in Knightsbridge and were extremely wealthy and unbearably snobbish.

"I didn't care for her shoes, at all. And that short skirt!"

"Don't you think she's put on weight?"

"Ten pounds, I'd say. And what about that guy she's seeing?"

"He looks gay to me."

"She says he's a doctor, but I think he's a fishmonger."

"I just love my new Jag. It's all white. It goes with anything."

"We stayed at Cambridge Beaches in Bermuda for a couple of

weeks in June and played mixed doubles with Roger Federer and Maria Sharapova. And do you know what? We nearly beat them. Even though Jeffrey was still on crutches and I played in high heels. (I made some of that up.)

After two large portions of tiramisu washed down with a couple of sobering espressos, we sauntered off. The oboist had stopped playing but was still standing in the square. We stopped, and I placed a few euros in the case at his feet. Then I said, "We really enjoyed your music. I really love the oboe."

"So do I," the tramp of a guy said in perfect English. "But this is a clarinet."

Another belly laugh could be heard all the way to Paris.

46

Vence:

Silly Little Teapot Cosies, a Wedding, and a Masterpiece

It was time to put Twingo through its paces on another scenic drive along winding roads cut into the craggy gorges of southern Provence. We headed north through Opio to the medieval village of Gourdon. Sightings of the village on its rocky hilltop appear at many bends along the approach, which provides photographers with opportunities for superb shots. We stopped in the village long enough to stroll through it and see the spectacular panoramic views of the surrounding countryside, especially from the castle and its beautiful gardens.

From Gourdon we drove many kilometres of narrow, twisting roads until we came to Tourette-sur-Loup where we stopped briefly before proceeding to Vence. If you enjoy scenic drives, this area of Provence has some of the finest.

Our guidebook described Vence as a former market town that snoozes in the green hills above Nice. Well, when we arrived at the large square, place du Grand Jardin, the only thing that was snoozing was a scruffy, old dog lying in the shade of a plane tree. Quite to the contrary, the town was very much awake. Vendors were standing in front of their market stalls shouting at the top of their voices, trying to outdo the competition in the hope of selling their wares: ham, cheese, fruit, vegetables, and bottles of wine and olive oil. A short guy with long, grey hair was ringing a contraption made up of rows of bells mounted on springs anchored to a wooden frame, his ponytail swaying to and fro over his hunched back. He was attempting to play popular tunes, but the tourists just walked on by, frowning. Close to the scruffy, old dog dozing under the plane tree were half a dozen kids with fishing rods sitting on the rim of a huge rubber dinghy that had been filled with water and some fish. The kids were screaming with excitement at the prospect of reeling in today's "Catch of the Day"—dare I suggest, perch—for the restaurants in the perched village above.

Climbing the hill, we entered the old town through a 15th-century stone archway—similar to the one at Mougins—and strolled into the pretty place du Peyra which, like many squares in Provence, is flanked by trendy art shops, boutiques, cafés, and coiffures operating from the ground floor of ancient stone buildings. While we were window shopping, I noticed that, of all the heterosexual couples, it was the woman who was bright-eyed and moved with a spring in her step, while the man plodded behind like a sad, old dog tethered to its owner by its leash, its tail between its legs. But it wasn't until we'd entered La Poterie du Peyra, a fabrics and pottery store, where I stood bored out of my mind while my wife looked at tablecloths, napkins, towels, pillow cases, bed sheets, duvet covers, patio seat cushions, placemats, and silly little teapot cosies, that I realized I too had become a sad, old dog.

I can run a ten-kilometre race or work out on a stair climber for forty minutes without feeling the slightest ache in my legs, but subject me to thirty minutes of window shopping with my wife and you'd better pass me the painkillers and a shot of brandy and sit me down in a comfy armchair. However, after ten minutes of staring blankly at a pile of linen napkins, a pretty young woman asked me in English, with a sexy French accent, if I needed assistance.

"No, thank you," I responded instinctively. "I'm with my wife over there," I added, like a faithful, old dog that has been let off its leash but trained to stay close to its owner. "This is a lovely store," I white-lied, feeling the ache fading from my legs.

"*Merci,*" she replied. "You must jus' lurve theeze, *n'est pas?*" She continued as she pointed to the pile of silly little teapot cosies.

"Yeah, they're really cute," I fibbed.

"*Oui,* they are only twelve euros each. We 'ave a spe-ci-al, today only, two for twenty," she smiled, fluttering her eyelashes faster than a hummingbird flaps its wings—the sales pressure rising as the old dog was offered a tasty bone. "They 'ave been spe-ci-ally made to cover these teapots over 'ere. Are they not *magnifique?*" she asked, pointing at a row of silly little teapots.

"Yes, they are," I mumbled, turning in the direction of my owner, willing her to shout me over, attach my leash, and take me walkies.

"They 'ave been 'andmade by *artisans.*" She placed a silly little teapot cosy over a silly little teapot and then smiled at me again. "Look at that. Eet ees a great *souvenir, n'est pas?* Ee-ma-jeen eet on your table at 'ome; eet would give you good memories. The teapots are only forty euros. You could 'ave two for seventy. You will save ten euros."

"Oh, there you are. What are you up to?" asked my owner, as she came to my rescue carrying six patio seat cushions that would require purchasing an extra suitcase to carry them home.

"This young lady was just showing me these lovely teapots and cosies," I said, pretending to be interested.

"Yes, they are lovely, but we've got one at home. Come on, let's go. I want to look in the cosmetics store next door," she said as she reattached my leash and led me outside. The Saleswoman of the Year moved swiftly across the store to another sad, old dog and, as I plodded behind my owner to the store next door, my legs began to ache again.

From the cosmetics store, we walked into another large square, the place Georges Clémenceau. On the left, we passed Le Clémenceau restaurant and its separate patio—a large, rectangular, canopy-covered island of tables holding platters of food and bottles of wine, and chairs holding hungry, happy, and inebriated people. Plodding around its perimeter was a dour-faced musician dressed in drab medieval clothing, which included a bell-shaped felt hat. He was playing an accordion and singing slow, mournful songs. Attached to one side of his rope belt, which held up his pants but not his overflowing beer belly, was another bell-shaped felt hat that was inverted, ready to accept cash from inebriated or partly deaf diners. Based on his dour expression and mournful tone, I presumed that he would be setting aside all cash donations to pay for his impending funeral.

The Hôtel de Ville borders the square; it's an attractive building painted yellow and orange. And close by is the Cathédrale de la Nativité de la Vierge, where a notice at the entrance advises visitors that the building, or parts of it—at least two stones—date back to AD 220. I wasn't particularly interested that the cathedral's design is a combination of Romanesque and Baroque styles or that inside the baptistery is a colourful ceramic mosaic of *Moses in the Bulrushes* by Marc Chagall or that on the floor is a baptismal font big enough for the total immersion of babies at their christening. But what I *did* find interesting, in an odd way, was that a large contemporary sculpture of a grotesque humanoid had been erected only twenty metres away. And in front of it was a sculptor chiselling an ornate pattern on a stone sundial that he'd created in readiness for sale to someone who prefers not to buy a wristwatch or a cuckoo clock. Standing wide-eyed in front of the artist, facing the action at chisel height, with stone shards splintering off in every direction at each hammer blow, was a young boy risking his sight. I was just about to call out to him to move away, and then hit the sculptor over the head with a five-kilogram, wooden mallet, when the boy ran off in the direction of a four-piece band that had paraded into the square.

The musicians were playing Provençal folklore music on ancient instruments: a bandonéon, a drum, pipes, and a lyre, and were headed to the cathedral's front entrance. Creeping slowly behind them was a chauffeur-driven maroon-and-black 1951 Citroën decorated in white ribbons and white roses. Sharing the black leather rear seat was a bride dressed in white and her proud father dressed in a black tuxedo.

"A wedding!" screamed my owner, letting go of my leash and shooting off in the direction of the cathedral's entrance, where the musicians had stopped, two either side of the entrance, and continued to play, although I wasn't convinced that they were all playing the same tune. When the Citroën came to a stop, the bride's father got out and strode around the car to open the door for his daughter, who was having difficulty getting out of the tiny bucket seat. A petite Flower Girl and a not-so-petite Maid of Honour rushed out of the shadows of the porch to lend a hand—four actually. And, just as it's much easier to sit down on a low couch than it is to get up off one, it took the three of them several minutes to uncork the bride. When she did pop out, rivulets of perspiration were streaming down her face streaking her mascara, and her veil had twisted around ninety degrees.

"Doesn't she look beautiful?" my owner asked when I came alongside, as any well-trained hound would.

"You've got to be kidding," I thought.

"What a huge dress," she commented casually.

"Oh yeah, like it's the dress that's huge," I muttered.

"Wouldn't you just love to get married all over again?" came her next expected question.

"I sure would," I said as the petite Flower Girl, the not-so-petite Maid of Honour, the out-of-tune folklore band, the bride in the big dress, and her tuxedo-clad father walked into the shadows of the nave.

"Really, do you really mean it?"

"Yes, I really mean it," I replied, with equal amounts of sincerity and pragmatism as I recalled the adage, "A happy wife, a happy life."

Leaving the Vieille Ville, we walked back down the road to Chapelle du Rosaire de Vence, an amazing building designed by the painter Henri Matisse. The story goes something like this. In 1941, he underwent surgery for cancer and, to help him through his long recovery at his home in Nice, he hired a pretty, young nurse, Monique Bourgeois, who took great care of him. During Henri's convalescence, Monique posed for him, and several of his sketches and paintings of her are still much sought after.

In 1943, with Henri's health improving, Monique moved to Vence, entered the Dominican convent, and became Sister Jacques-Marie. Not long after, Henri also moved to Vence, where he bought a home not far from the convent. One day in 1947, Monique visited Henri, told him about the plans that the Dominicans had to build a chapel, and asked if he would help with the design. Henri had never done anything like it before, but he agreed.

And so, at the age of seventy-seven, Matisse began the greatest project of his life, and during the next four years he designed the building, its stained-glass windows, its interior furnishings, its murals, and even the clergy's vestments. The chapel was built and decorated between 1949 and 1951, and was regarded by Matisse to be his masterpiece. All of which goes to prove that you *can* teach a sad, old dog new tricks.

47

Saint-Paul-de-Vence:

Eighty Galleries and Many Likes

You might be thinking that by now we would have tired of visiting medieval villages. Surely, once you've seen one, you've seen them all. And to some degree you would be right, as we began to have trouble recalling the one with the narrowest streets, the best views from the rampart, the best restaurant, the worst waitress, the best people-watching patio, the worst public toilet, or the one with the best art shops. The main attraction for North Americans to visit a medieval village is to observe the contrast in architecture. In North America, buildings of fifty years or more are often torn down and replaced by towers of concrete, steel, and glass, which is why "old" is given little chance of becoming "historic."

St-Paul-de-Vence did not disappoint, even though it offered many similar attractions to those of its twin town, Vence. Just as in Vence, we parked Twingo outside the rampart and made our way up to the old town. First, we passed several busy restaurants and a main square of red clay on which a dozen or so weather-beaten old men were sipping pastis and playing pétanque in the shade of bordering plane trees. I stopped to take a photograph just as a heated argument broke out over the measurement of the two metal balls (*boules*) that had come to stop closest to the white marker ball (*bouchon*), and then, just as we thought the argument was going to turn physical, there was a roar of laughter and the loser of the argument (likely of the game too) ordered a round of pastis, then another game began.

Ooh-la-la Land

At the tourist information centre, we discovered that St-Paul is one of the oldest fortified medieval villages on the French Riviera, and is well known for its contemporary art galleries, of which there are at least eighty selling paintings, pottery, and handicrafts.

Most women love to shop. My wife doesn't; she loves to browse. She loves to wander the aisles, looking at and touching things on shelves, on tables, on racks, and on mannequins. Always under the watchful eyes and alert ears of the store's commission-hungry sales clerks, she is often observed smiling and remarking that she loves the colour, the feel of the material, the great deal, that she really needs one, that she knows exactly where she would hang it or who she would give it to. And as she browsed the galleries in St-Paul, I could understand why the sales clerks might have misinterpreted my wife's enthusiasm as an imminent sale and wondered if it was going to be the biggest sale of the day. Disappointment awaited them.

"Like, he's so good-looking and so cool, he's *sick.* And, like, we had so much fun last night, absolutely. When he dropped me off at the hotel he kissed me, like, passionately. I asked him up for, ya know, like, a drink or something. He said no, which really, like, upset me and yet, like, it didn't. He said he'd give me a call, like, sometime real soon. He's so absolutely real, like, really. I keep checking to see if he's texted, like, every thirty seconds. Like, I'm going absolutely crazy," said the twenty-something American woman with the black fingernails and a tattoo of a scorpion on the left side of her neck.

"Don't worry, like, for sure he'll call ya or text ya. He will, like, absolutely. Wow! He sounds so cool, so hot, and so sick. You didn't tell him you're, like, an apprentice mortician did you? That might, like, turn him off a bit," said her twenty-something friend with emerald green hair and a large nostril piercing that made my eyes water just picturing the procedure.

"Yeah, I did, but that didn't seem to, like, bother him. He works at a meat-canning factory, ya know, like, in a slaughterhouse somewhere in Wyoming. Like, I think we've got a lot in common.

He's, like, absolutely hot. I'm going, like, absolutely crazy."

Such was the gist of the dinnertime conversation of the two young American women sitting at the next table in a far-from-typical St-Paul restaurant. The walls were decorated in a variety of unusual fabrics, all with weird patterns and clashing colours. Equally weird for a French restaurant was the screeching Middle Eastern music that drifted from the room's four corner speakers, countering what little romantic ambience had been created by the candlelit tables and single-red-rose centrepieces. After being seated at a window table, and while waiting patiently for our waitress to come into view, I continued to listen to our two young neighbours communicate in, like, some kind of code.

Hungry and near to collapsing from a severe drop in blood sugar after hours of window shopping, we were about to get up to leave when a dour-faced waitress (yet, another one), with bulging varicose veins, dropped a psychedelic-patterned menu with a small Union Jack at the top onto our table and then disappeared. We stared across the table at each other with eyebrows raised, wondering why we were, like, still sitting there, and, like, not heading for the door.

But before one of us could say, "Like, we're leaving," Madame returned with a carafe of wine and a basket of bread sticks, and announced, "Our spe-ci-al thiz even-eeng ees our famous French 'ome-style Italian ravioli. Eet ees,—'ow you say?—dainty pasta feeled weez fine meat and 'erbs, *avec* pesto sauce. You want, yehz?"

How could we resist? Who, in their right mind, could overcome the temptation of being served Italian ravioli by a dour-faced waitress in a French 'ome-style restaurant decorated in unusual fabrics with weird patterns and clashing colours, while listening to screeching Middle Eastern music and the coded conversation of two young American women, one of whom was convinced that her new boyfriend was so good looking that he was, like, sick?

48

Villefranche-sur-Mer:

A Work-Around Plan, a Near Miss, and Spectacular Views on a Dark Street

It was the sound of Cavity Phil playing *reveille* on his trumpet, and of his accompanists, the black canine trio, howling along to every piercing note that woke us from our deep sleep. We had overslept. Breakfast was well underway. Flaming Flora would be refilling coffee cups and replenishing bread baskets for our fellow guests.

To speed up our morning ablution process, I devised a work-around plan to eliminate the time-consuming struggle of showering single-handedly. To begin, I disrobed, stepped into the cubicle, and then passed the dangling shower head to my wife who stood just outside the open glass door. I turned on the water and adjusted the temperature, grabbed the soap in one hand and the facecloth in the other, and then my wife moved the shower head and directed the spray over the soapy parts of my body. She then rinsed off the remaining soap suds as I turned around one revolution—like a cupid on a music box turntable. Finally, I turned off the water and stepped out of the cubicle into the towel held in her outstretched arms.

Next, my wife disrobed and stepped inside the cubicle and we repeated the process. But there was a glitch, which I doubted would be resolved before we returned to Vancouver: land of large bathrooms, spacious shower cubicles, high-pressure hot water, and properly functioning shower heads. The glitch: the soap suds clung stubbornly to her skin, and I had to insist she turn around several more revolutions. While doing so, she complimented me on my thoroughness in ensuring that her skin was totally suds-free and was appreciative of my extra effort in reaching over and wiping away the most stubborn of bubbles with sensuous hands. The work-around plan took significantly longer than I'd envisaged.

At breakfast, the Kit-Kat twins were conspicuous by their absence. A new face at the table—a good-looking Australian guy with a golden tan, blue eyes, blonde hair, and a disc-jockey voice—told us that he'd had the pleasure of meeting them on their way out, and that one of them—he couldn't remember if it was Kit or Kat—told him they were going walkabout. "So they've hit the 'frog and toad'," my wife beamed, having recalled the Cockney rhyming equivalent for "road." I checked her pupils; they were dilated. Habanita de Molinard was still lingering, even after a four-revolution rinse cycle.

"Quick, I need a coffee real bad," I mumbled as I sat at the table next to I'm-a-Man Ika, who was nervously raising and lowering his left heel, pivoting it from the sole of his sandal, tapping it rapidly on the floor, his calf and knee in constant tremor.

The Babes from Beijing sat quietly eating, occasionally tittering behind raised hands as they studied the pages of their phrasebook and softly practised the pronunciation of English words. They tittered some more as one searched for "frog," the other for "toad." I waited for frowns of disbelief to appear at the Mandarin translations.

With caffeine surging through my bloodstream, I began to pay more attention. The black canine trio had entered the room. Pregnant Paws had taken up her usual position curled up in front of the fireplace. Terrible Terrier was sitting patiently at the feet of the DJ from Down Under who was looking down and smiling at the cute little glistening pink tongue and the two white fangs protruding through its mass of matted hair—its eyes not visible.

Attracted by the noise of the rapid tapping of I'm-a-Man Ika's right heel and turned-on by the blurry movement of his calf and knee,

Horny Hound bounded over and began sniffing it. But Ika was oblivious to the proximity of Horny Hound and to the impending attention his leg was about to receive. He'd been stricken by the good-looking DJ from Down Under. His eyes kept darting to the DJ's face—his golden tan, blue eyes, and thick blonde hair—and then at Svenn's face—a pair of black horn-rimmed glasses against a face whiter than pale. Svenn's eyes darted in the direction of his lover and then back to the DJ from Down Under. The jealousy was palpable.

The DJ from Down Under looked across at I'm-a-Man Ika and said, "I have to buy my girlfriend back home a pressie before I leave France. As a sheila of about her age and size, what would you suggest I buy her?"

"I'm a man!" Ika blurted.

The DJ's jaw-dropping reaction was our cue to leave.

"Well, we're off to Villefranche," my wife interjected as she pushed her chair back from the table. "I hope you all have a lovely day. *Merci, Flora. Au revoir,* everyone," she shouted.

And like a faithful, old dog, I got up and followed at her heels.

Fact: A recent model Porsche 911 Turbo can accelerate from zero to 60 mph in 3.4 seconds, and it can decelerate from 60 mph to zero in less than 1.7 seconds.

Fact: Villefranche-sur-Mer lies ten kilometres east of Nice.

Fact: It took a little over an hour to travel the seventy-five kilometres from Puget-sur-Argens.

Fact: Driving eastbound, directly into the morning's dazzling sunshine on the A8, presented a few tense moments of temporary blindness and one particularly heart-pounding "near miss" with a recent model Porsche 911 Turbo. It cut in front of us from the fast lane, missing Twingo by inches and reminding me of three things: How important it is to purchase the most comprehensive automobile insurance package available, especially when driving in France; how essential it is to have a Last Will and Testament in safe-keeping back home; and how unbelievably loud my wife can scream.

Stephen Foey

Fact: I'd gone from temporary blindness to temporary deafness in less than 0.65 seconds.

We snaked our way down the hairpin bends and found a parking space near Villefranche's harbour-cum-fishing port. The port, which lies within a large, beautiful bay just east of the Cap Ferrat peninsula, was full to capacity with all types of watercraft whose hulls were bobbing and masts swaying gently—another scene for a 5,000-piece jigsaw puzzle. After a stroll along the jetties, we made our way to the 16th-century Citadelle St-Elme, its impregnable, sloping stone walls standing guard over the bay. After crossing the wooden drawbridge, we escaped the blazing sunshine and entered one of the gallery-museums where, among many paintings and sculptures, a few of Picasso's works were on display. From there we climbed to the battlements and looked out over the harbour, the coastline, and the sparkling sea. The views were spectacular.

Farther along the waterfront we sought out the orange-walled and green-shuttered Welcome Hotel, where we were greeted by a friendly English-speaking young man at *Réception*. Happy to escort us on a short tour of the premises, he explained that the hotel had long attracted artists, writers, and intellectuals—some quite famous. He smiled, perhaps it was a smirk, and asked if I was an artist or a writer. Although I recalled my mother hanging one of my paint-by-number watercolours on her fridge when I was nine, I chose to tell him that I was only a writer but was quick to add that my wife was the most intelligent intellectual that I'd ever met. He smiled; perhaps it was a smirk. He informed us that legendary movie stars Evelyn Waugh and Richard Burton used to hang out at the bar until the early hours of the morning, and that Somerset Maugham once lived in one of the small rooms on the top floor, from which the views were spectacular.

With tourist map and guidebook in hand, we walked up to the well-preserved old city of tiny streets, many steps, and buildings that date back as far as the 14th century. We continued until we found rue Obscure (or Dark Street, in English), which runs parallel to the seafront and is covered with vaulted arcades. Halfway along Dark

Street, we sat in the shade of the bright orange awning of a *pâtisserie* and enjoyed mid-morning refreshments while people-watching and reading our guidebook.

So impressed by the beauty of a young woman passing by, my wife nudged my elbow and whispered, "Look at her. Look at those long, tanned legs. Isn't she beautiful?"

"Who, darling?" I asked, swivelling my head from side to side, pretending that I hadn't noticed her approaching in the brilliant sunshine that lit Dark Street. "Oh *her.* I guess she's beautiful. Well, sort of," I feigned, being careful not to overreact with, "Ooh la la! She's an absolute knockout." Or to ad-lib with a crass Cockney rhyming phrase like, "Cor, blimey! That skirt's so short I can see her Alan Whickers." Or, worse, "Her legs are so long they go right up to her Khyber Pass."

Sitting there in the bright sunlight on Dark Street, I reflected on the notion that all a man has to do is to sit at a café on any street in any town, anywhere in the world, and sooner or later a woman will come along and the view will be spectacular.

49

Beaulieu-sur-Mer:

A Damsel in Distress, Greek Goddesses, and a Smoke Break

No sooner had we opened Twingo's doors than another Renault Twingo screeched to a halt behind us—its right-turn signal flashing, its driver tapping the top of its steering wheel, as if playing bongo drums, impatiently waiting for us to vacate the most desirable pay-and-display parking spot in all of Villefranche.

Along the coast road just four kilometres east of Villefranche, lies Beaulieu-sur-Mer, where we stopped to explore and to change a few large Canadian dollar bills into fewer, smaller euro bills before heading down the Cap Ferrat peninsula. Less fortunate in finding a vacant pay-and-display parking spot on Beaulieu's busy, cramped streets, we parked Twingo in the car park of the historic and luxurious five-star Hôtel Métropole and proceeded to enter the hotel's lobby on the pretence of making enquiries as to availability.

"*Madame et Monsieur, un mo-ment, s'il vous plaît.* Let me see eef we 'ave," said the older gentleman dressed in an immaculate navy blue uniform, the jacket adorned with deep yellow epaulettes and piping, a gleaming gold name badge, and gold (possibly 24-carat) buttons. All that was missing was a row of gold medals dangling from colourful ribbons pinned to his chest and a ceremonial sabre sheathed in a silver scabbard at his side. "We may 'ave only one *suite*," he said, as he frowned and studied the computer monitor.

"*Oui,* you are ve-ree luck-ee. We 'ave jus' one. Eet ees *magnifique.* Eet 'as a king bed and sea view. Eet ees on floor fifteen. You weel lurve it," Monsieur Distinguished continued. "Eet ees a spe-ci-al price of 450 euros per night. Eet ees only available for two nights. *Madame,* for 'ow many nights do you stay weez us?" asked Monsieur Distinguished as I stared—mouth agape, throat constricting—at my wife's attentive expression and pondered with increasing trepidation the worst possible outcome of our charade.

"Oh darn, what a dreadful pity. That room would have been absolutely perfect, but we were looking to stay for at least five nights. Would you please check again?" my wife persisted, pushing her luck. Beads of perspiration were forming on my forehead.

Monsieur Distinguished scrutinized the monitor. "No, *Madame,* I am *so* sorr-ee. There ees no more room. Eet ees imposs-ee-bla."

"*Merci.* Thank you so very much for checking. Hmmm. Can you recommend a hotel close by?" my wife asked pleadingly, her voice cracking, her eyelashes fluttering.

"There are many hotels in Beaulieu, *Madame.* You can walk to them all from 'ere, but eet ees peak season. Eet weel be *difficile* to find a room for five nights. I weel phone for you, yehz?"

"*Merci, Monsieur.* But that will not be necessary. Please, don't trouble yourself, we will walk and make enquires. Oh, by the way, may we leave our car in your car park?" she asked while biting her bottom lip, just as you'd expect of a damsel in distress.

"*Oui, Madame, absolument!* No prob-lem. Yehz, of course you may leave your *auto* 'ere—all day, if *nécessaire.*"

The inhabitants of Beaulieu are called Berlugans—not to be confused with the inhabitants of the largest tank at the Vancouver Aquarium, the belugas: the massive and blunt-headed whales. The small town lies crammed between the cliffs of the corniche and the clear waters of the Med and is protected between Cap Ferrat and Cap Roux peninsulas. A little research revealed that this sheltered locale creates somewhat of a tropical microclimate, which is why an area of town is known as Petite Afrique. In the 19th century it was the place to "get away from it all" (and yet be seen doing so) by royalty and members of high-society who would stay at one of the grand hotels. The Prince of Wales, Empress Eugenie, and Russian nobility were once among the visitors to this resort-town. Today, visitors include your average man and a conniving damsel in distress.

We started our mini-tour of Beaulieu by checking out one of its beaches, la plage de la Petite Afrique, which is located just east of Port de Plaisance. It's a large crescent-shaped beach of soft sand and has an impressive backdrop of palm trees and high, craggy cliffs. I found it surprisingly attractive, as I did the many damsels in a state of undress. Scantily clad women, glistening in tanning oil, were everywhere we looked. Usually in pairs, they frolicked on the sand, tanned on sun lounges, splashed in the waves, posed for photos, and talked with muscle-bound men. Of particular interest to most men were the women who'd forgotten to bring along their bikini tops.

"Look at her. She's like a Greek Goddess. Just look at that bikini bottom. What a brilliant colour. See how it complements her tan. And it fits her so well, don't you think?" asked my wife as I pretended not to have noticed the *mademoiselle*, with the bronzed cupolas, who was standing less than six feet away posing provocatively for her Adonis with a little point-and-shoot. "I'm really curious to know if it's a thong. Let's wait to see when she turns around."

"Okay," I agreed nonchalantly and yet demonstrating the open and honest communication that is necessary to preserve a healthy, loving marriage.

"Look! It is. It *is* a thong," my wife exclaimed as the Greek Goddess turned and walked slowly towards the water's edge.

"I think I'd better sit down," I muttered as I felt the blood drain rapidly from my head.

Speaking of semi-clad Greek goddesses, there were several strikingly beautiful ones, statues sculptured from the finest Italian white marble installed in the popular tourist attraction, Villa Kerylos, which we entered after I'd recovered from my near-fainting spell on the beach. Equipped with rental audio players, we moved around the floors of the magnificent mansion like two synchronized tourists, just as we'd done in the palace in Monaco. Villa Kerylos's Greek-style beauty has been described as eye-popping, and we concurred with our guidebook that it should not be missed because it is one of the most unusual houses in the south of France.

We were also impressed by Beaulieu's other attractive buildings, especially its grand, old hotels and the Notre-Dame de l'Espérance church, which is worth entering, if not to say one's prayers then at least to see the impressive architecture and stonemasonry, and the strikingly beautiful stained-glass windows.

"There's a bank over there," my wife said, pointing to another large stone building on the other side of the street. Forgetting that we were not in Vancouver, where motorists often come to a screeching halt at the sight of a pedestrian just considering whether to cross the road, we jaywalked. Note to self: French drivers tend to treat pedestrians who have strayed as targets.

The bank's atrium was gigantic; its walls were faced with white marble; and its roof was a massive, multi-coloured, scene-painted dome with golden lantern atop. People were milling around, standing at tables and filling out forms, and sitting on wooden benches waiting to be served. That is, waiting for the number on their ticket to appear on one of the electronic displays mounted high on several of the huge marble columns. Judging by their drawn, expressionless faces, many customers had been waiting a long time. For some of the frail and elderly, heaven may have appeared before their numbers did. Several customers were eating packed lunches and some had dozed off. Some were reading, playing cards, or working on crosswords.

"*Excusez-moi. Parlez-vous anglais, s'il vous plaît?*" I asked.

"Yes, I do. Please, how may I help you, sir? I am the manager." The short, ruddy man, who was dressed in a midnight blue suit and a white-on-black polka-dotted bow tie and wore a pair of rimless bifocals on the tip of his nose, spoke the Queen's English like one of the Royals.

"Thank you. Where do we get a ticket?"

"Over there. The two dispensers to the left of the entrance."

"*Merci, Monsieur,*" I responded.

"You're welcome. Have a nice day," the manager replied, like a customer service representative from Harrods.

I pulled a ticket from the dispenser: B-167. I showed the ticket to my wife. We looked up at the four electronic displays and checked the numbers. "Look, there. A-112, she's going to counter number two. Now A-113, he's going to counter one, and A-114, he's going to counter three."

B-139 popped up. A young man, a tourist holding a book of crossword puzzles in one hand and a wad of US bills in the other, stood up and walked to counter number four.

"B-139, you've got to be joking!" I looked again at our ticket. "We're going to be here all day," I moaned.

My wife pointed to a space on one of the wooden benches. The *Daily Mirror* lay open at the crossword page. We sat down. She picked up the paper while my eyes darted from display to display.

"You've got to be kidding! Look, nearly all the numbers start with the letter A, and they're all going to the first three counters." I felt my blood pressure rising. "Look, they're already up to A-121. Our guy at counter four is still serving B-139. Why are all the numbers starting with *A* and not *B*?" I knew I was ranting.

My wife lowered the folded newspaper in her right hand; she held a pen in the other. She was frowning. "What's the land at the South Pole? It has ten letters and begins with *A* and ends with *A*?"

"Marvellous! B-140, at last, B-139 has gone. Why is there only one teller serving numbers beginning with *B*?" I whined.

"Three down: The capital of Thailand. Seven letters, begins with *B*," my wife said thoughtfully.

"Look, we're only at B-141. I'm going to complain to the manager. This is absolutely ridiculous! Service would never be this slow in Canada." I got up to search for Manager Harrod.

"I got it! 'Antarctica'," my wife shouted as I strode off, steam coming out of both ears.

"Excuse me. It's me again. The service here is dreadfully slow. We've been here for twenty minutes and the guy at counter four has only served two or three customers. We'll be here all day at this rate." We looked over at counter four. There wasn't a customer or teller. "Where has the teller gone?" I glared at Manager Harrod.

Manager Harrod looked over the top of his bifocals at his wrist watch. "Yes, he's gone on his break."

"What! He's gone on his break!" I yelled incredulously.

"I'm afraid so, sir."

"But for how long?"

"Fifteen minutes, sir."

"Is someone going to take his place?"

"I'm afraid not, sir. Union rules, sir."

"You've got to be joking!"

I returned to the bench, shaking my head in disbelief. "Can you believe it? Our guy at number four has gone on a fifteen-minute smoke break. Unbelievable! No wonder France is in the state it's in."

"By the way, 'Bangkok' was the answer to three down," my wife said in a matter-of-fact tone.

"Unions! You can thank the unions," I went on.

"Seventeen across—a port on England's northwest coast. Nine letters, second letter *I*, last letter *L*."

"Liverpool," I answered distractedly.

"Yes, you're right. It fits."

"Give me another."

"Seven down, five letters begins with *T*—a South Pacific island."

"Tonga."

"Wow! I never knew that you're good at crosswords. Isn't this fun?" I looked into her eyes. She smiled and kissed me on the cheek.

We left only two words incomplete. We would have finished the crossword, but unfortunately we didn't have enough time, as B-167 came up on the electronic display and we had to go to counter four and exchange our Canadian dollars for fewer euros.

50

Cap Ferrat:

Peninsula of Dreams

Cap Ferrat has been described as the jewel of the French Riviera and the peninsula of dreams. After retrieving our car from Hôtel Métropole's car park, we drove two kilometres down the narrow M25 and stopped at St-Jean for lunch: a pizza and a carafe of chilled rosé wine sitting in the shade on the second-floor patio of Le Saint Jean restaurant. The Calabrese pizza was excellent, the wine hit the spot, and the views overlooking the small pleasure port, the pretty crescent beach, and the sparkling blue waters of Beaulieu's bay were magnificent. However, there was one thing that wasn't right. An Englishwoman, sitting at a table upwind of us, was chain-smoking and, between puffs, chastised her two uncontrollable little brats who moaned, fidgeted, and fought continuously. The peninsula of dreams had been compromised.

Scenically, Cap Ferrat is a stunningly beautiful peninsula of rocky bays, soft-sand beaches, tropical gardens, and tall hedges that succeed in hiding its lavish villas. Its wealthy residents, who fiercely protect their privacy from curious onlookers, have no need to turn the pages of local newspapers in search of one-day specials on jumbo-sized boxes of washing powder or bran flakes, or to clip out coupons offering a 20 per cent discount on cartons of orange juice or family-sized tubes of toothpaste. St-Jean is a haven for the affluent, for those with yachts that glide in and out of its port, their passengers and crew shuttling from gleaming hulls to aroma-rich cafés and *pâtisseries* for pastries, and to *magasins de vins* and *charcuteries* for chilled bottles of champagne and duck liver pâté to enjoy back on their varnished teak decks.

We began our afternoon trek by walking around the port and then following the coastal path around the smaller peninsula that protrudes eastwards from St-Jean. We came upon plage Paloma, which is rated the best and, consequently, the most popular beach on the peninsula. We were somewhat disappointed that the beach was pebbly and not made up entirely of soft, easy-on-the-feet sand and that not all the sunbathers, like the waves, were small and soothing to the ear.

However, we were not disappointed with the natural beauty of Scaletta Cove. Less than 200 metres long, the cove is pretty and sheltered by pine-covered hills, and the views towards the steep cliffs to the east are picture-postcard worthy. Strolling along the warm water's edge, we came across more natural beauty in the form of two, young, topless women playing beach paddleball—another eye-popping, ooh-la-la sight. As we neared the young women, my wife stopped suddenly to avoid breaking their concentration, but I didn't and walked into the back of her, almost knocking her over. And that's how I suffered a painful split lip and a more painful tongue-lashing.

After I bathed my lip and pointed Percy at the porcelain in the only public toilet on the beach, we found boulevard du Général de Gaulle and headed south in search of the Grand-Hôtel du Cap-Ferrat. Unsure how to get there, I asked a young woman who was standing at a bus stop on the other side of the road.

"*Excusez-moi. Parlez-vous anglais, s'il vous plaît?*" I shouted, catching her attention, my fat lip barely impairing my pronunciation.

"*Oui,* I do," she shouted, looking at my wife.

"How far is it to the Grand-Hôtel?" I shouted, as I pointed down the road. A scooter went by with a hole in its muffler.

"*Pardonnez-moi?*" she shouted, still looking at my wife.

"Honey, why don't you cross over, so you don't have to shout?" my wife suggested.

I waited for a gap in the traffic, then jogged across.

"Hi. We want to get to the Grand-Hôtel. Are we still headed in the right direction?" I asked. She didn't turn to face me, but kept looking across the road at my wife.

Then she shouted, "Yes, *Madame*, you go in the right direction."

"Thank you, and where do we turn off?" I asked, looking at the side of her head.

"Go five 'undred metres more. Go past avenue de la Corniche, and you weel see a sign for the Grand Hôtel. Turn left there," she shouted, avoiding eye contact with me.

"*Merci*. Thank you very much," I said.

"You're ver-ee welcome. 'ave a nice day," she shouted, still looking across the road at my wife.

I crossed back over the road. My wife shouted, "*Merci*. Thank you. *Au revoir*." The bus came and the young woman was gone.

"What the heck was *that* all about?" I asked incredulously.

"It's your *fly*. It's wide open!" She burst out laughing.

I looked down at my open zipper and the tail of my white cotton shirt protruding through it. It was another eye-popping sight. The peninsula of dreams had been compromised yet again.

The Grand-Hôtel du Cap-Ferrat is indeed grand. It's one of the world's most iconic resorts, and although rated as a five-star hotel, it's known to those who can afford to stay there as the highest ranking of all the Riviera's *palaces*. Built in 1908, it's set amid seventeen acres of lush, tropical gardens on the bluff at the tip of the peninsula. It offers panoramic sea views and boasts seventy-three luxurious rooms, three fine-dining restaurants, a beach club, and an award-winning spa for those who become stressed at the thought of paying a palatial sum upon checkout.

The hotel's interior is elegant and understated, with cream and white marble and the occasional touch of colour, a Murano glass chandelier here, a vibrant tapestry there. The Residence Wing, which caters to royalty, movie stars, and business tycoons, features suites with massive glass-panelled sliding doors that open onto terraces and private plunge pools. Past and future co-exist, especially in such details as the glass funicular that sweeps VIP guests from the hotel down to the Club Dauphin and the Olympic-sized infinity pool at the beach, and then sweeps exhausted guests back up after swimming numerous lengths of the butterfly stroke—or after suffering a stroke.

Before entering the hotel, we stood in the shade of a plane tree in the front garden to comb our hair. My wife adjusted her sunshades; she applied a fresh coat of ruby red lipstick and two fine sprays of Habanita de Molinard. I checked my fly. The zipper was where it should be, nothing protruding from it. We entered the magnificent lobby and walked over to the attractive man behind the reception desk. My wife smiled and asked if we could possibly look around the hotel, its gardens, and the beach club.

It was obvious by the way we were dressed that we were not millionaires, CEOs, movie stars, or royalty. So there was no point in pretending that we were interested in a suite with a Murano glass chandelier here, a vibrant tapestry there, and a massive glass-panelled sliding door that opened onto a terrace and private plunge pool. There was simply no point in advising him that we would want the use of a glass funicular to sweep us down to the beach club, and that we were accustomed to living where the past and future co-exist.

No pretence was necessary, none whatsoever. For, as expected Habanita de Molinard had taken effect. The young man's eyes had glazed over before he managed a breathy, *"Oui, Madame.* Please, be my guest. Do as you wish."

Such words are always music to our ears, and so too was the sound coming from the back of the lobby. It definitely was not elevator music; it was a classical piece being played on a piano somewhere by someone with extraordinary talent. We turned the corner to investigate. We couldn't believe our eyes. We couldn't believe our ears. We came upon a vision, like one sees in a dream. But we were not dreaming in the grand lobby of the Grand-Hôtel on Cap Ferrat, the peninsula of dreams.

51

Cap Ferrat:

A Pianist, a Lover of Music, a Villa, and a Coronation Street House

The Steinway grand piano had been positioned on the left of the airy, semi-circular, rear section of the spectacular lobby. Five floor-to-ceiling windows looked out onto sunlit, manicured lawns and on, beyond the bluff and the beach, to the sparkling sea's horizon. Playing a classical piece was a beautiful, young woman. Standing behind her were two men and a woman—the pianist's parents and her publicist, we soon discovered. There were many empty upright chairs arranged in rows and facing the piano, ready to accommodate an audience, perhaps a recital later that evening. The mother looked and smiled approvingly as we sat down quietly in the back row and listened in awe.

Since as far back as I can remember, I have enjoyed listening to music, but not all music. I need a catchy melody that I can whistle to, a rhythm that I can dance to, and lyrics that are clear enough to learn and sing along to. The wonderful sound of the classical piece being played by the young concert pianist met none of these needs. I couldn't whistle or sing along to it, and I certainly couldn't dance to it, and yet I loved it. It touched my soul.

As a child growing up in England, my father had an old

gramophone and a collection of classical 78s—the fragile records that played on a turntable at 78 rpm and comprised a single track on each side. Many were produced by the record label His Master's Voice—today's HMV. Our old radio, which was large and full of dimly lit valves and whose antenna constantly needed twiddling, was usually tuned in to music on our favourite BBC station.

Later, my mother bought records of the soundtracks from musicals like *South Pacific, Oklahoma!* and *Carousel*, which we played on our ultramodern Decca three-in-one unit (a TV, radio, and record player) that was the envy of our neighbours. Made of plastic, these LPs (long players) with eight or more tracks on each side were played at 33 rpm, and still are whenever they're retrieved from boxes stored in the basement. I loved to sing along to them and can still recall the lyrics of most of the songs.

My two older sisters took piano lessons and practised frequently. I wasn't always sure when they played the wrong notes, but our dog sure did. Running from the room with its tail between its legs and its ears back were the telltale signs. At nine, I became a choirboy at our local church. Years later, my mother bought a small transistor radio, which I took everywhere while listening to pop music, especially to the pirate commercial radio broadcasting ship, Radio Caroline.

In my late teens, I was among the first to arrive and the last to leave the local discothèque on Saturday nights. Not blessed with my sisters' musical talent and patience, I failed miserably at playing the guitar and trumpet. I had, however, more success at playing the drums and, by twenty, I was playing the college circuit as the drummer in The Invaders, a five-man rock band. I practised several times a week at home in the living room, which was probably the cause of my father needing a hearing aid, my mother keeping earplugs handy, my sisters leaving home, and my dog running away to the local SPCA, where it was last seen barking at an official behind the reception desk, pleading for refuge.

☼

But I've digressed. We applauded enthusiastically when the concert pianist played the final note of the piece she was rehearsing. She looked across at us, smiled and nodded in appreciation. Then, as she started to rehearse another piece, her mother walked over and sat beside us.

"*Buongiorno,*" the mother said, smiling.

"*Buongiorno,*" my wife responded, to my surprise.

"*Parli Italiano?*" the mother asked.

"*Mi dispiace, no parlo molto bene italiano. Lei parla inglese?*" my wife asked as I looked on in bewilderment.

"*Si, Si,* I speaka Ing-leesh. She eesa my daughter. Her name eesa Chiara Opalio," the mother replied.

"I absolutely *love* Beethoven's 'Moonlight Sonata'. It's one of my favourites and she played it so magnificently," my wife stated. I nodded in agreement, as if I knew what she was talking about. "And now, Mozart's 'Rondo alla Turca' is another favourite," she added, as she looked in the direction of Chiara. I shrugged my shoulders and twisted my lips a little, indicating that I had a different opinion, that I had my own favourite. I wracked my brain trying to think of another famous composer, but I could only come up with Rachmaninoff. I was tempted to casually throw his name into the conversation but I'd forgotten how to pronounce it. So I just sat and listened to the music, and looked on, like a sad, old dog with no intention of seeking refuge in the closest SPCA.

What we learned from the mother, as we listened to another beautiful piece of work being played by the beautiful piece of work sitting at the piano, was quite amazing. Chiara Opalio was born in 1990 in Vittorio Veneto, just north of Venice, and began to play piano at the age of three. Three! How could her feet have reached the foot pedals? I could barely stand at that age. My thumbs were for sucking and my fingers were for pointing at things, prodding people, and for picking stuff out of orifices. She played her first recital when she was four and performed as a soloist with an orchestra for the first time when she was only eleven.

Her website revealed that she had won many prizes in national and international competitions, not the least of which was a "Special Mention" awarded at the Carl Czerny International Piano Competition in Prague, when she was just nine. When I was nine, my schoolteacher made a "special mention" to my mother at the end-of-term parent-teacher night: "Stephen's work is marred by carelessness, but he's a happy boy and a very good whistler."

At the age of fifteen, Chiara made her debut in Milan with the Orchestra dei Pomeriggi Musicali at Teatro Dal Verme. In 2012, she won First Prize at the Città di Padova international competition, playing in the Schumann Concerto finals under the baton of Maestro Maffeo Scarpis. In my case, as the drummer of The Invaders, I never had the opportunity to play under a baton, I simply relied on our rhythm guitarist, Maestro Harry Higginbottom, to nod at me, point his guitar at me, or shout an obscenity at me.

Since 2010, Chiara has been performing on piano with Italian cellist Giovanni Gnocchi. They recently won the prestigious "Bruno Premuda" prize from the Trio di Trieste international school. And as if that weren't enough, Chiara has also been playing violin for eight years and, since 2012, has been teaching piano at the Fondazione Santa Cecilia in Portogruaro. She has become one of Italy's most acclaimed musicians, both as a soloist and as a chamber music player. I'm still a very good whistler.

After leaving the splendour of the Grand-Hôtel, we walked the path to the cape's lighthouse, around the tip of the peninsula, and up the west coast while taking in the views across the Bay of Villefranche and drooling at the sight of the many beautiful cliffside villas. When it comes to rating pleasurable seaside walks, the best is reported to be the twenty-five-minute walk south from Beaulieu to St-Jean on the east side of the peninsula, which passes rocky beaches and lavish villas, including one right at the water's edge that was once owned by the late David Niven. However, the walk on the west side, which winds its way over white cliffs buffeted by waves and is shaded by pines, *has* to be a close second.

A kilometre or so north of St-Jean's port, at the narrowest part of the peninsula, we toured the Villa Ephrussi de Rothschild. For those who love large, beautiful homes full of precious artwork, tapestries, furniture, porcelain, Chinese vases, and fine Italian antiquities, this neo-Venetian-style house, built for Baroness Béatrice de Rothschild in the early 1900s, with a pink façade and seven magnificent themed gardens, should rank high on the list of "Must-See Tourist Attractions on Cap Ferrat."

The house was named "Île-de-France" after the Baroness's favourite French ocean liner, *SS Île de France*. The liner was built in France after the end of World War I and was the first liner to be decorated entirely with designs associated with the Art Deco style. While it was neither the largest nor the fastest ship ever built, it was considered the most beautifully decorated.

The themed gardens, which include the French, Spanish, Rose, Florentine, Japanese, Exotic, and Stone garden, are magnificent and deserve a stroll through to fully appreciate their tranquility and beauty; and a wide variety of beautiful trees provide a leafy canopy of shade. The large, formal French garden, which is symmetrical and runs north to south from the house, has a set of centrally located fountains that spray pulsating jets of water high into the air, dancing to the rhythm of piped music.

Strolling the gardens, I once again recalled my humble start in life. In contrast to Villa Ephrussi de Rothschild, I was raised in a two-up-two-down, neo-Coronation-Street-style row house. It too was built in the early 1900s but it had a dirty red-brick façade. It was named "One Charles Street," as it was the first of the row of houses on Charles Street. In the early days, it didn't have an indoor toilet or a bathtub but it did have a coal-burning fireplace, and our furnishings and carpets were well-worn. Though it lacked precious tapestries and artwork, we did have several porcelain piss pots, a paving stone front garden, and a concrete back garden. As for flowers, I recall that one late spring, a dandelion burst forth between a paving stone and our dirty red-brick wall. Sadly, its golden yellow petals bloomed for only a single day because Rover, the mongrel from number 17, cocked his leg and dowsed it with his stronger-than-weed-killer jet stream.

Back at the villa, we were tempted to have late afternoon refreshments in its glassed-in porch, which overlooks the grounds and offers spectacular views of the coastline, but we decided instead to save our appetites for a sumptuous meal—a final romantic dinner on the French Riviera—at Capitaine Cook's restaurant back in St-Jean. Who could have guessed the bizarre experience that unfolded there?

52

Cap Ferrat:

Potent Hooch, Nape Sniffing, and the Lush with the High IQ

By the time we'd returned to St-Jean's village centre, we were tired and hungry. It had been a long walk, my legs felt weak, even a little wobbly. Neither of us had spoken since leaving Villa Ephrussi de Rothschild. We hadn't stopped to admire the view, take a photo, or look in a shop window, and we hadn't even made eye contact with each other. I felt irritable; perhaps my wife did too. We both stared straight ahead as we plodded on. Without realizing it, we had entered a lover's danger zone. We had missed the red flags. One wrong word and look out! Tired, we hiked up the hill towards Le Restaurant Capitaine Cook, the delectable aroma of garlic sautéing in olive oil wafted our way and encouraged us to pick up our pace, like blinkered horses returning to their stables.

A modest building from the outside, Capitaine Cook was quite charming inside—somewhat rustic with an exposed stone wall and wooden ceiling beams. The hostess, who greeted us with a warm welcome in English, introduced herself as Nelly Pelletier: co-owner with her husband, Lionel, the chef.

"He's the cook, cooking in Capitaine Cook's," she beamed. "We 'ave been 'ere for twenty-seven years," she added.

It was not a large dining room, and it was busy. The candlelit tables were close together, and most were occupied by suntanned couples who were chatting, eating, and sipping wine while rubbing elbows with their neighbours. It was the cosiest and most intimate atmosphere that we'd experienced in Provence. And the aromas coming from Lionel's copper pans were mouth-watering.

"We 'ave *une terrasse*. The night is warm. *S'il vous plaît,* come." Nelly beckoned us to the outdoor patio. We collapsed into chairs and exhaled exhaustive sighs. Nelly lit the candle that was secured in an old wine bottle draped in layers of wax. Next to it was a glass vase holding several dahlias. Within seconds, Nelly popped a menu and a basket of sliced baguette onto our table. It wobbled. She pulled a plastic wedge from her apron pocket, knelt down, and slid it under a leg. "*Voilà!*" she said. She went back to her wooden desk, which was strategically positioned against a wall. From there she could observe the patrons and respond quickly to any request.

As I reached for a slice of baguette, my wife slapped the back of my hand. I looked up at her; it was the first eye contact we'd made in an hour. She took the piece and bit into it. I took another piece. We smiled at each other. We were out of the danger zone, the red flags had been replaced by amber ones, the green ones would surely be hoisted by the time the Côtes de Provence touched our lips.

Judging by the plates of food served to our neighbouring tables, portions were hearty. For starters, my wife ordered the avocado salad with shrimp, and I ordered the salmon ravioli. And, like young lovers who have never entered a danger zone or seen red flags flying, we shared each dish, feeding each other forkfuls across the table. For our main courses, we ate grilled sea bass served with vegetable *au gratin* and a *bouillabaisse*. And our dessert, fruit salad with raspberry sorbet, was followed by a cheese platter and espressos.

When we'd finished eating, Nelly appeared with a bottle encased in a block of ice, set within a glistening ice bucket. "*Madame et Monsieur,* you 'ave a *digestif? Oui?* Eet ees 'omemade. A Capitaine Cook *surprise*. You weel enjoy." We didn't protest; we just smiled as

she poured. "I 'ope you are not dri-veeng. Eet can make your legs—
'ow you say?—wobbly." Two beautiful women sitting at the next
table, sipping from liqueur glasses, laughed softly. "Eet ees based on
passion fruit and Marc de Bourgogne," Nelly explained, and then
returned inside, topping up the two Beauty Queens' glasses en route.
They looked across at us, smiled, and raised their glasses. We
returned their smiles, raised our glasses, and said, "Cheers!" and we
all took a sip.

It took several minutes for me to stop choking and gasping for
air. The two Beauty Queens laughed, my wife giggled, and I managed
a weak smile—happy just to be alive.

"What the heck was that?" I croaked, my oesophagus ablaze.

"It was the Marc de Bourgogne. It's a French spirit made from
pressing the skins, pulp, and seeds that are left over after grapes are
processed into wine." My wife took another sip of her passion fruit
juice mixed with sulphuric acid. "It's called a pomace brandy, albeit
one of the more polished versions. As you just discovered, the taste is
far from subtle. Some describe it as a considerably potent, well-aged,
pedigreed hooch." The Beauty Queens were eavesdropping as they
sipped the toxic concoction. Astounded by my wife's knowledge, but
somewhat suspicious that she'd experimented with home-distilling
equipment during pre-Steve days, I didn't interrupt her, "Aficionados
vehemently argue that Marc de Bourgogne is not bathtub-still swill,
but rather it enjoys the distinction of an appellation."

The trouble with sipping potent hooch after consuming a bottle of
Côtes de Provence was that I became numb to its fiery afterburn, to
my inhibitions, and to my wife's encyclopaedic knowledge. What I
hadn't become numb to was the fragrance of a perfume that wafted
our way from the Beauty Queens' table. One of them had just
returned from freshening up while I'd been listening to the brew
master with the high IQ sitting across from me.

"Excuse me, what's the name of that perfume you're wearing?" I
startled myself by asking, forgetting that they may not speak English.
My wife looked surprised at such a brazen question.

"Which one? We 'ave not the same parfum," replied the blonde. Her smile revealed perfectly formed white teeth. Her eyes sparkled. I shrugged my shoulders and suddenly felt awkward.

"I'm wear-eeng Shalimar by Guerlain," smiled the brunette with dark brown eyes, "She ees wear-eeng Givenchy's Very Irresistible," she added, nodding at her friend. Both of them were wearing low-cut, ooh-la-la tops that were difficult to ignore.

"You may sniff and compare, if you like," suggested the blonde.

I couldn't believe my ears. What an invitation! I looked across at my wife ashamedly, like an old dog that knows it's misbehaved. She laughed and nodded. "Go on. Check them out. See which one you prefer, and then you can treat me to a bottle." She laughed again. The green flags were flying high.

She'd thrown the ball for me and I set off after it. The blonde flicked back her long hair, exposing her neck. I leaned over and sniffed. The fragrance smelled divine. Then the brunette presented her neck. I moved over, leaned in, and sniffed. It too smelled divine. My legs started to wobble.

"Which you like?" asked the blonde.

"Hmmm. I'm really not sure," I responded somewhat truthfully.

"You moost smell again," the brunette insisted.

I looked across at my wife. She nodded again between sips of hooch. I repeated the sniff test, but lingered longer, nose to napes, to make absolutely sure that I could conclusively proclaim a winner. It was the brunette. No, I mean it was Shalimar. As I wobbled back to our table, my wife had flicked back *her* hair proffering her neck. I leaned over and took a sniff, and then collapsed into my chair. We had a new indisputable winner: the beautiful lush with the high IQ.

53

Au Revoir, Le Mas du Centaure:

Hangover Symptoms, a Soprano, and a Cowboy

We'd become accustomed to waking up to the morning sunshine streaming in, illuminating our yellow-and-white room. And our last morning at Le Mas du Centaure, our last morning in southern Provence, our last morning on the French Riviera, was no exception. Accompanying the warm shaft of sunlight was a soft, sweet breeze as we stirred and stretched and kicked aside the cotton sheet. I had a splitting headache. Pleasant but somewhat vague memories of eating a delicious meal and sipping several glasses of Côtes de Provence, and then, regrettably, downing several glasses of Marc de Bourgogne, and sniffing the napes of two women—total strangers—crept back into my throbbing head.

My hangover was crying out for freshly squeezed orange juice, caffeine, and extra-strength acetaminophen tablets. Until then, I'd have to refrain from looking into the bright sunlight, avoid loud noises, and be extremely careful what I said to my wife who, I assumed, would be suffering similar symptoms. But no, she jumped out of bed, said she'd slept like a baby, exclaimed that it was a beautiful morning, and began singing the Beatles' "Good Day Sunshine" in perfect pitch and rhythm as she stepped into the vertical coffin to shower. It was very annoying.

I just wanted to be quiet, to be left alone, to suffer in silence. I was thankful that the black canine trio wasn't barking and that Cavity

Phil wasn't playing his trumpet or driving around on his bulldozer. But I cursed him later, after banging my forehead on the hot water knob when I bent over to retrieve the shower head that had slipped from my grip as I struggled to shower single-handedly.

I also cursed the person who invented the small, foot-operated, flip-top, cylindrical garbage receptacle in the corner, just to the left of the pedestal basin. Why? Because I banged my bony shin on it, that's why. Or, I should say, it banged me. I'd had my challenges with this ineffective gleaming receptacle during previous morning ablutions but had survived unscathed because I hadn't consumed Nelly's oesophagus-corroding concoction the night before. However, on this occasion, discarding an empty toothpaste tube, I placed my foot on the black pedal and depressed it, but instead of the silly lid flipping open, the entire receptacle sprang forward, its rim cracking hard against my shin bone. My scream aggravated my throbbing headache and deteriorating mood, but it brought some relief when my annoyingly happy wife handed me a glass of water and two extra-strength acetaminophen tablets.

"Here, take these, *please*," she implored.

With a stinging bruised forehead and left shin, and a persistently throbbing headache, I clunked down the staircase behind a light-footed soprano who had switched to singing "Oh, What a Beautiful Mornin'" by Rogers and Hammerstein. She hadn't listened to *Oklahoma!* as a child, which is why she couldn't remember all the words. Consequently, she kept singing the first two lines over and over. It was very annoying. I wanted so badly to prompt her with the next two lines, "I've got a wonderful feeling, everything's going my way." But alas, I had a lousy feeling that nothing was going *my* way.

The blur of Flaming Flora's long, red hair flashing from the kitchen to the dining table reassured me that she was, as usual, serving guests at supersonic speed and that it would be a matter of seconds before she'd place a freshly squeezed orange juice and the first of several cafés au lait in front of me. And, no matter where I sat, I knew that a small basket of croissants and a jar of homemade jam would be within reach before I could ask.

"*Bonjour,*" my wife said enthusiastically. She smiled at all the guests, waved in the general direction of the red blur in the kitchen, and sat next to the DJ from Down Under.

I smiled a weak smile and sat down. I didn't make eye contact with anyone other than Horny Hound and Terrible Terrier, who were eyeing their prey from the far end of the room. Both were salivating as they sat alert, either side of Pregnant Paws who was curled up pretending to be asleep in front of the fireplace. I shot the two of them a three-second glare that conveyed in no uncertain terms that I was not to be messed with—or else!

As the caffeine and the tablets started to have their desired effect, I began to make eye contact with our fellow guests. Svenn was sitting to my right, and to the right of him was, I'm-a-Man Ika. He was pointing to the flower arrangement on the table and describing the fragrances that he'd distinguished—reminding me of the "nose" at Molinard's perfumery. And the slight vibration of his teaspoon tinkling his cup and saucer was evidence that his present state of nervousness had triggered another bout of the incurable under-the-table, rapid-heel-tapping, oscillating-knee syndrome.

Sitting across the table, opposite my wife, was a new arrival: a forty-something guy dressed in blue jeans, a plaid shirt, and a paisley neckerchief. His blue eyes, mop of blonde hair, and bushy blonde moustache complemented his clothing, creating a cowboy image and reminding me somewhat of Brad Pitt in *Legends of the Fall*. I glanced around at the coat stand by the front door to check if he'd hung up his white ten-gallon hat and his two holstered, ivory-handled Colt 45s before moseying on over to the table to order a pot of coffee and a plate of baked beans. I was surprised, almost shocked, to discover that he was a fellow Canadian, hailing from the oil-rich, cattle-rich province of Alberta. Unlike most Canadians, he was outspoken and boastful. And if that wasn't irritating enough, he had the habit of starting every sentence with "Listen" or "Look."

"Just wait a second, let me switch on my hearing aid and remove my blindfold, and then, if you wouldn't mind, please repeat your question," I was tempted to respond, but didn't because I'm your normal polite Canadian.

"Listen, what was that song you were just singing?" asked Brad Pity, smiling at my smiling wife.

"It's called 'Oh, What a Beautiful Mornin'','" she gushed.

"Look, have you ever sung professionally?"

"No, I haven't," she replied, hopeful of receiving praise.

"Listen, with a voice like yours, and such a pretty face, I'm absolutely certain you could go places," the cowboy continued, as he opened his mouth and popped in a piece of chocolate croissant—or was it chewing tobacco?

"Do you really think so?"

"Look, let me give you a piece of advice. You should audition when you get home. Listen, I'm absolutely positive that if you find the right agent, you could *really* go places."

I shot a sideways glance at Svenn. "I wish *he'd* go places, the farther the better," I muttered with a wry smile.

Thankfully, my headache succumbed to the caffeine and the tablets, and by the time I'd slurped down my third café au lait, I'd been miraculously delivered from the temptation of making further sarcastic comments and wry smiles, and was back to being my congenial self, cracking jokes and recounting some of our humorous experiences and ooh-la-la escapades on the French Riviera. And, while Flaming Flora's espresso machine hissed in overdrive, conversation flowed uninhibitedly, punctuated by bursts of raucous laughter, and the noise grew to an all-time crescendo. Even the Babes from Beijing managed to break through the "whisper" level, but, still, they did so with hands covering their mouths. At one point, I noticed Pregnant Paws raise her head, prick up both ears, and raise one eyebrow before returning to her feigned slumber. In spite of the caffeine-fuelled chatter, I realized that the side-effects of Habanita de Molinard had worn off, as my wife declined Brad Pity's request to regale everyone in the room with another rendition of "Oh, What a Beautiful Mornin'."

Suddenly, I felt a pang of sadness at the thought of leaving the French Riviera: Ooh-la-la Land. And yet this fleeting feeling was countered by a rush of excitement at the thought of returning home to Vancouver—land of beautiful scenery and large bathrooms.

We packed our suitcases, closed Cigales' door, lumbered down the circular steel staircase for the last time, loaded up Twingo, paid our bill, said goodbye to Flaming Flora, and set off down the dusty, bumpy lane to exit the property, leaving behind Le Mas du Centaure. Curiously, I believe we would have felt cheated if Terrible Terrier hadn't escorted us off the property, running alongside, snapping at our front tire. The sound of a rapid three-beep horn coming from the far end of the paddock and the sight of Cavity Phil waving from his front-end loader was the final gesture of farewell from the proprietor-cum-dentist, who could manufacture, assemble, install, construct, and repair anything and everything, single-handedly.

54

Au Revoir, Ooh-la-la Land:

An Old Pack Mule and the Green Grass of Home

Remarkably, I'd become accustomed to the high-risk driving habits of the locals. In fact, I believe I'd adapted extraordinarily well. My rapid transition from nervous driver to Formula 1 racing pro began by imagining that Twingo was an armour-plated Ferrari and that I was vying for the lead in the Monaco Grand Prix, taking all necessary risks to win.

And so, with one foot heavy on the gas pedal, the other poised above the brake, and a trigger-happy hand positioned over the horn, I attacked the route to the airport, reacting to avoid oncoming cars and death-defying motorcyclists performing wheelies. The fact that Twingo remained dent-free and that I hadn't spent time in hospital or behind bars or popped a single blood vessel was proof enough that I'd adapted and blended in. I had become just one more maniac amid the frenetic French Riviera traffic.

Unconcerned at the sound of screeching tires and blasting horns, and the lurching of her upper body against her seatbelt as Twingo accelerated, swerved, and braked hard, my wife flipped the pages of a fashion magazine that comprised full-spread photos of ridiculously skinny women wearing ridiculously tight dresses, hiding ridiculously long legs. In among the pages of the ridiculously thin air-brushed beauties, I deduced that there were also several photos of ridiculously handsome men looking bored and in need of a clean shave, wearing ridiculously expensive suits.

"I wonder if that same guy will be at the Renault rental counter," my wife remarked casually while staring at a photo. She sighed.

"Why?" I asked, as memories of Captain Good-Looking came flooding back.

"Oh, I just wondered."

As soon as I'd parked Twingo in the Renault-designated parking area, Captain Good-Looking rushed out of the terminal building to greet us. Correction: to greet my wife. His white uniform and brilliant white teeth contrasted against his deeper-than-deep tan—the result of many more hours lying prone (probably in a Speedo) on a sun-drenched beach.

"*Bonjour, Madame.* 'ow was your viz-eet?" he asked with that sexy French accent. My wife had lowered her window, smiled, and given him a little wave. She hadn't even opened her door when he reached for her hand and kissed the back of it softly. "*Enchanté.*"

"Wash that hand in hot water and extra-strength disinfectant as soon as you can get to a washroom," I thought of saying.

He opened her door and smiled. The sun reflected off his teeth and momentarily blinded me as I witnessed the performance.

"*Merci, Jean-Claude.* Our holiday was marvellous. Thank you," my wife responded—her smile much brighter, her hand hanging limp; his kiss had rendered it immobile.

"Ah ha!" I thought, noticing she'd had no problem recalling his name and how easily "Jean-Claude" had rolled off the tip of her tongue, when only moments earlier it was, "*that same guy.*"

"*Oh là là*, you 'ave much sun," he said as he leaned in to help my wife unbuckle her seatbelt. "You 'ave a lurv-lee tan. Ees eet all over?" he asked flirtatiously. My wife looked puzzled. "Ees your tan all over?" He laughed, she giggled, and I almost threw up.

I got out of the car and set about unloading our luggage while Captain Good-Looking assisted my wife in retrieving the rental documents from the glove compartment. Apparently, in France, it takes two people to execute such physically demanding and complex tasks. With suitcases unloaded and placed to one side, I waited for Captain Good-Looking to perform the usual walk-around inspection of Twingo's body. But no, that didn't happen. He didn't even kick the tires. The only inspection he was performing was that of the tanned body exiting demurely from Twingo's passenger side. Perhaps he'd check the car later, but his immediate priority was building client relations—Frenchman-style. It was all part of the ser-veece.

"'ere, take my arm," he insisted. "I weel escort you across the road to my off-eece."

"Well, thank you very much. That's very kind of you."

"Eet ees my ple-zure. Eet ees my doo-tie. Eet ees my privi-large to be of ser-veece." He flashed his teeth, she giggled, and I choked back breakfast as they set off, walking arm-in-arm in the direction of his office. Resorting to my familiar role, I staggered some distance behind loaded down like an old pack mule wobbling on its last legs.

"*Voilà!* All ees een order," said Captain Good-Looking after running back to check Twingo for damage and mileage. "I 'ope you are 'appy and come back next year," he said, as he kissed my wife on the back of her other hand. "*Enchanté, Madame.*" He smiled and flashed his teeth, my wife giggled, and I yawned and popped in an antacid tablet.

"*Oh là là!*" he muttered, and was gone. Out of the corner of his eye, just after releasing my wife's limp hand, he'd spotted another car entering the Renault parking lot and had dashed out to greet its occupants: two young, scantily clad, sun-drenched women. And by the time I'd put away the paperwork and my wife had stopped sighing, Captain Good-Looking was making his way back across the road, arm-in-arm with a smiling client on either side.

My wife looked at me—the sad, old dog, the pack mule on its last legs—and said, "You know, you're much more handsome than he is."

☼

Ooh-la-la Land

The sky was the richest shade of blue, but then it usually is at cruising altitude, and it remained that way even as we started our descent over the spectacular Rockies. Thankfully, the easyJet flight to Liverpool's John Lennon airport, and the connecting WestJet flight back to Vancouver were zombie-free and alien-free, and we spent most of our time recounting our unforgettable escapades in Ooh-la-la Land.

On final approach to Vancouver airport, scrunched together against the window, craning our necks to enable a better view behind the wing, we peered down in wonder and excited anticipation at the beautiful sight of home: the downtown skyline, Stanley Park, the Pacific Ocean, the mountains, and golf courses, all set amid the lush greenery of the British Columbian rainforest. Just before touchdown, my wife squeezed my hand and whispered, "It's been a wonderful vacation. I love you so much—you're the best."

"I love you too." I kissed her softly on her cheek and then on the back of her hand, and whispered, "Eet ees all part of the ser-veece."

Stephen Foey.

Bibliography

These are works I've consulted and drawn from for factual information:

Word for Word by Andrew A. Rooney
Putnam Publishing Group
Penguin Random House
New York, NY, USA
www.penguin.com

Baedeker's
FRANCE
Prentice-Hall Press
New York, NY, USA
www.baedeker.com

DK Eyewitness Travel Guides
PROVENCE & THE CÔTE D'AZUR
DK Publishing, Inc.
New York, NY, USA
www.dk.com

Insight Guides
THE FRENCH RIVIERA
Apa Publications UK Ltd
London, UK
www.insightguides.com

Fodor's
PROVENCE & THE FRENCH RIVIERA
Penguin Random House
New York, NY, USA
www.fodors.com

Lonely Planet
France
Lonely Planet Publications Pty Ltd.
Footscray, Victoria, Australia
www.lonelyplanet.com

Stephen Foey

Featured Accommodation:

Hôtel Miramar
67, Chemin de la Plage,
06160 La Garoupe
Cap d'Antibes - France
Tel: +33 (0)4 93 61 52 58 - Fax: +33 (0)4 93 61 60 01
E: miramar.antibes@orange.fr
www.lecapdantibes.com/miramar

Hôtel Beau-Site
141, Boulevard John Fitzgerald Kennedy
06160 Cap d'Antibes - France
Tel: +33 (0)4 93 61 53 43 - Fax: +33 (0)4 93 67 78 16
E: contact@hotelbeausite.net
www.hotelbeausite.net

Le Mas du Centaure
83480 Puget sur Argens - France
Tel: +33 (0)4 94 81 58 25 or Cell: +33 (0)6 72 55 14 98
E: contact@lemasducentaure.com
www.lemasducentaure.com

Featured Transportation:

Renault Car Rental / Buy-Back

European Cars Service (Toronto)
Tel: (1) 416-366-2413
E: andre@european-cars.net
www.european-cars.net

RENAULT CANADA (Montreal)
Tel: (1) 514-735-1808 or 1-800-361-2411
www.renaultcanada.com

RENAULT EURODRIVE (Europe)
www.renault-eurodrive.com

WestJet (Canada)
www.westjet.com

easyJet (UK)
www.easyjet.com

Stephen Foey

Ooh-la-la Land

Inexpensive — Amusing — Gloriously Warm

Published by WorkPoint Ventures
E: workpointventures@shaw.ca